Capacity Building and Restructuring of Library and Information Centres

Capacity Building and Restructuring of Library and Information Centres

Edited By

Rabindra K. Mahapatra

Ess Ess Publications
New Delhi

Capacity Building and Restructuring for Library and Information Centres

ISBN: 978-81-7000-621-3

Rs.950/-

First Published 2010

Published by:
Ess Ess Publications
4837/24, Ansari Road,
Darya Ganj,
New Delhi-110 002.
INDIA
Phones: 23260807, 41563444
Fax: 41563334
E-mail: info@essessreference.com
www.essessreference.com

Cover Design by *Patch Creative Unit*

Printed and bound in India at Salasar Imaging Systems.

Dedicated to

Prof. Krushna C. Panda

Professor and Head

Department of Library & Information Science

Sambalpur University

Contents

PREFACE

Capacity building is an emerging concept applied to the revamping and restructuring of any kind of organizational set up all across the world. Application of this concept in developing organizations has generated tremendous impact upon the efficient and effective operation of their activities. The non-government organizations which are result-oriented enterprises, are utilizing the concept of capacity building more and more for their overall growth and development. The management experts have also considered the concept of 'capacity building' as the most effective tool in developing the enterprise. Hence the concept holds good and dynamism in present day development scenario.

Experts in LIS are trying to find out new ways and means for development of library and information centers. Due to the emerging digital scenario, managing knowledge in libraries appears to be an arduous task for the librarians. The application of capacity building is an emerging concept with far-reaching consequences upon the development of library and information systems.

Libraries need to improve the acquisition of information, strengthen the organizational capabilities and enhance the quality of information services. The emerging role of the libraries is to empower the users with information which is used in research, teaching and learning. In the emerging technological environment the libraries need to develop various systems and services for which the greater need for manpower, infrastructure, finance, ICT application, collection building, services, resource sharing, digitization and new trends of subject gateways, open access initiatives, institutional repositories, electronic publishing, networking and continuing education activities are to be strengthened. However, the most important aspect is the concept of 'managing men' in library & information centers. In effective operation of all such initiatives and efficient operation of library activities the concept of capacity building appears to be a successful management mantra for libraries. In order to explore the new avenues of the concept of capacity building a seminar was organized, the culmination of which is the reproduction of this book which is the collection of papers presented by the authors.

Rabindra K. Mahapatra

1
Capacity Building of Libraries: Issues and Challenges

Rabindra K. Mahapatra

INTRODUCTION

The Present era has witnessed tremendous changes in knowledge management scenario while managing knowledge for development. A number of institutions and organizations are responsible for development of the society in which the role of the library plays a very significant role. Since knowledge is acquired, organized and disseminated in libraries, the efficient and effective management of knowledge rests on the successful restructuring and capacity building of libraries. In order to accomplish the task of developing a good library system and its successful management, certain newly emerged techniques and principles are applied. Capacity Building is such an emerging concept that has far reaching consequences upon the development of library information systems. The term "capacity building" is now taking over as the new umbrella term for these approaches. This term was brought into popular usage by "Agenda 21", the global action plan for environment and development adopted by world governments at the Earth Summit in 1992. Specifically, **"Capacity building** as defined by the New Mexico State University... is the development of an organization's core skills and capabilities, such as leadership, management, finance and fund-raising, programs and evaluation, in order to build the organization's effectiveness and sustainability. It is a process of assisting an individual or group to identify and address issues and gain the insights, knowledge, and experience. Capacity Building encompasses the country's human, scientific, technological, organizational and resource capabilities. A fundamental goal of capacity building is to enhance the ability to evaluate and address the crucial questions related to policy choices and modes of implementation among development options; based on understanding of environment potential and limits of the needs pursued by people of the country concerned (UNCED, 1992). Capacity Building is one of the essential components of enhancing the profession of particular system, such as, library and information science. The main thrust of the concept is to develop the capability of the persons already working and strengthening the training needs of the professionals. According to UNDP, the Capacity Building is a long term continuous process, in which all stake holders participate and make a policy framework for overall development of organizational excellence to solve problems and implement change. Capacity building is facilitated through the provision of support activities, including coaching, training, specific technical assistance, and resource networking".

AREAS OF CAPACITY BUILDING IN LIBRARIES

Capacity building is a holistic approach for all round development of an organization, such as library and information centre. The concept has sincerely invoked the application of the theories and practices of human resource development, organisational development and an institutional framework development. While human resource development is the crux of the problem in libraries in modern era where digitization is the order of the day, proper modernization and digitization needs right selection and recruitment of right professionals. The process of recruiting good professionals in the library environment ensures the growth of the libraries. Right recruitment procedures with adequate pay-packages for the library professionals ensure a good environment for library professionals and status of the librarians. Proper human resource development in libraries ensures the skills, capabilities of the professionals. Developing continuing education and training enables them to perform diligently and most effectively. In India library professionals are not treated as mainstream professionals in an organization rather they are treated as supporting staff which hinders their attitude towards work and their performance. Library is treated as inseparable part of an academic, research and public institute. Therefore, position of library professionals should be given utmost significance in an organizational hierarchy. In order to develop good work culture in libraries there is a greater need of effective human resource development.

While management principles aim at the basic requirement for organizational development, the libraries are no alien to those principles. Library is an information organization, and its effective performance needs the right application of management principles. Many management theorists have suggested that libraries are management organizations and all the principles and practices of management are applied to its effective performance. In order to promote organizational development of libraries there is a greater need for effective management, structure, processes and procedures. But it is realized that library information centres have least used those management principles and practices. As a result libraries do not get its desired growth and development. However, there are few research organizations in India where their library is treated with equal status with other departments. The library professionals in CSIR laboratories are well placed in terms of salary, promotion and status. The National Institute of Rural Development is an exemplary institute where its head librarian is designated as professor. It is required to see libraries as service institutions in a so far as management perspectives are applied to achieve the glory and credibility in information environment.

Another aspect of capacity building is the institutional framework development which refers to the growth of the institute and its agencies at all levels. While the principles of capacity building are to ensure the improvement of capabilities of all components of the system, it is to again ensure that all sections of the library system need to be improved. Adequate care is to be taken to ensure that all individuals working in libraries must be given equal importance and the growth of those individuals rests on the overall growth of the libraries.

NEED FOR CAPACITY BUILDING IN LIBRARIES

Capacity building is a systematic, planned effort to increase organizational performance through purposeful reflection, planning and action. In particular, capacity building looks at where an organization/ institution stands in comparison to where it hopes to be in future, and develops the skills and resources to get there. Every organization/ institution needs to build up necessary capacity to enable it to achieve its goal. Thus, capacity building refers to the actions that enhance an organization's/ institution's capacity to go towards its mission. The issue of capacity building has enormous implications for development of an institution such as, the library. But it is felt that adequate attention has not yet been paid for library sectors to improve the capacity building of libraries. There is an appreciation problem for libraries in which the implication of capacity building is at the minimal level. All library administrators must realize the implication of capacity building and its realistic application for development of library and information centres. It is understood that there is no provision of adequate funding for libraries to develop its capacity building scenario, there is a greater need for such support. If a drastic change in the structure and functions of the libraries are to be seen, the concept of capacity building is to be evolved and implemented in library sectors. There is a communication gap which hinders the realistic approach of implementing capacity building principles and practices. Another lacuna is that we do not recognize the alternative ways of capacity building for improving the library situations. On the whole, the methods utilized for capacity building may be evolved for library information centres and adequate attention should be paid to improve the library situation.

CAPACITY BUILDING IN LIBRARIES

Libraries are primarily characterized as service entity by providing due supporting role towards achieving greater objectives of the organization. Their role is to empower the users with information which they use in research, teaching and reading. While catering to the needs of the various types of users, libraries need to develop various systems and services for which there is a greater need of manpower, infrastructure, finance, ICT application, collection, services, resource sharing, digitization and implementation of the new trends like subject gateways, open access initiatives, institutional repositories, electronic publishing, networking and continuing education activities such as seminars, conferences, training workshops.

It is an established fact that without proper human resources no organization can exist. Since library information centers are professional institutions, the consideration of trained and skilled manpower plays the most vital role in effective management and functioning of the libraries. In the present era where ICT rules the world, the libraries are not left untouched. There is a growing demand for ICT based services in libraries and generation and use of e-resources by the user communities. In order to cope up with the task of developing an e-environment in libraries there is a greater need of competency building among the library staff. Libraries must undertake various programmes of activities for continuous professional development. The library staff should be given adequate opportunities to attend workshops, seminars, refresher courses and visit other libraries to observe the best practices. National Institute of Science Communication and Information Resources (NISCAIR) and Indian Council of Social Science Research (ICSSR) through its documentation centre NASSDOC are doing an appreciable job in regularly supporting manpower training programmes. In social science sector ICSSR is providing funding for organizing seminars, workshops, publishing books and supporting the research work at PhD level to library professionals in continuous manner. If other leading organizations such as, CSIR, ICAR, ICMR, DBT, and other leading organisations promote similar activities, the library professionals working in all sectors will be immensely benefited and real capacity building of library man power will be successfully achieved.

Infrastructure is the key component for effective operation of library services and functions. A suitable library building with standard furniture is essential requirements for a good library. In bigger organizations an independent building is more suitable for a library. Sufficient stacks and bay-guides in the storage area should be provided. Provision of sufficient light and air in reading and stack area makes it convenient for easy reading. Cleanliness inside the library premises improves the better environment for readability. Special ramps for disabled persons should be provided in the libraries for their easy access. The physical infrastructure of the library should be augmented to comply with the users requirements so that every library can adopt best practices for the greater interest of the organization.

Managing finance is the crucial question in real capacity building of libraries. Barring few research institutions and universities in India, there is scenario of financial resource crunch in every library. Libraries are the target of continuous reduction of fund in its budget provision. Since library is a growing organization, every unit of the library system grows. There is growing trend of increasing prices of documents, and subscription prices, increase of electronic information prices; increase of man power which gives the impression that library needs regular enhancement of funds in its annual budget. But the reverse is much vividly experienced. The library authority must realize that reducing financial provision for the library is the bottleneck of library's real growth which needs to be seriously considered. Most of the good libraries have developed marketing of information products and tried to generate financial resources. It is now required to determine the unit cost of library services so that the actual expenditure is earmarked for the libraries. Mobilization of resources is the order of the day in which the library is no exception to it. There are certain standard practices in financial management of library that need to be followed which in turn can ensure the actual growth of the library.

The latest technology has given birth to the ICT and its uses in library environment. All library and information centers have accepted the change of technology application, but due to several factors such changes are not yet realized. The concept of e-library has already been emerged and on-line data-bases invoked in most of the leading libraries. The concept of digital library has taken its place in leading libraries. There are several library automation softwares available in India for automation of library. Some open source softwares are available to develop digital library system. E-journals and online digital books are subscribed by many leading libraries in India. While scientific and technological libraries are able to effort the cost of electronic information the libraries existing in social science, humanities and some state universities have limited funding to afford such electronic information. Since ICT is the key to modernization of library systems and provides best possible services in given environment, constant effort should be made to improve the ICT environment for all type of libraries irrespective of size and strength.

The advent of internet has made dramatic change in functioning and providing services in library environment. The web has enabled the libraries to develop different types of electronic services within the libraries and networking systems among different types of libraries. On-line services are faster, easier and cheaper and highly accessible to the users. A number of open source softwares have come up and by downloading such packages libraries are able to make automation of their respective libraries. The use of e-journals has dramatically changed the information needs and seeking behaviour of researchers. Through the use of different types of search engines the users are now able to browse a variety of sources of information of several libraries. The capacity building of present libraries has been really increased with the internet base resources in library information centers.

COLLECTION DEVELOPMENT

Collection development is the crux of the problem in library information centers irrespective of the type of libraries. The services of libraries really depend upon the collection development of the libraries. The library gains its popularity due to quality resources. The collection development policy of the libraries needs to be strengthened and right principles are to be followed to ensure a proper collection development. The present situation has given rise to the need for e-resources. Since, users have changed their attitudes towards electronic information systems; all libraries should be having access to valuable e-resources and databases. The existence of e-journals consortia has enabled the libraries to get full text access to thousands of e-journals. In India most of the consortia are centrally funded and managed by leading organizations. However, some other sectors like social science and humanities, the consortia are not well developed nor properly managed. There is a need for more open access portals which will be more useful for research pursuits in library environments. The library should look forward to other e-resources which are freely available in the internet such as DOAJ (Directory of Open Access

Journal), Open J-gate etc. A number of e-databases have developed such as PROWESS, CAPX, and Indiastat.Com. by private information producers which are available in market. Such databases are very often required for research use. Those databases should form the part of the collection development in libraries. The most dynamic form of publications are e-books which are going to replace the traditional books. Although the e-books are less in number, the significance of those books are now realized in libraries for different user groups.

The new web technologies such as web 2.0, RSS feed, Blogs, wikies, instant messaging are emerging which appear to be highly useful in providing services to the users. All libraries should welcome such emerging technologies for capacity building of systems and services of the libraries.

SERVICES

Information service is the core of the library system. The popularity of the library depends upon the quality of services provided. The present era has witnessed the increasing user expectation of the libraries. In order to fulfill the needs and expectations of the users all libraries should take up the onus for assessing the demand for quality base library products and services. At this point of time the library can be able to justify its existence for the society. The librarian must visualize the new innovation in library operation and services and develop new avenues of value added services. In most of the libraries, the users are not aware of the information systems and services for which there is a greater need of introducing information literacy programmes in libraries. Because, a better information literate is a greater user of the library services. Always users- centric approaches are to be developed so that the desired services from the

Library and information centers are directed towards satisfying user needs.

NETWORKING AND RESOURCE SHARING

Internet has created the opportunities to share the resources in many libraries. New dimensions of resource sharing has been emerged enabling several libraries to develop resource sharing networks. Such networks be expanded for various subjects and specialization of libraries irrespective of size and strength. It is high time to develop collaborative digitization programme among libraries to avoid duplication, cost, time and money. It is also similarly important to develop the union catalogue of resources the fine example of open index initiatives. The modern libraries must practice the staff exchange programme among libraries to improve the skill and capability of professional library staff.

CONCLUSION

Capacity building is a buzzword in management practices. In order to improve organizations effectiveness, the concept of capacity building is being used. Library and Information Centres are service institutions aiming at providing information services up to the entire satisfaction of user community. In order to improve the existing information environment, both physical and service aspect in libraries continued endeavour should be made to utilize the principles of capacity building. In this knowledge driven capacity the library information centres are required to augment their services capacity to fulfill other exact requirement of users and diversify various innovative services to attract more users. Leading libraries in research organizations in India such as CSIR, ICMR, ICSSR, ICAR, IITs, IIMs and leading universities should come forward in designing the capacity building programmes for library development in their respective subject oriented libraries. Other information organizations in India should also take initiatives to monitor the endeavours towards capacity building in whatever way possible to them. The end result of such efforts will have far-reaching consequences upon the overall development of library systems and services.

REFERENCES

1. Capacity Building, Wikipedia, 20 Sept. 2009 <http://www.gdrc.org/uem/capacity- define.html>
2. Capacity Building, New Mexico State University. 20 Sept. 2009. <http://planning.nmsu. edu/taskforce/glossary.html>
3. Ahmad Ishak, M. S. and Amira S. Firadaus. *Importance of Capacity Building in Digital Content Industry in Malaysia*. 20 Sept. 2009 <http://portalfsss.um.edu.my/portal/upload Folder/pdf/Importance%20of%20Capacity%20Building%20for%20the%20Digital%20Content%20Industry%20in%20Malaysia.pdf
4. Rowland, F. *The Librarian's Role in the Electronic Information Environment*. 1998. 20 Sept. 2009. http://bodley.ox.ac.uk/icsu/rowlandppr.htm

2

Capacity Building for LIS Professionals in Digital Environment

Kunwar Singh
Krushna C. Panda
Mrutyunjay Sethy

INTRODUCTION

Capacity-building is a key feature of LIS education in that focuses on recognization and reconstruction of libraries. At grass-roots level, it is necessary to train LIS teachers and LIS professionals the new skills related to the unusual and stressful situation, and often to train many inexperienced teachers the basics of education. Project management staff and LIS education advisers drawn from national or refugee communities need guidance and training, with the objective of increased self-reliance and/or effectiveness. At the level of implementing agencies and field staff of India, there is a need for greater awareness of the special features of education in situations of emergency and in post-conflict situations.

There is also a need to strengthen international standby capacity, especially in respect of LIS education for post-conflict reconciliation and reconstruction. As may be seen from the foregoing, there is a substantial workload in the coming years to permit the needed development of the field of education in emergency and reconstruction. The strategic dimension, assessment and capacity-building are generally neglected. There is a clear gap that UNESCO can fill, focusing over the longer term on capacity-building, development of training materials and training teams in field operations. UNESCO therefore seeks to promote capacity-building within the organization itself, within the Indian system and in the field of Library and information Centre.

CAPACITY BUILDING

"Specifically, capacity building encompasses the country's human, scientific, technological, organizational, institutional and resource capabilities. A fundamental goal of capacity building is to enhance the ability to evaluate and address the crucial questions related to policy choices and modes of implementation among development options, based on an understanding of environment potentials and limits and of needs perceived by the people of the country concerned". Capacity Building is much more than training and includes the following:

- Human resource development, the process of equipping individuals with the understanding, skills and access to information, knowledge and training that enables them to perform effectively.
- Organizational development, the elaboration of management structures, processes and procedures, not only within organizations but also the management of relationships between the different organizations and

sectors (public, private and community).

- Institutional and legal framework development, making legal and regulatory changes to enable organizations, institutions and agencies at all levels and in all sectors to enhance their capacities.

WHY THE CAPACITY BUILDING NEEDED AND ITS CORE

There are three core dimensions as follow:

- Printed resources to electronic resources
- Mode of services
- Professionals/Staff Development and continuing education

Primarily, Printed resources are less preferred to electronic resources. Information technology has gone under several changes since its invention, particularly in electronic and digital era. Starting from the formation of clay tablets in Babylonian civilization it has traveled for its evolution through paper age, punched cards up to electronic media, particularly the computer. The important features that have affected the quality of information are accuracy, comprehensiveness, freshness and time. The Information technology can be used in libraries to support technical functions associated with technical processing and circulation work, to support information storage, retrieval and dissemination systems, to support management of information services in libraries, and extension services.

In electronic era, the information technology has different fields that have impact on the life of human being as well as the information management; but the most important technologies which are being utilized for the library activities such as digital products (CD-ROMs and

DVDs), web resources, multimedia and the networking.

The modern libraries with large facility, tremendous enrollment and huge resources are in a position to make significant contributions in the area of social sciences, humanities and science and technology. In a developing country like India, it is expected that organization should produce people committed to development of the nation and its service. In older days library was regarded as storehouse of reading material collected for the purpose of preservation. Libraries role in educational process was marginal. But today library is considered as integral part of organization.

Secondly, Mode of Library Services is the most significant aspect very often considered.

The library offers the following services to its users group.

- Lending services
- Online Public Access Cataloguing Service (OPAC)
- Online bibliographic and full text database services
- Internet browsing
- Reprographic services
- Books exhibition
- Resources sharing & Electronic document delivery service
- Content base services
- Conducting technical film shows
- Consultancy service

Thirdly, Professional staff development and Continuing Education is apparently necessary for overall development of the library system. Staff development and personnel development are often used interchangeably or synonymously. Professional staff development at the University/ Institute library falls into two categories. First and foremost, there are in-house training programmes- the most prominent being staff orientation, regular and periodic rotation of staff, staff meeting, subject responsibility, research and publications. The other includes professional activities outside the University/Institute. Notable among these are attendances at conferences and seminars, both at home and overseas, training courses and workshops, sponsorship for higher studies in library and information science and sabbatical leave. The whole staff development package involves training and retraining on a continuing basis.

- Staff Orientation
- Staff meetings
- Subject responsibilities
- Research and Publication
- Professional activities
- Training Programme
- Membership of Professional Association
- Sabbatical Leave
- Future trends

Skills Required for LIS Professionals in Digital Environment

Skill is a measure of a professionals expertise, specialization, and supervisory capacity. Skilled professionals are generally more trained, higher paid, and have more responsibilities than unskilled professionals. The library and information professionals are needed to have some of the basic skills. Some of the skills are as follow.

Effective Communication Skills

Effective communication skills are most important and necessary at all levels of management. Communication is the way library leaders can bridge the gap, stay in touch, build trust, monitor performance and attain the concrete division. Proper communications helps in controlling misunderstanding conflicts and improving co-ordination in the groups. Reading, writing, learning, speaking, listening, presenting are also the important parts of effective communication skills.

Library Management Skills

Library and information professionals developed basic knowledge about handling of resources and key concepts of cataloguing and classification. Learned about the policies and procedures required for library management. Library and information professionals should learn how to evaluate, review their own performance and career development planning.

Resource Building Skills or Collection Development Skills

Resources building skills is one of the important skills of library and information professionals. Not many years ago, most libraries acquisitions were limited to books, serials, microforms, and audiovisual materials. Today library patrons expect access to virtual documents as well as to physical items, and the concept of a library "collection" is being redefined. Leased electronic resources are made available to patrons without being acquired for the library. Intangible resources, such as the full text of articles, are provided through "pay per view" arrangements, and are used or taken away by patrons without ever being added to the library's permanent collection.

Technical/ Technology Skills

It involves specialized knowledge and analytical ability with in that specialty, and facility in the use of the tools and techniques of the specific discipline. Technical skills such z39.50 protocol for cataloguing, open source software applications, OAI and metadata harvesting etc. Vocational and on the job training programmes largely do a good job in developing the skill. These skills basically involve the use of knowledge, methods and techniques in performing a job efficiently and effectively. For example to become a librarian a person must have formal education in library and information science with some experience and technical degree.

Leadership Skills

Leadership skill can be considered to be the personal qualities, behaviors styles and division of the leader. The function of leadership is to produce more leaders not more followers. Leadership skills are very important for 21st century's library professionals.

Decision Making Skills

Decision making skills are very important to library professionals. No decision will be successful without the co-operation commitment and enthusiasm of other colleagues, team or users. Making a decision begins when we realize that something's need to be done. The decision should be firm to achieve the objectives in right direction.

Performance Skills

Performance management is a term being used

increasingly to cover a number of personal techniques. Performance development provides a means of communication what is happening with the organization and demonstrating its future direction in a way that has immediate meaning to the individual members of staff. Library and information professional performing the quality services within stipulated time limit is called truly LIS professionals.

Time Management Skills

S. R. Ranganathan's fourth law "save the time of the user", indicates about the time management for library professional and users like. In this turbulent world we never seem to have enough time. Working long hours is not necessarily a sign that you are overloaded with work. It can mean that you need to develop your time management. Strategy and planning is a vital element of time management.

Public Relation Skills

A public relation (PR) is concerned with the reputation of an organization or individual: creating it, safeguarding it, representing it to the public, and potentially promoting products and services as part of this. Public relation skill is very important in marketing of library services and attracts the outside users to generate the revenue.

CONCLUSION

Today, Libraries and Information centers are undergoing great transformation from single medium static conventional Libraries to multimedia dynamic hybrid libraries facing variety of critical challenges. The role of library and information professionals in the 21st century is changing very fast. Library and information professionals are becoming more and more custodian of print-based and digitized archives and special collections. They are likely to be the administrator dealing with the purchasing and delivery of information services. The Information Technology has given an opportunity to the librarians to become a teacher of information literacy and related skills to the students and faculty. The future activities of library professionals will have a role in teaching and developing researchers in various aspects of academic and professional practice. The global trend is that the librarians are involved in effective dissemination of research generating and managing research output involved in providing inputs on research skills and techniques that demands the true. Capacity building through professional development.

REFERENCES

1. Elliott, L., *"Professional staff development in academic libraries", Journal of Librarianship*, Vol. 15 No. 4, October 1993.
2. Thompson, J., *An Introduction to University Library Administration, 3rd ed.*, London, p. 46.
3. Osei, I., *"Library instruction at the University of Science and Technology (UST): a need for new approaches", Journal of the University of Science and Technology*, Vol. 13 No. 2, June 1993, pp. 67-72.
4. Osei, I., *"The functions of the university library: a consideration of the role of the University of Science and Technology Library, Kumasi, Ghana", Journal of the University of Science and Technology*, Vol. 12 No. 3, October 1992, pp. 116-19.
5. Jackson, M.M. (Ed.), *Contemporary Developments in Librarianship: An International Handbook, The Library Association*, London, p. 10.
6. *http://www.gdrc.org/uem/capacity-define.html*, Retrieved on 20th August 2009.
7. *http://www.managementhelp.org/plan_dec/str_plan/str_plan.htm*, Retrieved on 24th August 2009.

8. *http://www.cilip.org.uk/training/training/2009/libinfo/essentialskills.htm*, Retrieved on 28th August 2009.

9. *http://targetjobs.co.uk/advertising-and-pr/articleview-48s_3a_1653.aspx,Retrieved* on 29th August 29.

10. http://en.wikipedia.org/wiki/Skill_%28labor%29, Retrieved on 30th August 2009.

3
Capacity Building and Restructuring of Libraries and Information Centers : A Spotlight

Bibhu Prasad Panda
Dillip K. Swain
Kamal Lochan Jena

INTRODUCTION

In the parlance of LIS, capacity building promises a great reformation, restructuring and renovation of systems, services, information infrastructures of library and information centers for meeting the topical elevated needs of users' community. In conformity with the cardinal principles of capacity building, library and information professionals need to come out with novel ideas of restructuring and refurbishing their information infrastructure, systems, services, and all sorts of library operations for the fulfillment of comprehensive needs of each and every clientele pin-pointedly just in time. Therefore, it is quite essential for the information professionals to understand as to what constitute library capacity building. We have attempted to put focus on some of the key considerations for capacity building and restructuring of libraries.

CAPACITY BUILDING: CONCEPT

"Capacity building", sometimes used interchangeably with "institution building", "institutional and organizational development" and "institutional capacity building" (***Jones and Blunt, 1999*; Tadele and Manyena, 2009**). Specifically, capacity building encompasses the country's human, scientific, technological, organizational, institutional and resource capabilities. A fundamental goal of capacity building is to enhance the ability to evaluate and address the crucial questions related to policy choices and modes of implementation among development options, based on an understanding of environment potentials and limits and of needs perceived by the people of the country concerned"(*http://www.gdrc.org/uem/capacity-define.html*). The WCO defines capacity building as "activities which strengthen the knowledge, abilities, skills and behavior of individuals and improve institutional structures and processes such that the organization can effectively meet its mission and goals in a sustainable way. "It is, however, important to put into consideration the principles that govern community capacity building (http://en.wikipedia.org/kiki/Capacity building).Besides, the following web definitions of capacity building are worthy of evaluation:

- A coordinated process of deliberate interventions to: (i) upgrade skills (ii) improve procedures, and (iii) strengthen organizations. Capacity building refers to the investment in people, institutions and practices that will enable countries to achieve their development objectives.

- To increase the operating efficiency of a government or non-government institution, a community based organization, a community per se or an individual through training (increasing knowledge), changed operating procedures, restructuring, etc.
- Training lays foundation to ensure that the interaction of and between actors and services is crucial for the improved organization of agricultural services.
- Capacity-development focuses on improving the expertise and skills of personnel in relation to the responsibilities and tasks which they will carry-out. It is generally considered to be a specific part of institutional strengthening activities (see also: Institutional Strengthening).
- Increasing the potential to gain maximum results/ benefits for the community.

The synthesis of all of the above definitions implies that capacity building involves investment in people, organizations and services to enhance operating efficiency, expertise and skills of personnel towards the achievement of organizational excellence.

NEED FOR LIBRARY RESTRUCTURING

Libraries provide key support to economic development through direct job creation, contribution to cultural development of the local area, education, training and skills development, and the development of social capital and social inclusiveness **(Ashu and Clandening, 2007)**. One of the things that can make life interesting for information professionals is the way in which libraries are structured. Structure contributes to the successful implementation of plans by formally allocating people and resources to the tasks which have to be done, and by providing mechanisms for their co-ordination. However, there are about as many ways of organizing or structuring libraries as there are libraries. Organizations should adopt certain characteristics to make them more efficient and effective, **(Ibegbulam and Olorunsola, 2001),** but it is a matter of consideration that how well the respective organization supports the trend.

In the case of academic libraries, a feasible plan to enhance user services is to organize a library into subject divisions, with professional librarians located at each one of them. This plan is targeted to increase gradually the subject expertise of librarians working in each subject division through their experiences with users. To carry out this new modified organization, the conventional library setting needs to be changed from placing books according to their forms (e.g. monograph publications, periodicals and reference books), to organizing them according to their subjects (e.g. philosophy, economics, law, physics, computer science). The subject librarian will, at the same time, take care of reference services, SDI, DB instruction and book selection on the same subject. Previously existing discord between the book collection, user service librarians and users will, thus, be removed, as the new setting will permit interconnection of work within the same subject. For the users it would mean a one-stop service and also a realization of user-centered services. Taking the transformation a step further would be to allow technical services to be taken care of within each subject library as well **(Shin, and Kim, 2002)** and this is a stepping stone to capacity building since restructuring and reorganizing can make room for amending the chance of scattering of information by the process of integration and reorganization of the prolific mess of information under the specific subjects for effective and efficient traceability.

LIBRARY CAPACITY

Library capacity consists of the people in the library, its culture, attitude, environment and appearance. It requires commitment to training to develop people skills. It requires libraries to identify and take advantage of opportunities and strengths. How does one recognize that capacity is being built? *The Community Development Handbook* identifies factors that confirm capacity is being built. "People are active, interested and participating in what is going on. People may also be questioning, challenging and debating – but they will be debating what should be done, not complaining that nothing will ever change. More people are getting involved, helping to identify key issues, and taking action. Results are becoming obvious and the abilities, esteem and resources of many communities are growing as capacity grows." These factors may also be used to indicate when library capacity is being built (**Ashu and Clandening, 2007**).

Library capacity is basically focused on community building since it offers community meeting space, facilitate access to computers and the internet, provide public access to desired set of information needed for community building, Therefore, libraries can bring experience in restructuring and reorganizing information sources for the community's development.

LIBRARY AS CAPACITY BUILDING INITIATOR

Library as a community connector is rightly regarded as the capacity building initiator. Initiation of capacity of any set up can take its fuel from library. It can accommodate community meetings, discussions, forums, and events and activities as a catalyst for community building.

In this digital age, as libraries are making great efforts to deliver information services to users' desktops, they are also facing a serious dilemma: fewer users are physically visiting libraries as a response to the unprecedented development of technological innovations and as the traditional library as a physical space has less to offer today's students. How can libraries continue to justify their occupation of physical space in this climate? **(Sidorko and Yang, 2009)** as a remedy to this effect, libraries can fill an important role in building the skills needed to use the new technologies and in local access and training to use e-government initiatives. The digital divide isolates people who cannot afford the technologies and lack digital literacy skills or motivation to develop these skills **(Ashu and Clandening, 2007)** and it is the library which can initiate the process.

DIGITAL LIBRARIES AS CAPACITY BUILDING INDICATOR

Witten, et al.(2002) identify the following **five** key important areas where digital libraries can promote human development as a capacity builder:

1. Dissemination of humanitarian information: Digital libraries, by decoupling production and distribution costs from intellectual property charges, offer a desperately needed lifeline. More broadly, increasing the level of education through knowledge and technology transfer, particularly for doctors, teachers and other professionals.

2. Disaster relief : Natural disasters such as earthquakes or hurricanes, and man-made ones such as terrorist attacks or nuclear accidents, demand immediate and informed response in an environment where the local infrastructure may be unpredictable or severely damaged. To this effect digital library technology allows organized collections of information, graced with comprehensive searching and browsing capabilities, to be created very rapidly. Intelligence specific to the nature of a disaster, the geographical region and the logistic resources available for the relief effort can be gathered into a built-to-order digital library collection that combines targeted knowledge with general medical and sanitary information.

3. Preservation and propagation of indigenous culture : Libraries and their close relatives, museums, have always been involved in preserving culture. These institutions collect literature and artifacts, and use them to disseminate knowledge and understanding of different times and cultures. Digital libraries, however, open up the possibility of far more flexible and coherent multimedia collections that are both fully searchable and browsable in multiple dimensions, and permit more active participation by indigenous people in preserving and disseminating their own culture. This strengthens individual cultures, promotes diversity and reduces the dominance of English in the global information infrastructure.

4. Locally-produced collections of information: Digital library applications in culture preservation have the advantage that the relevant information is, of necessity, readily available locally.

5. New opportunities to enter the global marketplace : Countries such as India, Romania and the Philippines have long undertaken low-level information-processing tasks like data entry and OCR – indeed. The varied demands of digital library development, such as manual metadata extraction, collection organization, cataloging and information presentation, will greatly expand the range of tasks that the developing world can undertake, creating valuable new export markets.

THE TECHNOLOGICAL INFRASTRUCTURE

Proliferation of modern information communication technology has changed the way in which information is delivered and how users want to receive information. Asking for librarians to search databases was no longer necessary as the search process became easy enough for users themselves to conduct. A trend for direct searches of all kinds of information featured in academic publications, graphs and data is growing. Academic libraries need to satisfy these kinds of users in a variety of ways, including such measures as wider utilization of Inter Library Loan and Document Delivery Services (**Shin and Kim, 2002).** Anticipating the demand of network access; the structure and organization of digital libraries are rearranging their distribution media. Library websites are being regularly updated and free access to users is provided at all time. OPAC features are modified with vivid references and cross references. CDs/DVDs are properly preserved, organized and distributed.

Computers in developing countries tend to be low-end, often with poorly-installed software. The computing environment is quite outside the control of system developers, and may lack network access, CD-ROM drives, browser software, adequate disk storage and main memory **(Witten, 2002).** Additionally, the online catalog is capable of providing wide-ranging information service since it has potentially infinite linking power that can direct and connect library users to forever growing electronic resources, as well as physical collections. With the globalization of the online catalog, the catalog is no longer just a tool, as it used to be, when it meant stacks of static cards stored in separate little drawers; it has become a dynamic gateway to increasingly expanding information resources through constantly extending networks of hyperlinks. It is still important, as ever before, for us cataloging librarians to adhere to prescribed standards and rules when working on bibliographic records, but we also have to adopt a user-centered and user-friendly approach to assembling, maintaining, and enhancing the online catalog according to library users' needs **(Huang and Wong, 2006).**

CONSTITUENT ELEMENTS OF COSTING PROVISION OF LIBRARY SERVICES

Provision of efficient and effective library services depends on both materials and human resources. Costing elements should thus be based on a thorough analysis of what is provided, what should be provided, how it should be provided and by whom, with clear indication of quality (qualitative and quantitative) assessment indicators and the cost involved in each case. As library capacity building is a continuous process, elements of this continuity should also be built in and clearly reflected in the costing exercise by allowing a certain percentage in the budget. Thus, in order to be comprehensive, costing should be divided into thematic themes, related to major components of a library: staff and staff development, collections and buildings, general operational costs, or along any budget lines that cover all activities undertaken by a particular library, both capital and operation based **(Nawe, 2004)**. The budgeting estimation should be clear cut and goal oriented.

STRATEGIES FOR ENHANCING PROVISION OF SERVICES THROUGH EXTERNAL SUPPORT

Strategies for enhancing provision of services through external support fall under two categories. The first category is that of colleagues elsewhere in the library profession. Libraries all over the world depend on each other as no single library can meet all the needs of its users at any given time. Through forming links, consortia and other forms of cooperative relationships, libraries can cut a lot on individual spending through sharing of resources. However, a precaution is needed when considering cutting on costs and meeting strategic needs of core users, although this element in this era of ICT may be irrelevant when the connectivity problem is resolved. Nonetheless, copyright issues will need reconciliation. Apart from building capacity in the area of information provision, cooperation can also contribute significantly in human capacity building through exchange of staff or exchanging experiences and publishing through the Web **(Nawe, 2004)** and this in turn can be instrumental in strengthening the organizational efficiency.

CONCLUSION

Capacity building considerably depends on successful innovation within an existing set up that is operated through procedural and systematic desertion of old practices and services. Library capacity building though constitute restructuring and reorganizing, however, it is not an easy enterprise since there are infinite methods of revamping and re-engineering of systems and services of libraries that come to the forefront as issues. Whatever may be the case, in order to keep pace with the progressive trends of ICT and information highway, the urge of the hour is to opt for library capacity building for expanding the horizon of information preservation, processing, and subsequent utilization.

REFERENCES

1. Ashu, M and Clendening, L. (2007), "It takes a library to raise a community", *Partnership: the Canadian Journal of Library and Information Practice and Research*, Vol. 2, No 2, available at: *http://journal.lib.uoguelph.ca/index.php/perj/article/viewArticle/241/569*, accessed 23 August, 2009.
2. Capacity Building-Agenda 21's definition*(Chapter 37, UNCED, 1992.) available at: http://www.gdrc.org/uem/capacity-define.html accessed 21August, 2009*
3. Witten, I H, et al.(2002), "The promise of digital libraries in developing countries" *The Electronic Library*, Vo.20 No.1, pp.7-13., available at: *http://www.emeraldinsight.com/Insight/ViewContentServlet?contentType=Article&Filename=Published/EmeraldFullTextArticle/Articles/2630200101.html*, accessed 24 August,2009.
4. Ibegbulam, I. J. and Olorunsola, R.(2001), "Restructuring academic libraries in Nigeria: issues to consider", *Library Management*, Vol 22 No 8/9, pp.381-386, available at: *www.emeraldinsight.com*, accessed 27 August, 2009.
5. Huang, J and Wong, K.(2006), "Technical services and user service improvement", *Library Management*, Vol.27 No. 6/7, pp. 505-514, available at: *www.emeraldinsight.com*, accessed 27 August, 2009.
6. Shin, E. J. and Kim, Y. S.(2002), "Restructuring library organizations for the twenty-first century: the future of user-oriented services in Korean academic libraries", *Aslib Proceedings*, Vol.54 No.4, pp. 260-266, available at: *www.emeraldinsight.com*, accessed 27 August, 2009.
7. Sidorko, P. S. and Yang, T.T.(2009), "Refocusing for the future: meeting user expectations in a digital age", *Library Management*, Vol.30, No. ½, pp. 6-24, available at: *www.emeraldinsight.com*, accessed 27 August, 2009.
8. Sidorko,P. E. and Yang, T. T.(2009), "Refocusing for the future: meeting user expectations in a digital age", *Library Management*, Vol.30 No.1/2, pp. 6-24.
9. Nawe, J.(2004), "Strategizing financing of public university libraries in East Africa", *Library Management*, Vol.25 No.8/9, pp.381-385.

10. Tadele, F. and Manyena, S.B.(2009),"Building disaster resilience through capacity building in Ethiopia", *Disaster Prevention and Management*, Vol.18 No.3, pp. 317-326, available at:www.emeraldinsight.com, accessed 27 August,2009.

11. Jones, M.L., Blunt, P. (1999), "Twinning as a method of sustainable institutional capacity building", *Public Administration and Development*, Vol. 19 No.1, pp.381-402

Websites

- *web.worldbank.org/WBSITE/EXTERNAL/TOPICS/EXTPOVERTY/EXTPSIA/0,,contentMDK:20433436~menuPK:2453409~pagePK:210058~piPK:210062~theSitePK:490130,00.html*
- *www.acil.com.au/glossary.htm*
- *www.naarm.ernet.in/NAIP/Consortia%20concepts.doc*
- *www.mos.gov.pl/mos/publikac/Raporty_opracowania/manual/glosry_1.html*

4
Determining the Value of Library and Information Services: A Methodical Approach

Sabitri Majhi
Bulu Maharana

INTRODUCTION

Valuing a Library and Information Service is a complex and difficult process. When an LIS manager is asked to prepare a valuation of their service, they will realize only too soon how hard it is going to be. Even if they are well organized and have researched the appropriate and copious professional LIS literature on the subject, they will soon be overwhelmed at the variety of methods and practices that can be used. None seem to be for the whole department and which might be the most appropriate for their circumstances. This paper describes a suitable methodical approach for valuing the library and information service, without using money as the measuring rod.

It is very difficult to identify libraries' contribution from an economic perspective, in terms of money i.e. "for each dollar or rupees investment in the library, the university received how much rupees in return". Hence this article provides a framework to evaluate library and information services based on users' assessments.

WHAT IS VALUE?

Value is an indispensable intermediating concept for establishing & guiding actions, relations, Priorities & exchanges.

Dealing with value is a challenge in any field .The field of library and information services is also not behind this challenge. We can turn to philosophy and economics to clarify the meaning of value & can synthesize some of the major views from these two fields that seem most relevant & useful in establishing a framework for study of value in library and information services.

2.1. Philosophers consider value as the worth of something, and the process of valuation as an estimate, appraisal, or measurement of its worth. In their works, worth seems to be an undefined primitive term. They consider that value is related to, but no' synonymous with, "good," "desirable," or "worthwhile," and that it can be positive or negative.

In philosophy values are distinguished like below.

Intrinsic value, being good or worthy in and of itself. It is basic to all the others. Health or good experiences might be considered as intrinsic values.

Extrinsic or instrumental value, which is a means to, or contributes to something that is intrinsically valuable. Often relates to an activity. An example might be exercise that contributes to good health.

Inherent value, something whose experience, contemplation, or understanding contributes to intrinsic value. Often relates to an entity. An example might be aestethic value of a work of art that contributes to good experiences.

Contributory value, something that contributes to the value of a whole of which it is a part and which may be contingent on the existence of other parts or activities. Often relates to a constituent. Utility or usefulness of a product used for a given purpose might be an example.

We can extend these concepts to information and to information services like:

- If "being informed" has intrinsic value, similar to health or good experiences, then we may consider that information may have extrinsic or instrumental value because it may contribute to or advance a person's state of "being informed" (or better informed) .
- An information service has contributory value if it provides such information. In particular, it may have contributory value if the information provided is connected to some application or decision by an informed person.
- Finally, something that may "carry" information, such as an information object (i.e., an object potentially conveying information) , a well-written article, or a well designed book, may have inherent value.

In other words, the value of being informed is intrinsic. The value of information is extrinsic or instrumental. The value of an information service is contributory. The value of an information object may be inherent.

- The economists consider value as the worth of something that contributes to wealth. It is a concept at the foundation of economics. Adam Smith's classification of value in exchange and value-in-use remains valid, with, of-course, some modern elaboration on the theme. Dealing with measurement of value-in-exchange in economics is considerably easier than in other fields.

Unfortunately, in considering value of information and information services this measuring rod can't be easily applied. For most library and information services there is not a market in the economic sense, where money is exchanged directly, and hence we can't use the measuring rod of money. Hence for the most, we must deal with value-in-use, which can extend the economic treatment of value to intrinsic value, dimensions such as demands, wants, usefulness, satisfaction, pleasure, pains, and the like.

SIGNIFICANCE OF STUDYING VALUE

Clearly, libraries and information system, and the services, they provide, have been valued for a long time. They were supported by society, communities, organizations, institutions, and users because it was implicitly believed or explicitly stated that they provide unique value, most often intangible or even symbolic, rather than monetary in nature. Recently, the importance and urgency of determining value of library and information services in a more utilitarian, explicit and specific way have increased for a number of reasons.

- The social role of information is changing, represented by the evolution of the "information society ". Information is as you mean an ever more central role in every aspect of life. As a consequence, roles of and expectations for library and information services are also changing.

- Library and information centers are in transition along several dimensions .They are sifting from the "just-in-case" model of collection completeness to the "just-in-time" model of providing excess to information resources located any where . Electronic information resources and network are providing new ways of access and use.
- Many new "players" enabled by modern information technology and networks, are beginning to provide information services and they are competing directly with library and information centers. This growing competition confronts libraries information system with heightened need for justification and valuation.

VALUING OF LIBRARY AND INFORMATION SERVICES

Libraries have a long tradition of evaluation, which started with the emergence of modern librarianship at the end of the 19th century, and concentrated for a long time thereafter on evaluation as to compliance with established standards and best practices, related to holdings, representation, arrangements, space, staff, operations, etc. Criteria derived from standards and best practices did not reflect dimensions of value. Evaluation of IR systems began in the 1950s and concentrated mostly on relevance. By the end of the 1970s, a number of studies have emerged that used diverse perspectives and criteria for evaluation of Libraries and information systems. The approaches to evaluation of library and information services have been often dichotomized into system- and user-centered. While there is and shouldn't be any conflict between the two—they are very much related—there is a strong school of advocacy for the need for user-centered evaluation, because main motto of the library is to satisfy the user.

User-Centered Studies have been conducted using a variety of criteria and associated measures, among them: satisfaction, success, utility, relevance, completeness, specificity, accuracy, timeliness, impact, effort, difficulty, failure, frustration, and the like (Baker & Lancaster, 1991; Kantor, 1984; Robertson & Hancock-Beaulieu, 1992; Saracevic, 1995; Saracevic & Kantor, 1988) . A number of these criteria and associated measures reflect one or another dimension of value, but multiple dimensions are needed to capture the richness of value-in-use.

A large study sponsored by council on Library resources developed a derived taxonomy of value-in-use of Library & information services with multiple dimensions based on user's assessments & proposed methods & instrument for valuing library & information services in general.

TAXONOMY OF VALUE IN USING LIBRARY & INFORMATION SERVICES

The present taxonomy of value in using Library and information services provides the overall structure with description of major general classes and subclasses in detail. The General classes or facets are like below:

A. REASONS for using a library or information service

  A.1 For a TASK or project

  A.2 For PERSONAL reasons

    A.2.1 Cognitive reasons

    A.2.2 Affective reasons

A.2.3 Reasons for substitute choice

B. INTERACTION with a library service

B.1 RESOURCES-availability, accessibility

B.2 USE of resources, services

B.3 OPERATIONS and ENVIRONMENT

B.3.1 Policies, procedures

B.3.2 Facilities. Organization

B.3.3 Staff performance

B.3.4 Equipment performance

C. RESULTS of using library services

C.1 COGNITIVE results

C.2 AFFECTIVE results

C.3 ACCOMPLISHMENTS in relation to tasks

C.4 EXPECTATIONS met

C.5 TIME aspects

C.6 MONEY estimates

GENERAL CLASSES OR FACETS

Description of Major Classes and Subclasses

Class A: Reasons : This class covers the causes motives, bases, purposes, and/or rationales underlying the use of library services. Why do users use the library and information service? What do users want to get from the service? We have subdivided Reasons into three subclasses:

A.1 Task or project: Activities, work, or problems in which the user is engaged that are the direct cause for using the library service. What are the users doing that prompted the use of the service? What were the users working on or wanting to work on? What problems brought them to the service? Included are tasks such as: research, compiling a bibliography, class assignment project proposal, and a host of others. Most of the times there is some tangible element in Tasks, an element that is directly reflected in the responses.

A.2. Personal reasons : Private, individual reasons for using the library services. Most of these are intangible. What is the motivation of the users foe using a library service, as far as knowledge or emotion is concerned? The Personal reasons are further subdivided into subclasses:

A.2.1 Cognitive reasons, related to various aspects of learning and knowledge, staying current, or orienting oneself;

A.2.2 Affective reasons, related to a person's own emotional feelings or desires for using the services. Like relaxation, stress reduction, feeling of satisfaction.

A.2.3 Reasons for substitute choice, related to a personal decisions to use the given library or information services instead of some other choice.

A.3 To get an object, information or perform an activity : Covered are reasons or objectives associated with what users intend to request from a service or what activities they intend to request from a service or what activities they intend to engage in at the library. What do the users actually want to get from the service? What will they do in the library? This subclass is further subdivided into:

A.3.1 Physical (tangible) objects : Reasons or objectives related to getting a book, article, or other objects available from a library service;

A.3.2 Intangible objects: Reasons or objectives related to getting information, facts, data; being directed to other sources of information;

A.3.3 Perform an activity or work: Studying,

searching, browsing and other activities a user intends to perform. It includes non library activities, such as the use of a computer, if available for general use.

Class B: Interaction : This class covers the assessment by users of the qualities of various aspects of library services. How does a user assess or evaluate the encounters with the library while seeking and using a service? We have divided interaction into the following subclasses:

B.1 Availability and accessibility of resources, services : Covers availability, accessibility, and quality of given materials, items or services. A availability asks: Does the library have a given resource, item or service? Does it have a given book or journal and is it available for use on this occasions? Accessibility asks: How readily can the access to the service be obtained? Quality asks: How current, timely, complete is a given resources or service?

B.2. Use of resources, services : Covers a number of aspects connected with user experiences while using a resource or service. How convenient is it to use the service? What effort is required or how easy is it to use? What is the degree of frustration in using it? How much effort is required to get from one service to another (e.g., from searching for and finding references to getting articles)?

B.3 Operations and environment : Covers the experience of user in relation to the working performance and environment of the service. Four subclasses are included:

B3.1 Policies, procedures : How clear, convenient, reasonable are they?

B3.2 Facilities, organization : How adequate or of what quality is the apace, physical layout, intellectual organization? How comfortable are the facilities?

B.3.3 Staff performance: How knowledgeable, helpful, efficient is the staff?

B.3.4 Equipment performance : Technical functioning; instructions; difficulty; user friendliness?

Class C: Results : This class covers users assessment of outcomes. What did a user do out of the services? What expectations were met? How is the service related to time and money? Six subclasses are included:

C.1. Cognitive results : What was learned? Getting ideas? Reinforcement / Serendipity?

C.2. Affective results : Degree of satisfaction? Failure? Confidence? Comfort ? Frustration?

C.3. Accomplishment in relation to task(s) : Degree of contribution? Fulfilling assignment? Next step?

C.4. Meeting expectations : Getting, obtaining what needed? Too much, too little? Uncertainty?

C.5 Time aspects : Saving time? Wasting? Speed of service? Sufficiency of allocated time?

C.6 Money estimates : Estimate of dollar value obtained. Saved? Spent? Lost if service not available?

Above taxonomy helps a lot for evaluating the library and information services. The objective of this paper is not to evaluate the services involved; it only provides suggestions for applying these tools and techniques for evaluating the library and information services.

CONCLUSION

It is important to study value of library and information services in more specific term than ever before because such services are in transition and faced increased competition.

Hence this is the time when librarians can assess their position and create some strategies for change in order to survive and possibly come out strong. Librarians are always asked to provide statistics of usage but are not asked to valuing the services on those classes and sub classes. If the policy makers and the administrators for whom the librarians are working would know the fact they might take further step for improving the service pattern.

REFERENCES

1. Assessing the value of library services Online at **http://** info.emeraldinsight.com/librarians/management/viewpoints/ measure.htm?PHPSESSID=6p12bcsprj526oujon1llkobe3&part=3
2. Ahituv, N. & Neuman, S. (1986) . Decision making and the value of information. In: Principles of information systems for management. analysis: (pp. 36–73) , Dubuque, IA: Brown
3. Baker, S. L. & Lancaster, F. W. (1991) . The measurement and evaluation of library services (2nd ed.) . Arlington, VA: Information Re-sources.
4. Bawden, D. (1991) . User-oriented evaluation of information systems and services. Brookfield, VT: Gower.
5. Roslyn, Donald(2000) valuing Library Services. Online at http:// www.insitepro.com/donald2.htm
6. Tefko Saracevic and Paul. B. Kantor (1996) Studying the Value of Library and Information Services.Part I. Establishing a Theoretical Framework online at *http://comminfo.rutgers.edu/~tefko/ JASIS1998value1.pdf*

5
Capacity Building of Library Professionals with Reference to Application of Information and Communication Technology

Prasanna Kumar Barik
D.B.Ramesh

INTRODUCTION

ICT has profound effect on the progress and development of human civilization .The emergence of ICT is one of the wonderful gifts of modern science and technology which has brought tremendous changes in Library and Information Science. Application of ICT to library and information work has revolutionized the traditional concept of libraries from a store house of books to an intellectual information centre. The application of ICT has brought a phenomenal change in the information collection, preservation, and dissemination scenario of the world. It becomes the blessings in disguise for the library professionals. According to Encyclopedia of computer science, "information and communication technology is an imprecise term frequently applied to broad areas of activities and technologies associated with the use of computers and communications. Mahapatra, M and Ramesh, D.B. defined ICT as "information communication technology is the result of the technological convergence of existing single isolated technologies via, computer technology, communication technology, information processing, publishing technology etc." The term, information and communication technologies (ICT) refers to forms of technologies that are used to create, store, share or transmit, exchange information. This broad definition of ICT includes such technologies as: radio, television, video, DVD, telephone (both fixed line and mobile phones), satellite systems, computer and network hardware and software; as well as the equipment and services associated with these technologies, such as videoconferencing and electronic mail. (UNESCO 2002)

NEED OF ICT IN LIBRARIES

Various factors have contributed to bring about change from traditional to ICT based library operations. Basically ICT is needed in libraries for the following two main reasons:

In terms of various problems faced by the traditional library systems : The manual performances of library functions were getting difficult because of the following main reasons:

- ***The size of recorded information*** is ever growing

whereas space available at the disposal of each library is limited. No library can think of getting additional space every year , although the collection will grow continuously ;

- Due to ***knowledge explosion*** , the library has faced a great problem of storage capacity;
- ***Library operations*** due to potential growth of information ,could take many by hours to perform manually;
- Due to ***information explosion***, all sorts of house keeping jobs and information works can be performed manually with less effectiveness and less accuracy

In terms of various facilities provided by computers and related technologies : The various facilities of using computers and other telecommunication media/ devices in managing libraries are manifold. Some of the facilities are as follows:

- ***Speed*** **:** A computer can carry out an instruction in less than a millionth of a second. Searching of information, compilation of bibliographies, and preparation of current awareness bulletins, indexing and sorting can be processed by a computer in a few hours.
- ***Storage*** **:** Human brain can store pieces of information to some limitation whereas computers can store voluminous data.
- ***Accuracy*** **:** Computers can perform functions very accurately
- ***Reliability*** **:** Computers and all related technologies have long life if maintained properly. The data gathered in it are reliable
- ***Repetitiveness*** **:** A computer can be used repetitively

to process information

- ***Compactness*** **:** The present day computers are laptop / palmtop, which do not occupy more space.

COMPONENTS OF ICT IN LIBRARIES

ICT refers to the devices and tools used in the generation, gathering processing, storage, retrieval, communication and delivery of information. It is the convergence of computers, communication and micro-electronic base technologies. In recent years, IT has expanded so rapidly to include a wide array of devices information products and services that transformed the role of a library into a gateway of accessing global information resources. The components of information technology, which frequently used in library and information center are - **Computer Technology, Communication Technology** and **Reprography & Publishing Technology**

Computer Technology : The wide spread use of computer technology has made dramatic developments in the information transmission process in every field of human life. The current developments in computer technology include: Mainframe Computer, Super Computer, Mini Computer, Personal Computer, Microchip Technology, Artificial Intelligence, Software Technology, and CD-ROM Technology.

Communication Technology : Communication or telecommunication technologies are used to transmit information in the form of signals between remote location, using electrical or electromagnetic media as carriers of signals. Communication technologies include - Audio Technology, Audio-visual Technology, Motion Picture, TV, Videodisc, Videotext, Teletext, Telephone, Fax, E-mail, Voice mail, Teleconference, Satellite Technology, Internet, and

Network Technology.

Reprography and Publishing Technology : Reprography and Publishing Technology is used to identify that field of information processing which concerns with technologies and equipments for the reproduction of documents. Micrographic is that field of information technology which concerns making use of microforms. It includes optical media for the high density recording and storage of optically encoded information .Printing Technology is another device for the reproduction of document. It is a device that converts computer output into printed images.

IMPACT OF ICT ON LIBRARIES AND LIBRARIANS

Today, Libraries have wide range of opportunities and variety of challenges offered by the rapid development and wide application of information communication technology. ICT has become integral part of all library operations and information services. This movement of using ICT in libraries has dramatically changed the ways by which data acquisition, processing and access has been carried out and the libraries have provided information services. ICT usage in Indian Libraries has gained considerable momentum in recent years which is going to increase at much faster rate in future. The benefits of using ICT and information centers may be consolidated as to:

- eliminate duplication of efforts,
- facilitate effective utilization of funds,
- facilitate to market library services.
- improve accuracy and control,
- improve collection management,
- improve efficiency of library operations,

- increase image,
- improve management information,
- improve quality of existing services,
- improve uniformity and standardization,
- increase ability to share resources,
- introduce new services,
- perform tasks not possible by the manual system, and
- rapid communication.

WHY ICT IN LIBRARIES

The main points of application of ICT in libraries are as:

- To capture , store , manipulate , and disseminate information;
- To introduce and provide new services , revive the new services by providing faster access to the resources , by overcoming the space and time barriers;
- To provide need –based browsing and retrospective search services to the users;
- To have large number of databases in CDs;
- To avoid routine and redundant activities;
- To utilize the staff for providing better information services;
- To upgrade/ develop the library professionals for coping with the frequent changes in ICTs;
- To encourage networking and resource sharing in local level;
- To have access a large number of national and international journals those are being published only in e-form;

- To digitize the documents for preservation of cultural heritage and also for space saving;
- To support library functions, other office works and developing in-house databases;
- To retrieve and disseminate information in users defined format;
- To access other library catalogue databases through library networks;
- To improve the efficiency of the library functions and professionals and
- To improve the cost effectiveness of library operations.

AREAS OF ICT APPLICATION IN LIBRARY

Many libraries mainly concentrated on the house keeping functions consist of acquisition, serial control, cataloguing, circulation, reference etc. In some libraries, it has expanded on the library management system to incorporate OPAC, Web OPAC, CD-ROM networks, etc.

Acquisition System : In a computerized library, the acquisition process from book requisition to procurement is done by the computer. It is easier and automatic to maintain bill register, expenditure register, and vendor directly etc. Online queries may be made on titles, order invoices, vendors and budget heads. Various reports such as approval request form; purchase orders; overdue notices; budget and expenditure analysis; payment requisition report, accession register, and bill register can be generated and printed on requirement.

Cataloguing System : Cataloguing is one of the important functions, which link user's requirements to the documents in a library. In cataloguing, we take into account the various approaches of users in searching for a book in the library and make catalogue entries in order to ensure that each major search approach of a user is satisfied Computerized catalogue is the most efficient tool in retrieving information about the documents in a library easily and quickly .

Classification System : Call number of the book is to be assigned manually and relevant call number for each book is to be fed in the computer through keyboard. Computer can help in alphabetical classification only by taking key words from acquisition module. It helps the professionals to improve accuracy and speed in classification.

Circulation System : The use of technological devices such as computers, barcode scanners and its software in circulation help in performing these routine operations easily and quickly. An automated circulation system provides information about the location of the item on loan , at the bindery, on reserve , being re-catalogued , details of items on loan to a borrower , a reserve ; print recall notices ,renewal ,calculation of fines, printing of fine notices, printing due date slips, automatically generating orders for lost books and provision for inter library loan transactions.

Serial Control System : Serial includes periodicals, newspapers, manuals, journals, proceedings, transactions, etc. of societies and monographic series. An automatic serial control system provides the following benefits:

- Ordering new journals; Renewal/discontinuation; sending reminders; Receiving the journals;
- Preparation of a list of periodicals received; preparation of a list of periodicals cancelled; preparation of a list of holdings; List of holdings with their status i.e. on shelf, in binding, in circulation etc.
- Bindery management; recording and accessioning

bound volumes and

- Keeping track of amount spent on subscriptions, binding etc; Estimation of the budget for the next year; announcement of the missing serials for recording the same.

Article Indexing System : The article indexing system facilitates indexing and abstracting of articles from various journals, technical reports, conference proceedings, monographs etc. It includes scanning of articles entry of citation and online searches on author, keywords / descriptors and even word-based free text searches . This system also provides periodic documentation SDI, bibliographies on specific subjects etc.

OPAC System : The library staff and the public can usually access it at computers within the libraries or from home via the Internet. OPAC terminals began to replace card catalogue in many libraries in the 1980s. In its most simple form, a library OPAC could consist of nothing more than a simple index of the bibliographic data catalogue in the system. OPAC modules rely on pull-down menus , popup windows , dialogue boxes , mouse operations and other graphical user interface components to simplify the entry of search commands and formatting of retrieved information. OPAC system also provides the facility to request acquisition of titles, to reserve materials, and to send personalizes SDI, overdue /recall/collect notices. The concept of Web OPAC is recent origin and it is serving as a gateway to the resources not only held by the respective library but also to the holding of other participating libraries without limiting to local collection but going beyond further to regional ,national and international levels .

Bulletin Board System : Bulletin board is a facility to display/ view in an electronic bulletin board, news announcements, etc. with constant updating of information .Several bulletin boards can be made available in the network for each of specific categories of users, node types, staff, disciplines, etc.

Storage Technologies : For century's paper has been considered as the appropriate medium for storing of information .But now the new technologies have succeeded in storing information on various media. Mass storage is necessarily to meet the following needs:

- providing large volume digital storage for archival management;
- providing users with immediate access to the rapidly growing volume of data and information that is stored in digital information system and is likely to be distributed on optical media in the future;
- providing users with access to multimedia information quickly and interactively through the integration of technologies ; and
- Transferring large volumes of data and / or files from one system to another

Multimedia : Multimedia is media that uses multiple forms of information content and information processing (e.g. text, audio, graphics, animation, and video, interactive) to inform or entertain the users. Video conferencing, voice chatting computer animation, desktop publishing are some of the finest testimonies of the growing importance of multimedia. Multimedia technologies are designed to enable users to integrate and manipulate data from diverse sources on single hardware platform.

CD-ROM : Many libraries depend more on CD-ROM databases than the online systems because CD-ROM needs only a fixed annual charge and there is no need to rely upon telecommunications networks. Online searches are used just to supplement the information obtained from CD-ROM .The popularity of some CD-ROM databases and the presence of local or wide area networks in many organizations along with the increasing availability of networking solutions have provided librarians with an impetus for exploring the feasibility of simultaneous multi user access.

DVD (Digital Video Disc or Digital Versatile Disc) : DVD is an Optical Disk Storage media format that can be used for data storage, including movies with high video and sound quality. Some of the benefits of DVD are:

- its utility as a single file system for all disc types
- its backward read compatibility with existing CD and future compatibility with read or write and WORM disc
- to represent more multimedia elements and to integrate many reference sources on a single DVD disc.
- its low cost
- DVD can deliver the data at a higher rate than CD-ROM
- better security of data
- its high performance for sequential and non-sequential data

Library Networks : Library networking is meant to promote and facilitate sharing of the resources available within a group of libraries in order to provide maximum information to users. Several models have emerged that provide specific services. Numerous library networks have been in place and are still in existence, through out the world. Application networks which are set up by or for a specific community or for serving well- defined end- users. Networks like online computer library center (OCLC), Information and library network centre (INFLIBNET), Developing Library Network (DELNET), Calcutta Library Network (CALIBNET),

Bombay Library Network (BONET), Ahmedabad Library Network (ADINET) and Madras Library Network (MALIBNET) are examples of this category.

Library Consortium : The term consortia has been defined as "cooperative arrangement among groups or institutions or libraries" .A library consortium is a formal association of libraries not under the same institutional control, but usually restricted to a geographical area, number of libraries , use of materials , or subject interest established to develop resource sharing among members. With the advent of the Internet, it is possible to provide instantaneous access to the sources available not only within the organization, but other institutions that participate in the consortia program. The committee of Experts on Consortia-based subscription to Electronic Resources for Technical Education system in India listed the following benefits:

- consortia-based subscription to electronic resources would increase the access base more e-journals at substantially lower cost
- consortia-based subscription provides rational utilization of funds.
- provides qualitative resource sharing and effective document delivery services.
- increases user base access from desktop of users
- provides electronic contents licensing for providing access to Bibliographic , database e- journals , full text reports , conference proceedings etc.
- facilitates inter library lending and document delivery.

Internet Technology : The Internet is an exciting and intellectually stimulating social medium of communication and information. Internet has become an indispensable resource for libraries world wide to enhance the collection, improve services and operations. Internet has made easy access to information sources like books, journals, electronic publications etc. The internet can be successfully utilized for providing reference service because various primary and secondary sources of information are available online.

Smart Card : A smart card, chip card or integrated circuits card, is defined as any pocket sized card with embedded integrated circuits which can process information .This implies that it can receive input which is processed by way of the ICC. Memory cards contain only non-volatile memory storage components, and perhaps some specific security logic. Microprocessor cards contain volatile memory and microprocessor components. Application of smart card in library delivers increased efficiency by providing a means of regularity updating the library's inventory and maintaining an accurate control of borrowing records.

RFID : Among the many uses of RFID technologies is its deployment in libraries. This technology has slowly begun to replace the traditional barcodes on library items. However, the RFID tag can contain identifying information, such as a books title or material type, without having to be pointed to a separate database. The information is read by an RFID reader, which replaces the standard barcode reader commonly found at a library's circulation desk. RFID was first proposed in the late 1990 as a technology that would enhance workflow in the library setting. Rockefeller University in New York may have been the first academic library in the United States to utilize this technology, whereas Farminton Community library may have been the first public library, both of which began RFID in 1999.

CAPACITY BUILDING OF LIBRARY PROFESSIONALS

Capacity building of Library professionals will be the key to the widespread infusion of ICT enabled practices in the library system. In service training of library professionals will comprise of Induction Training as well as Refresher Courses. The refresher trainings should be carried out every year to enable the library professionals to share, learn and keep abreast of the latest trends in ICT based service and management of the library. Training in ICT will be integrated with general training programme organized for Library professionals at all levels in order to popularize its use and to demonstrate effective practices in ICT. Professional participation in the digital content development process will catalyze its broad based usage in the library activities. Library professionals' capacities will be developed in instructional design, selection and critical evaluation of digital content, and strategies for effective use of digital content to enhance users satisfaction by providing right content to the right reader at right time.

NEW SKILLS AND KNOWLEDGE REQUIRED FOR LIBRARY PROFESSIONALS

Information sources and services being provided by libraries to their users need to adapt to the electronic information environment being experienced by most information end-users. In addition to the traditional library and information management skills and expertise , more so in the use of modern information and communication technologies , automated information service , electronic publishing , digital information management . New information professionals should acquire technological skill, commitment to continuous improvement of skills, techniques and strategies and sensitivity to network environment. In modern ICT based library services, the information professionals handle various types of activities in relation to the use of computers and other new information technologies. Therefore, in order to cope with such changes the library professionals must be acquired some sort of knowledge about the following skill :

- Managerial skill;
- Preservation skill;
- Technological skill –(i) Internet and Networks using ; (ii) Computer & IT Tools using (iii) Information Retrieval
- Communication skill.

CHALLENGES FOR LIBRARY PROFESSIONALS

The use of ICT in libraries has raised a number of challenges. These include:

- Changing role of libraries and librarians;
- Funding for libraries
- Copyright management
- Information access
- Preservation of digital information resources
- Legal deposit

CONCLUSION

Today computer and related technologies has brought revolutionary changes in the whole world of information .Perhaps , this is the most exciting period in the history of human race when world's most population is shifting from 'techno-illiterate' to techno-literate'. The society is undergoing a kind of transformation. With the passing of each day, we find that ICT has affected almost every sector of our life, bringing a change in the case of people's think, interaction etc. This revolutionary change is also true in the case of libraries and information centers. Libraries and information centers can hardly function today without computers and information technologies. A well-equipped library with the facilities of modern information infrastructures and technologies could satisfy the maximum demand of the present technology conscious users.

REFERENCES

1. Babu, T.A. 1999. Automation of public Libraries. Herald of Library Sci., 38: 47-53.
2. Blurton, C. 1999. New directions in education. In: UNESCO's world communication and information 1999-2000 , Paris ; UNESCO : 46-61
3. Chisenga, J. 2004. ICT in Libraries: An overview and general introduction to ICT in libraries in Africa. Paper presented at INASP ICT workshop, held at Johannesburg, South Africa on 21-23, July 2004. Available at: *http://www.inasp.info/lsp/ict-workshop-2004/session1-chisenga.ppt.*
4. Chidnandappa, S and Dharnendra, P. ICT tools for building digital learning environment. DRTC-ICT Conference on Digital Learning Environment, Bangalore, 2006.
5. Haneefa, K. Application of wireless technologies in libraries. Proceeding of the second International CALIBER on road map to new generation of libraries using emerging technologies, 23, 3; 2003; 4-5.
6. Henderson, F. 1992. Relationships with users. In information technology in special libraries; Margaret Britting (Ed.), London, Routledge, pp 98-106.
7. Mahapatra, M and Ramesh, D.B. ICT in Libraries. Bhubaneswar, Reproprint, 2006.
8. Mercelle, 1998. Available at : *http://www.education.pwv.gov.za/content/documents/143pdf*
9. Nasiruddin, M. and Roknuzzaman, 2002. Technological Influences

on Library Environment: Contemporary challenges for the professionals of Bangladesh, Rajshahi University studies, part-c .10: p23-39.

10. Pradhan, M.R. 2004. Developing Digital Libraries: Technologies and Challenges, Library Herald, New Delhi , 42 . 100.
11. Ramana , P.V. Information Technology applications in libraries. 2004. Ess Ess Publications; Delhi.
12. Rao, I.K.R. 1992. Library Automation, New Delhi; New Age Intl. , pp. 1-7.
13. Saraf, V. 1998. Dynamics of the Information Technology and Its Implications for Library and Information Education in the New Millennium. Study presented at an international seminar entitled Library automation: Problems and Prospects" held at University of Dhaka, Dhaka, Bangladesh, pp. 1-10.

6
Capacity Building for Library Professionals using Web 2.0

Rosalien Rout
Bulu Maharana

INTRODUCTION

The information environment of libraries is changing faster than ever happened. The digital revolution driven by ICT innovations has transformed the library and redefined the role of LIS professionals fundamentally. The emergence of Internet and especially the web has brought in a communication revolution enabling every one to access, retrieve and send information anywhere easily, instantaneously and inexpensively. The Web has transformed the way libraries functioning and providing library services to the user community. World Wide Web or in short the Web provide an unparallel media for delivery of information with greater speed and economy.

In recent years with the evolution of web application the latest buzzword in the Internet world is Web 2.0. It describes the changing trends in the use of WWW technology that aim to enhance creativity, communications, secure information sharing, collaboration and functionality of the Web. It is a user-centered application enabled by the emergence of platforms such as Wiki, Blogs, Social Networking, RSS, Podcasts, Instant Messaging, free images and video uploading etc. that collectively allowed easy content creation and sharing by everyone.

The question which inevitably arises for us is: how does the concept of Web 2.0 relate to the library world? Many experts including Notess, Farkas, Maness, etc., have opined that, Web 2.0 is of vital interest for libraries as it involves users through interactive and collaborative activities such as adding tags, contributing comments and rating different library items. Abram portrays the image of the new librarian, Librarian 2.0. The librarians understand the power of Web 2.0 opportunities; investigate and ultimately adopt these tools. Librarians 2.0 connect users to experts' discussions and to communities of practice; they develop social networks and encourage users to develop content and metadata. Librarians 2.0 understand the 'wisdom of crowds' and the new roles of the blogosphere and wikisphere. Maness adds that Librarian 2.0 acts as a facilitator. The paper discusses the role of Web 2.0 tools in building capacity for the LIS professionals.

WHAT IS CAPACITY BUILDING?

Capacity Building can be broadly defined as, '*the set processes, both external and internal, that help people as individuals and as groups to manage their changing environment and enhance their capacity to address the challenges related to development in a sustainable manner*". In the context of Capacity Building, capacity is defined as the broad ability of a person or a group to take up responsibilities.

Capacity building is the development of an organization's core skills and capabilities such as leadership, management, finance and fundraising, programs and evaluation, human resource management, service delivery, external relations in order to build the organization's effectiveness and sustainability. Effective capacity building embraces all three aspects of development that is human resource development, organizational development and institutional development. It is an on going process of continuous learning, adaptation and innovation in dealing with anticipated problems or issues. A process where issues today must be dealt with efficiently and effectively, but relevance for future work must also be considered.

Just like other organization professionals, capacity building for LIS Professionals becomes a key issue for adapting new changes. Libraries need to focus on building their capacity if they want to maximize their effect on the research and development community. LIS professionals need to dedicate themselves to raising capacity building to the same level of importance as that of their organization's critical functions. However, LIS professionals must identify core competencies need to work effectively in a new environment. The possible avenues for training and development for LIS Professionals are workshop, refresher/ orientation, conferences/seminars, courses at universities and institutions, distance education programmes, online training courses, self-learning etc.

WEB 2.0 AND LIBRARY 2.0: THEIR DIMENSIONS

The term **'web 2.0'** was officially coined in 2004 by Dale Dougherty & Tim O'Reilly during a brainstorming session of a conference organized to discuss the future of web and emerging techniques. It is being defined differently by the experts, few say it is a technology which provides experience to the users while using the internet and few say it is an advance stage of Internet or Web. Actually, web 2.0 is not a new technology or new set of rules, it is an idea. At the heart of this idea is a web platform where users control their own data from where scalable services are offered .Web 2.0 is about services rather than packaged software and it is about offering compatible with many devices.

Broadly speaking, the term web 2.0 refers to the second generation of web development and web design that facilitates information sharing, interoperability, user-centered design and collaboration on the World Wide Web. It refers to the set of tools that enable web users to easily conduct two way communications, while web1.0 primarily allowed individual web users to find information. Web 2.0 tools such as blogs, wikis, forum & social-networking sites have transformed web usage into two way communication, enabling to interact with prospects, customers and others.

Library 2.0 is "*the application of interactive, collaborative, and multi-media web-based technologies to web-based library services and collections*". It refers to the application of Library 2.0 theory to aspects of librarianship.

Features of Web 2.0

- Web –based applications can be accessed from anywhere.
- Simple application solves specific problems.
- Values lies in content not the software used to display content.
- Data can be readily shared.

- Distribution is bottom-up, not top-down.
- User can access and use tools on their own.
- Social tools encourage creating, collaborating, editing, categorize, exchange and promote information.
- Network effects are encouraged; the more people who contribute, the content gets.

Characteristics of Web 2.0

- The Web 2.0 **as a platform** which permits the building virtual applications, drawing data and functionality from a number of different sources as appropriate, that means they can be used from any location .
- The Web 2.0 as **'participative architecture'** meaning that, the Web doesn't depend on large organization to have contents, but the user collaborate.
- The web 2.0 **as a decentralized** system in its architecture, participation and usage to make room for the majority of users that can use very specific services and websites. It is about communication and facilitating community.
- The web 2.0 application **are modular**, with developers and users able to pick and choose from a set of interoperating components in order to build something that meets their needs.
- The web 2.0 **applications work for the user** and are able to locate and assemble content that meets our needs, rather than forcing us to conform to the paths laid out for us by content owners or their intermediaries.
- The web 2.0 as an expression of **collective intelligence**, users edit and publish contents that are

linked from other users, creating and interlinked network.

WEB 2.0 TECHNOLOGIES

The technologies used in web 2.0 are

AJAX (Asynchronous Java Script and XML) : It is a combination of XML and java script that allows for the creation of dynamic & interactive web applications. It enables web 2.0 sites to behave dynamically, so that they feel more like computer programs than static web pages.

API (Application Programming Interface): It is a software , communication interface ,which is a set of functions and procedures that allow different software to communicate with each other.

MASHUP: It is a hybrid web application that uses content from other web applications to crate a new complete content.

RSS (Really Simple Syndication): It is a data format or protocol used to syndicate or distribute contents to subscribers of a new website. it is the technology which facilitates users to keep track of new updates on selected websites. It makes it easy for computer users to receive content from their favorite providers whenever the content is updated. Instead of having to remember to visit a website to read a favorite column.

BLOG: It is a periodically updated website that compiles texts or articles from one or several authors in chronological order. It is a simple content website created with inexpensive self-publishing tools.

WIKIS: this is a type of website where users create, edit, delete or change content; this is an interactive, easy and quick way to make a webpage. A clear example is wikipedia.

SOCIAL NETWORKS: it is the most promoting and most talked technology of present days .This allows people to create virtual communities (personal or professional) over the internet for interaction .social networks are online communities where people meet, socialize, execute digital files etc. Face book, Myspace, Orkut, Plick and Flick are few popular examples of social networks.

IM (Instant Messaging): in simple words it is known as chat. It is a form of real time communication between two or more people based on typed text, images etc.

POD CASTING: it defined as "a digital media file" or collection of files that is distributed over the internet by syndicated download, through web feeds, to portable media players and personal computers .The file be played back on a computer or personal player i.e. ipod or mobile etc.

TAGGING: A tag is a user generated key word used to describe online content. tags make it easier for both humans and search engines to find relevant and related information

USES OF WEB2.0 TECHNOLOGIES IN LIBRARIES

The development of libraries and permanent evolution of web applications provide an opportunity to redesign the services offered by libraries with the aim of improving their quality and fomenting user participation. Below we will show some of the services and ways of implementing/using current web 2.0 trends into libraries.

Name of the Web 2.0 tool	Use of Web 2.0 tools in libraries
Blogs	The use of blogs in libraries can be extensive and is only limited by the type of library and the users. Some of the applications of Web 2.0 in libraries include: • Librarians can start their blogs to encourage interaction amongst users and library staff. • Blogs can serve as a platform where the users can file concerns, quries and suggestions regarding the services and activities of library. • Blogs can also be used for the collection development where the users request the resources • It allows users to share ideas, opinions and contents, serves as a discussion forum It can be used as a tool for posting Minutes of the Meetings for necessary actions.
Wiki	• It helps in creating collaborative spaces for users to generate and update information. • Libraries can open their webpages in wikis and can provide social interaction and discussions among librarians and library users. • Wikis can also be used by the users to share information and enhance the content, and a record of these transactions is archived for future references. • Wikis can be used for creating subject guides, subject gateways. • Reference resources wiki can be built.

Really simple syndication (RSS)	Some possible uses off RSS include: • Providing a selection of RSS services related to the users topics of interests. • Implementing of RSS services for OPAC with the aim of automatically seeing the latest books in the catalogue. • It is a tool to broadcast the library's activities. • It helps in dissemination of the contents of new journals issues arrived in the library. • Integrating library services through RSS feeds. • Announce availability of new research and learning opportunities in various academics/research departments.
Social Networking	Some possible uses of social networking are • Libraries can start their social network about latest books or documents of libraries where users can discuss or put their comments on the contents being contained in the documents.

NEED OF CAPACITY BUILDING FOR LIS PROFESSIONALS

In the new digital age, the Web has revolutionized the way content is created and the way people access, use and contribute information and have opened up new possibilities in information retrieval and dissemination. LIS professionals cannot ignore the changing shape of digital environment .The transition of traditional collection to digital or virtual collections presented the LIS professionals with new opportunity, not in a threat & to play a new dynamic role and serve the information based society in better way.

Application of web 2.0 technologies in libraries has taken the libraries into next generation. It make libraries user centric which provokes libraries to share the resources collectively. It has changed the fundamental roles, paradigms and organizational, culture of libraries & LIS professionals. It is important for the LIS professionals to experience web 2.0 tools from a user's perspective and use these tools in modernizing library services. Therefore, LIS professionals have to techno–savvy in today's world of information and technology.

Presently, library professionals are functioning under great pressure to become more efficient to deliver more effective services to the users in the web environment. They need to be confident and competent that they can prepare for new challenges, deal with emerging technologies, and manage change effectively and claim new professional roles. The LIS professionals with better personal, professional and technological competencies have great opportunities and bright future in the modern libraries .Therefore, there is a great necessity on the part of LIS professionals, to learn a great variety of professional skill and competencies for developing & managing libraries and to accomplish the role of LIS professionals in the constantly changing challenging web environment.

For successful implementation of web2.0 technologies in libraries, it is essential that LIS professionals are well trained and posses' requisite knowledge & skill in this respect.

Knowledge and skill

LIS professional need to know and understand

- Meaning of web technology & the recent trends.
- Blog, wikis, social networks, twitter, Ajax-css, mash-ups.

- Pod casting
- Face book
- RSS feeds
- Semantic Web

TECHNICAL KNOWLEDGE REQUIRED

Digital literacy : capacity to read and understand text and audiovisual content.

Media literacy : capacity to produce content and services based on freely available applications, such as blog, wikis, social network and all free software which does not require install

Running a server skill : capacity to install software on a server and customize

Coding skill : can write code and conceive and develop applications

COMPETENCIES THAT REQUIRED TO POSSES IN LIS PROFESSIONAL

- Acceptance of change
- Provide quality service
- Be adoptive, flexible and resistant
- Create awareness among the users, make them accept the changes

CONCLUSION

Library and Information professionals should add new Web 2.0 skills to their current capacity in order to help the users overcoming their anxieties about the new world of networked and digitized information, and to assist them to navigate through the vast amount of information. The greater capacity of the professionals would lead to greater productivity in terms of information analysis, organization, communication and meeting users' need for information effectively and efficiently. .

REFERENCES

1. Mohmed, Hanif N Need foe Web Technology for the libraries: 7th international CALIBER-2009,at Pond cherry University. Pond cherry, feb25-27, 2009. <*www.inflibnet.ac.in/caliber2009/ CaliberPDF/40.pdf* >
2. Saha, Nimai Chand, De Suman, and Paul, Nirmalendu Application of web 2.0 in the Library and Information Sciences; With Special Reference to RSS: 6th convention planner -2008, Nagaland University. Nagaland, Nov06-07, 2008.
3. Rao, Nageswara K and Babu, KH"Role of Librarian in Internet and World Wide Web Environment". Information Science. 4 .1(2001).
4. Ramana, Venkata P The changing Role of Librarian In a Challenging Dynamic Web Environment 4th international convention CALIBER-2006 Gulbarga. Gulbarga feb2-4, 2006.
5. Kanamadi ,Satis, Kadli and Koganuramath,Muttaya" Capacity Building In The Knowledge Environment: A Human Resource Development Approach" < library.igcar.gov.in/readit2007/conpro/ s1/S1_1.pdfdrtc.isibang.ac.in >
6. Burke, Liz. "The role of librarians in the virtual library environment ".The Australian Library Journal. (2001)
7. Sharma, P.L" changing Role of Librarian s in Digital library Era and need of professional Skills,Efficiency & Competency."< drtc.isiblang.ac.in>.
8. Miller, Paul. "Web 2.0: Building the new Library "Ariadne issue45 2005, Sunday, 30-october-2005 <*http://www.ariadne.ac.uk. issue45/miller/intro.html.*>
9. Levy,S & Stone, B "The New Wisdom of the Web". 14 august 2006 *http://www.msnbc.msn.com/id/12015774/site/newsweek*
10. Anderson, P."All that gliters is not gold: web 2.0 and the librarian." Journal of Librarianship and Information Science, 39.4(2007):195-198

7
Capacity Building of Libraries to Achieve Excellence in Digital Era: An Overview

Sunil Kumar Satpathy
Bijalaxmi Rautaray
Chandra Kanta Swain

INTRODUCTION

It is seen that the Library and Information Science discipline have borrowed many concepts and terms from other disciplines has as computer science, management, economics, statistics etc. The popular terms which the LIS discipline has borrowed from computer science are networking, digital library ,web 1.0,web 2.0,web 3.0 etc. Similarly many terms have been borrowed from management disciplines such as corporate governance, stress management, walk life balance, knowledge management, and capacity building and so on. Among various such terms, capacity building has become a buzz word in library management. But in reality we have not been able to use this concept in libraries in its true or wider context. Only we have been able to use this concepts in its narrower context which have lead the modern libraries to a house of misconception and misinterpretation of these terms and the library & information science professional as a joker of all these modern technology and concepts. This has resulted in the poor performance of the libraries and people are not able to see a vast change in library environment in true sense in spite of several slogans on change in library environment due to the rapid development of Information Communication Technology.

WHAT IS CAPACITY BUILDING?

Capacity building in literary terms is to increase the capacity of an organization or individual by which it will be able to perform extra responsibilities in a perfect way. It is not only to enhance the system or services of libraries but also to reach in a state by which it will be able to contribute for the development of other libraries and the society as a whole

NEED FOR CAPACITY BUILDING

Library, may it be academic, public or special has to ply as a service institution. Since the target users have no expectation limit, libraries have to increase its capacity in terms of collection, organization and services to satisfy their users. Further, the importance of such capacity building is much more in the age of Information Technology, where it is not possible to acquire all materials needed for their users due to information explosion but to satisfy the changing demands of users. In this context libraries have no other option than to adopt capacity building programme and to adopt collaborative mode of living through library networking, resource sharing, formation of consortia etc. The basic need for capacity building in libraries can be summarized as follows.

a) **Rapid development of ICT & its use by libraries** : The developments of Information Communication Technology have affected all walks of libraries and libraries are remarkably affected by this development. Due to this, the traditional manual libraries have been changed to computerized libraries, then automated libraries, digital libraries and more recently virtual libraries. Accordingly the collection, organization and services of the libraries have also been changed to a great extent. The library collections are becoming more and more electronic and digital day by day, so also the organization and dissemination process of such information have changed.

b) **Increase in the expectation of users**: The expectation of users have changed tremendously keeping in pace with the social changes, which is highly influenced by the use of Information communication technology. The IT has made the whole world into a small village, so that everyone is aware of the development of other parts irrespective of places ,In this situation ,one library cannot restrict the expectation /need of its users in the name of non availability of information resources, finance, manpower etc because the users know what is happening in other libraries and what type of services are being provided by other libraries

c) **Availability of large amount of literatures in every field of knowledge:** The generation of huge amount of literatures(both print and electronic) in all field of knowledge has posed problems for libraries and libraries are yet to find a suitable solution of this. The financial constraints, shrinking library budget, infrastructural facilities for better organization of library materials etc have compelled libraries to rethink on their collection development policies to satisfy its users in a better way.

d) **Ever increasing price rise of both print & electronic resources**: Over past few years, the prices of both print and electronic resources have increased remarkably; as a result libraries are facing a lot of problems in acquiring required library materials within the limited budgetary provision.

e) **Shrinking/static library budget:** It is a fact that library budgets in most libraries is seems to be static and in some cases shrinking taking into consideration the induction of new IT based systems and services by libraries. Libraries, being the non–profit service unit/ organization are mostly neglected by the parent bodies in all aspects more particularly, in providing necessary funding to carry out its function smoothly.

f) **Contribute for organizational excellence**: Although libraries are not recognized properly by parent bodies, these are considered as an important organ, more particularly in academic setup. It has become a trend for academic institutions to be accredited by various national bodies such as NAAC, NBA, ISO etc to claim as an institute of excellence. In this context, libraries being part of the academic institution has to contribute for organization excellence by streamlining its system and services.

CAPACITY BUILDING BY MANAGING LIBRARY RESOURCES

Capacity building of libraries can be possible by managing its basic components such as collection, human resources and finance properly.

Management of Library Collection

Over past few decades, along with print resources, resources such as electronic and online have occupied a significant place in library collections. Thus the library's collection of today is of hybrid nature consisting of print resources, non-print resources, electronic resources, online resources etc which need to be managed properly through systematic procurement, organization and dissemination. Some methods of effective management of library resources are as discussed below.

Library Automation/RFID : Generally library automation means the works and services of libraries are automated with the help of any software package through computer. It makes the library system systematic & error free which is not possible manually. Automation enables libraries to provide services very efficiently, rapidly, effectively, adequately and economically. Besides, it reduces the time of both library staff and users in handling the routine work of the library such as issue and return, information about documents and users etc, there by helps in managing the library resources. The automation work can be carried out by either commercial software packages available in the market or can be developed indigenously. Similarly RFID, that stands for Radio Frequency Identification technology is the latest technology, used for library transaction, inventory functions and theft detection system and thus helps in the proper management of the library resources.

OPAC/Web OPAC : Online Public Access Catalogue (OPAC) and web based OPAC have become important tools in automated library environment. It provides access to the library s' holdings through various catalogues and indexes such as author catalogue, title catalogue, subject catalogue and the classified catalogue. Besides the basic search strategies, OPAC also provides information on new additions of books and serials. All these tools facilitate proper management of library resources.

CD/DVD Mirroring : This is helpful in arranging the CD and DVD collection of the library .A number of Mirroring software are available in the market for this purpose.

Creating Gateways for Web Resources : Now a days a large number of web courses are being developed by learned societies, R& D organizations in electronic form. One of the best web courses available in the field of Engineering & Technology is the web course developed by the IITs and IISc, Bangalore through NPTEL project. These web courses can be accessed simultaneously by users through a gateway.

Creation of Digital Libraries : The traditional concept of libraries is gradually becoming obsolete and a new concept of "digital library" is entering slowly. In this changing world of digital library emphasis is more on technology i.e. computer hardware, software, storage format, network connectivity etc than the physical organization of documents. The rapid proliferation of information in the networked digital environment poses challenges as well as opportunities for the digital libraries. Digital library is a library of digital objects of any types having facilities for organization, maintenance and dissemination of information in a suitable and effective manner. Many libraries have already created digital libraries in their institutions and a good number are in progress.

Creation of Institutional Repositories : Institutional Repositories is a set of services offered by an organization or group of organizations to its members for the management and dissemination of scholarly materials in digital format created by the organization and its community members, such as theses, dissertations, technical reports, teaching materials etc. For this purpose libraries are using different open source software. Many open source software are available now a days for this purpose.

Management of Human Resources

Human resources of libraries are the total skills knowledge, creative, abilities, talents and aptitudes of its workforce as well as the values, attitudes, approaches, and beliefs of the individuals engaged in the organizational affairs. These are the most vital element apart from technological, financial, physical or any other resources. Without this, no organization including library can achieve its objectives. Therefore, proper management of these vital resources is to be made for its better and effective utilization towards achievement of organization's aims and objectives. Some steps in this regards are discussed below.

Recruitment of skilled/competent manpower: The library environment has undergone tremendous change in recent years in term of collections and services. Accordingly skilled and competent manpower is required to manage the library smoothly satisfying the user's needs.

Recruitment of professionals as per needs: The library structure and services differ from library to library. Accordingly the requirement of library staff varies among libraries. It is also advisable to estimate the requirement of library staff as per the library building, types of collection, types of users and types of services.

Motivate employees properly: Motivation has a direct link with employees performance and motivating staff in libraries is a critical challenge before every manager. Motivation refers to the way in which needs and aspirations of an individual direct and controls his behavior in the organizational context. Motivation implies that one person induces others to perform work properly by ensuring them to satisfy their needs and aspirations. A number of steps can be taken to create motivational environment, major ones of which are :

- Developing quality of work life.
- Human Resource Communication.
- Human Resource Counseling
- Employee Empowerment
- Employee Participation.

Identifying training needs & making provision for training : The training and development of human resources of libraries includes several dimensions such as human resource development system, career planning and development, personal development and organizational development. Both on-the-job and off-the- job training can be provided to library staff.

Performance Appraisal : Performance appraisal is a method of evaluating the behavior of employees in the work place, including both quantitative and qualitative aspects of job performance. It is a systematic and objective way of evaluating both work-related behavior and potential of employees. It is a process that involves determining and communicating an employee how he or she is performing the job and ideally, establishing a plan of improvement.

Creation of loyalty/belongingness towards libraries : It is seen that the loyalty and belongingness of library staff cannot be developed by providing sufficient motivation .It has created problems for library authorities and libraries are unable to retain good library personnel for a good period of time. It can only be achieved if library staff will be involved in library matters, hence necessary steps need to be taken by the library authorities to encourage library staff in this regard.

Management of Library Finance

Libraries, being the non-profit service organization are ever neglected by the parent organization. As a result the library budget remains almost static and seems to shrink in the context of increasing price of library resources, library technology etc. Hence it is highly necessary to manage the available finance of the library economically and purposefully to run the library smoothly. Following steps may be taken in this direction.

Promotion of ILL service : Inter Library Loan (ILL) system is highly significant on the view point that no library is able to procure all available library resources to satisfy their users. Hence for rarely used resources, libraries need to adopt ILL system .However a set of justified agreement needs to be made among the participating libraries for its success.

Participation in library networks : Library networks are good platforms for library cooperation and resource sharing. A good number of library networks are available at national and regional levels. Every library must participate in these networks as per its suitability.

Formation of library networks : New library networks need to be formed at state level among similar types of libraries which will better facilitate resource sharing **and** consortia mode of acquisition in a better way.

Consortia mode of subscription : Consortium is an association of independent libraries established by formal agreement, usually for the purpose of cooperative acquisition of library materials. Membership may be restricted to a specific geographic region, type of library or subject specialization. To meet the high expectations of users with a limited financial resources ,ever raising price of journals/ books by publishers, libraries have shifted from individual collection development policy to consortia based collection development mainly for e-journals and books. A good number of consortia are available in India to serve the purpose.

Motivating users towards the use of open access journals : Open access journals are peer-reviewed journals and are available freely to the world. But the question arises is how it is free when it consists of many expense such as peer review, manuscripts preparation and server space. The answer is OA journals meet these expenses in the similar way broadcast television and radio stations do. Besides sometimes OA journals gets subsidy from the hosting university or professional bodies, charge a processing fee on accepted articles which is to be paid by authors or sponsoring body and also generate income from other publications, advertising, auxiliary services etc. Now a days a good number of OA journals are available in all field of knowledge and the libraries should motivate their users towards these resources.

Participation in open access movement : The main barriers to access information are the lengthy & traditional peer reviewed process of established journals, the irregular periodicity of publication, exponential increase in the prices of journals and ever decreasing financial provision of the library etc. All these have created problems for libraries & information centers to maintain their collections. Even well financed libraries of reputed institutes are badly affected for the access problems. Now the question arises how to overcome this problem. The only solution to this vital problem is to make research output free accessible i.e. without any restriction of the author, publisher, time, price and access. In other words open access to scholarly information is the only solution to address this issue nowadays.

SUGGESTIONS

The capacity building of a library mainly depends on its library staff. Therefore the LIS professionals need to develop positive attitudes towards the changes which occur in the library environment with the passage of time. Some suggestions for LIS professionals for capacity building in libraries are as follows.

a) Keep update on latest developments
b) Share your ideas with other professionals through web based forums, blogs, Wikipedia
c) Create an environment where everybody feels the existence of library
d) Formulate plans for the development of existing system and services both manually and with the help of technology
e) Develop positive attitudes to serve users
f) Helps other libraries to grow

CONCLUSION

In the present digital era, libraries cannot remain ideally and merely as a store house of books and other documents, rather they have to reach at a state of excellence which is possible through only capacity building to serve their user communities and society. The LIS professionals need to accept these new challenges and find out solutions for their successful existence in the competitive IT age.

REFERENCES

1. Collection building and archiving of e-resources in libraries: issues and concern, by S.K.Satpathy, C.K.Swain & B.Routray.In Digital Libraries (Prof.R.K.Rout Festschrift volume).Mahamaya Pub.House;New Delhi,2008.P.183-96.
2. Open access initiatives by libraries: an overview/S.K.Satpathy & B.Rautray.*In* Libraries in digital environment: problems & prospects/S.K.Satpathy, C.K.Swain & B.Rautray, *Eds*.Mahamaya Pub.House; New Delhi, 2008.P.180-190.
3. Creation of Institutional Repositories using D Space: an experiment/N.K.Mahanta, R.K.Bhoi & S.K.Satpathy.*In* Libraries in digital environment: problems & prospects/S.K.Satpathy, C.K.Swain & B.Rautray, *Eds*.Mahamaya Pub.House;New delhi,2008.P.191-216.
4. Digital Libraries: A need of the Twenty First century C.K.Swain, K.C.Panda & S.K.Satpathy. In Librarianship in 21st Century/ K.C.Panda, Ed. SBG Publication; Bhubaneswar, 2007.P.106-113.
5. Library Automation: What, Why & How in Academic Libraries, by S.K.Satpathy & R.K.Rout, Seminar paper presented in National Seminar on Recent trends in Library & Information Science, DLIS, Sambalpur University, 25-26 Nov.,2001

8

Capacity Building and Leadership in Social Science Research Libraries in India

Sunil Singh Chandel

INTRODUCTION

Social Science(s) deals with the specific study of social phenomena. This does not mean that knowledge gathered from other sources does not provide information about society, social events and social phenomena, however the knowledge gained through scientific studies is considerable, reliable and useful than the knowledge from other sources like authority (parents, teachers, experts of various fields, religious priests etc.), tradition, common sense, media myths, personal experiences etc. Social sciences such as "anthropology, sociology, psychology etc. involve the study of people and their beliefs, behaviour, interaction and several problems produced by human beings. Therefore social science is the system of producing knowledge about the society. In other words it can be said that social science is a method of producing social knowledge through specified procedures involving testing of theories.

The Central and State both the governments have paid special attention for development of research in social sciences. After independence India's contribution towards the development of the social sciences has widened. In this connection, Indian Council of Social Science Research, New Delhi was established by the Government of India with its main mandate to promote social science research in India. In addition there are many organizations and funding agencies supported by national and International organizations, which support researches in social sciences. There are 27 research institutes and six regional centers working in all over India. Apart from these, other organizations have also established and become learned social science research institutions in our country.

The research in social sciences is an important aspect in the society for the development of the society itself. The research in social sciences merely is carried out with the help of libraries. As we know the libraries are the storehouse of recorded knowledge in various forms and provide a platform for improving the quality of research through its services. There has been a tremendous explosion of data and information in recent years, particularly in the field of social sciences, with an increase in the number of research and development institutions at the national and international level. Some of the research institutions and universities possess excellent libraries and information centers and sharing their resources in a right manner. At the same time some of the libraries are facing with multiple problems. Because there is little access to the right information at the right time, it has become difficult to libraries to collect the data and information that are required by policy makers, administrators, researchers and scientists. Thus capacity building for the libraries is the dire need of today. The capacity building for the libraries in social sciences may be governed only through a dynamic leadership.

CAPACITY BUILDING VIS-A-VIS LIBRARY LEADERSHIP

Capacity building is an ongoing process through which individuals, groups, organizations and societies enhance their ability to identify and meet development challenges. The Capacity Building defined as "Specifically, capacity building encompasses the country's human, scientific, technological, organizational, institutional and resource capabilities. A fundamental goal of capacity building is to enhance the ability to evaluate and address the crucial questions related to policy choices and modes of implementation among development options, based on an understanding of environment potentials and limits and of needs perceived by the people of the country concerned" [1]. In terms of libraries, capacity building is much more than training of library professionals and it includes the following: human resource development, the process of equipping individuals with the understanding, skills and access to information, knowledge and training that enables them to perform effectively. The capacity building also encompasses organizational development, the elaboration of management structures, processes and procedures, not only within organizations but also the management of relationships between the different organizations and sectors (public, private, community and other libraries). It consists of institutional and legal framework, development, making legal and regulatory changes to enable organizations, institutions and agencies at all levels and in all sectors to enhance their capacities.

NEED FOR CAPACITY BUILDING AND LEADERSHIP IN SOCIAL SCIENCE LIBRARIES

The needs for capacity building are always changing. There are no ready solutions, and any programme must be appropriate for the present situation of the libraries. The capacity building activities for libraries are based on the key elements: Exchange programme and Resource Sharing, Organizational development, Strengthening libraries and library professionals. The state and central both the government need to improve their capacity to plan, organize and manage the role of libraries in various part of the country. The government plays an increasingly important role in enabling library personnel to enhance the capacities and effectiveness.

Leadership is a central concept related to the theoretical as also the practical forces that set institutions in motion. Many a sound constitutional power structure has been nullified in the absence of sound leadership. It is leadership that transforms the visualized theoretical perspective into real achievements. The success of democracy and development depends on the quality of leadership and the style of their functioning. Decentralization being the major tool in promoting participatory development process, leadership at different level acquires added significance not only politically but also for socio-economic upliftment and equity. Leaders are studied for the functions they perform in view of their position in the power structure. Leaders are thus expected to mobilize, direct, guide and control their groups i.e. their local communities. In this role leaders are expected to have the capability to encourage their community for voluntarily cooperating in the venture of identified common goals. Leadership in this sense refers to specific qualities of leaders and their performance in development.

Development being accepted as sine qua non of sustainability, equity, human dignity, social justice, peace and people's participation it dominates all development studies. Leadership as a driving force of development in concrete situations relates to the influence one has in community decision-making and in extracting people's voluntary cooperation in implementing those decisions.

For this leadership is expected to be intelligent, vibrant, responsive, convincing and likable. Leaders may follow varied methods of mustering people's cooperation, but one thing is certain that the attitude of domination or headship does not yield the required result. Hence, in their activity of organizing people's participation, leaders have to assume the roles of key communicators, catalyst, and development agents for constructive change. For achieving development goals people also have to be taught to help themselves and at the same time hold them accountable for the results of the use of power and responsibilities devolved on them. In the context of libraries it is herculean task for the library authorities to take leadership to perform the strength of the libraries.

There are several bodies working for the betterment of the libraries in India. Knowledge commission is established to solve the problems of the libraries and librarians as well.

SCENARIO OF THE SOCIAL SCIENCE RESEARCH LIBRARIES IN INDIA

There are a number of libraries working for the social science research. Out of which ICSSR leads 27 research institutes and six regional centers in the country itself. It is very disheartening fact that there is no similarity in ICSSR institutes for recruitment process and promotion policy, rules and regulation for the libraries, designation for the library personnel, strengthening the library resources and the process of capacity building. It is noticeable point that head of the NASSDOC is designated as a Director in the scale of Deputy Director. This fact is not justified. However there is a provision of all scales in ICSSR and ICSSR institutes for Professor, Reader and Lecturer. ICSSR evaluate the ICSSR institutes for a certain period. For this, a review committee is being constructed but there is no space for library experts.

CAPACITY BUILDING THROUGH E-JOURNAL CONSORTIA

The concept of library consortia has been introduced in India since a decade. Though it is the need of the hour, Indian libraries have yet to move in a definite direction in this regard. Strong resource-sharing activity among libraries, a prerequisite for the right attitude towards consortia activities, has not been as present in India as could be desired.

The E-Journals have become the largest and fastest growing areas of the digital collections for most of the libraries. For instance, the E-Journals a few years ago numbered just few hundreds of titles, are now running in many thousands and the rate of growth is phenomenal as well as amazing. The advancements in digital technologies and the recent proliferation of E-Publishing across the world have brought in a revolution in journal publication, subscription, access and delivery mechanism. E-journals are the electronic equivalents of their print counter parts possessing numerous additional features. E-Journals often referred to interchangeably as *Electronic Serials*, *Online Journals* and *Electronic Periodicals*.

NASSDOC has made endeavors to provide consortia based journals to ICSSR institutes and called meeting to offer a range of potential advantages to libraries and end-users but the number of libraries are not able to subscribe the e-journals even after the subsidized rate. The ICSSR is ready to pay fifty percent of the amount for e-journals through J-STOR and others but some of the institutes could not manage the remaining amount for the said purpose.

STRENGTHEN LIBRARY, INFORMATION RESOURCES AND OTHER RELEVANT SYSTEMS

Library and information professionals have to learn to scan, filter, interpret, analyze, repackage, and deliver information from a variety of sources in ways that are meaningful to their users.

Harrods's Librarians' Glossary defines information system as an organized procedure for collecting, processing, storing, and retrieving information to satisfy a variety of needs.

According to Bowman, four different components can be identified:

(1) A store of useful information that has been accumulated over a period of time;

(2) a series of techniques used for adding material to and retrieving information from the store upon demand;

(3) a group of people who operate the system and are responsible for selecting information to be added, answering questions, organizing the store, and for implementing and modifying the techniques for both storage and retrieval; and

(4) the user.

The ultimate test of any such system is the degree of satisfaction it gives the user who has specific information needs.

In the purview of the above said activities library professionals must be trained regularly by the technology experts. For this ICSSR has already involved and organized training workshop frequently in different regions of the country.

The Library resources are collection of relevant materials developed specifically to respond or to fulfill the needs of the users. The ICSSR provides library resources to all the institute's libraries regularly free of cost. The idea behind this is to build a body of knowledge and experience that will evolve continuously and provide current information to the researchers of social sciences and to the others involved in order to support social science research.

The institutes' libraries collect material from several different sources in various forms like books, journals, monographs, lectures etc. The library is an evolving, dynamic entity and will therefore continue to grow and expand as the processes develop further. The library resources support capacity-building efforts and create awareness, learning process, practices for gaining knowledge, training and exercises for capacity-building for different purposes.

DIGITIZATION OF INFORMATION SOURCES

Research publications are vital for any professional discipline, and it is crucial to preserve and provide access to them. Due to the amount of important information published in journals, conference proceedings, and reports, these efforts must be on a par with similar initiatives in other countries. Permanent preservation and enhanced access must be ensured vigorously now by the applications of new technology for digitizing and electronic access to valuable contents. Digitization provides unhindered access to information via computer and communication networks, justifying the need for using it for studying literature. At present, very few copies of conference volumes, journals, and reports are published, and these are exclusively distributed to subscribers. The institutions involved rarely encourage readers to subscribe personally to such literature, thus placing it out of the reach of a large number of readers.

SUGGESTIONS

There is a need for networking among the ICSSR Institute's libraries and information centers in the country for optimum resource sharing. Resource sharing and networking in libraries would be powerful tools both for increasing productivity and enhancing services to meet the changing needs of library users. The proposed network ensures effective bibliographic control, document delivery, cooperative acquisition of serials and other literature in the field, and dissemination of relevant information.

There should be uniformity in all the ICSSR's institutes regarding selection procedure, salary structure and promotion, rules and regulation for the institute, and the process of organizing information, document delivery system, computing and communication infrastructures, etc. There should not be discrimination in terms of facilities, salary and social status for library staff with other staff. The library personnel must be treated as the academic staff. This kind of approach may be helpful for improving the quality of research in social sciences.

Keeping all of these points in mind, the rules and regulation for the appointment of head of the NASSDOC must be restructured. The designation of the NASSDOC Director must be updated in terms of salary at par with the Professor. The constitution for the members of the review committee should be restructured consisting of a member for a library expert. A library expert must be exists in the review committee for fair evaluation of the library activities.

CONCLUSION

The leadership for capacity building for libraries is of great importance. The government of India needs to be convinced of the usefulness and utility of library system. It is not just storage and borrowing facilities. The libraries may be helpful in preventing the duplication of research also. As far as the human resources engaged in libraries are also efficient, intelligent and more qualified. Nothing can be developed in a vacuum. The development of human resources is also important in terms of education, training, working and their financial achievement.

It is necessary to emphasize that in the absence of such people, the information system will not function properly. A large amount of research talent and resources will be wasted. It is hoped that the ICSSR institutions and scientists engaged in social research will be able to impress upon the government of India for an early formulation and implementation of an amended policy for ICSSR institutes.

The capacity building activities in India are of recent origin and are fast evolving. The NASSDOC called several meetings of ICSSR institutes at national level for library consortia. These activities are part of the capacity building for libraries in social sciences. As the consortium initiatives demand active involvement of the LIS professionals as well as the promoting / beneficiary institutions, it normally evolves and grows with hardships and bottlenecks. The subscription of E-Journal itself is a complex and complicated process, which adds up problems to the consortium activity in multiple ways. Naturally there will be a host of issues and problems that keep haunting libraries involved in consortia activities.

The leadership approach for capacity building for the libraries bring number of benefits to the said libraries. This strong approach may be helpful to solve the problems like higher investment burden, ensuring uninterrupted access to E-Journals, enabling perpetual access to the early subscribed content for future, increasing the institutional intellectual capability and scientific productivity, opportunities for long term preservation of scholarly materials through state-of-art archiving strategies may be solved easily with the mutual cooperation and learning.

REFERENCES

1. Capacity Building - Agenda 21's definition (Chapter 37, UNCED, 1992.)
2. ICSSR (*www.icssr.org*)
3. Raymond Prytherch and L. M. Harrod, Harrod's Librarians' Glossary of Terms Used in Librarianship, Documentation, and the Book Crafts, and Reference Book, Gower Pub., U.K., 1987.
4. C. M. Bowman, The Development of Chemical Information Systems, in
5. Chemical Information Systems, J. E. Ash, and Ernest Hyde, eds. (Chichester, U.K.: Ellis Horwood, 1975).

9
Capacity Building for Library Professionals in SCERTS, SIES, DIETS of North Eastern Region

P S Kawatra

INTRODUCTION

The North East (NE) India comprises of the seven sister states of Arunachal Pradesh, Assam, Manipur, Meghalaya, Mizoram, Nagaland and Tripura. They form part of the East Himalayan region which extends from Sikkim eastwards and embraces the Darjeeling Hills of West Bengal.

Education

The NE Region comprising seven states has a high literacy level and is rich in ethnic cultural heritage with linguistic diversity. However, the region lacks infrastructure and facilities in educational institutions across sectors and there is a need to improve the quality of education imparted.

Access to educational institutions promoting skill development is a prerequisite for providing trained man power. As per 1991 census literacy rate of NER was 58.09% (all India 52.2%), while in 2001 it was 68.5% (all India 64.8%). Mizoram has the second highest literacy rate in India. The following table gives the number of educational Institutions in the NER.

Prim + UP	*Sec + HS*	*Arts/Sc. Colleges*	*Engg.*	*Medical*	*Uni.*	*Poly-technics*	*ITIs*	*IIT*
56677	7716	497	6	6	13	18	49	1

Source: Draft Report of the Task force on Development Initiatives for the NER, Sept. 2005.

SCERTs, SIEs & DIETs in North Eastern Region

The 1986 National Policy on Education, recommended the creation of State Council of Educational Research and Training (SCERT) in each State as a measure of decentralization of functions of quality education, research and training. SCERTs have been established to bring in qualitative improvement in school education by providing meaningful in-service training to teachers, preparing educational materials like "Teacher's Manual", "Text books", "Question Bank" for teachers and students and undertaking research activities aimed at understanding the problems in the field of school education and finding suitable solutions to them. SCERT is the nodal agency recognized for the admission, examination and certification of Elementary and Nursery Teacher Training courses of two years duration.

The functions of DIETs as spelt out in the PoA (1992) are :

a) Training and orientation of elementary school teachers, headmasters, heads of school complexes, officials of

Education Department, members of VECs, youth, adult and NFE personnel and resource persons for all of the above target groups.

b) Academic and resource support to the elementary (and Adult & NFE) education systems in the district by

- extension activities and interaction with the field;
- providing a resource centre for teachers;
- development of locally relevant teaching aids, evaluation techniques and tools, etc.
- serving as an evaluation centre for elementary schools and programs.

Action research and experimentation to deal with specific problems of the district related to elementary education.

In North Eastern region there are 07 SCERTs and 36 DIETs. In Assam the number of DIETs are 16, Manipur 16, Mizoram 1, Nagaland 2, Arunachal Pradesh 6, Meghalaya 4, Sikkim 1, Tripura 1.

DEFINING CAPACITY BUILDING

UNDP defined 'capacity building' as the creation of an enabling environment with appropriate policy and legal frameworks, institutional development, including community participation, human resources development and strengthening of managerial systems, adding that, UNDP recognizes that capacity building is a long-term, continuing process, in which all stakeholders participate.

Planned development of (or increase in) knowledge, output rate, management, skills, and other capabilities of an organization through acquisition, incentives, technology, and/or training.

Capacity building is defined as the "process of developing and strengthening the skills, instincts, abilities, processes and resources that organizations and communities need to survive, adapt, and thrive in the fast-changing world." (Ann Philbin, Capacity Building in Social Justice Organizations Ford Foundation, 1996)

Capacity Building is much more than training and includes the following :

- Human resource development, the process of equipping individuals with the understanding, skills and access to information, knowledge and training that enables them to perform effectively.

In its broadest interpretation, capacity building encompasses human resource development (HRD) as an essential part of development. It is based on the concept that education and training lie at the heart of development efforts and without HRD most development interventions will be ineffective. It focuses on a series of actions directed at helping participants in the development process to increase their knowledge, skills and understandings and to develop the attitudes needed to bring about the desired developmental change.

Professional education in India has two components – training before joining the profession and skills gained through mid career programmes.

The first component –pre service education – consists of BLIS / MLIS needed for professional jobs in libraries.

In-service training is more informal and is administered both through classes of variable duration offered by the government and professional institutions and through workshops.

NEED

The needs for capacity building are always changing. There are no ready solutions, and any programme must be appropriate for the local situation and organization. Hence the Process of Capacity Building should include steps that ensure assessment, implementation and monitoring that enables development of newer capacity development strategies from time to time.

The Teacher's Training Institutes Libraries in the North - East Region are ill-equipped and unorganized. Reader's services are either non-existent or of below standard. Because of non-availability of classification schedules and cataloguing codes in TTI Libraries, the Librarians find themselves helpless in organising / processing collection. This renders the collection unclassified and uncatalogued.

It is also noticed that various techniques, methods, rules and procedures currently being followed in Teacher's Training Institutes Libraries are obsolete and quite cumbersome and serve no purpose whatsoever. It is now absolutely essential to revise or design them afresh without any further loss of time.

ORIENTATION PROGRAMME FOR LIBRARIANS/ INCHARGE LIBRARIANS OF SCERTS, SIES, DIETS OF NORTH EASTERN REGION (2006-2007)

Realizing the above needs, NCERT organised the training programme "Orientation Programme for Librarians/ Incharge Librarians of SCERTs, SIEs, DIETs of North Eastern Region" from 12th – 16th March. 2007 to fulfill specific objectives, which are as follows :

Specific Objectives

The objectives of the orientation – cum – in-service training to the Librarians / Teacher Incharge of SCERTs, SIEs and DIETs were :

- to inculcate reading habits among users;
- to plan new services and enhancing the existing services using IT;
- to sharpen and up-date LIS professionals skill & knowledge;
- to develop model libraries using the latest technology within the limited resources; and
- to create a forum for interaction among library and information professionals to keep abreast of the latest developments in the field of information science and related IT applications.

PLANNING THE TRAINING PROGRAMME

Requesting the States to Depute Participants

Director, SCERTs & Principals, DIETs were requested to depute participants for the training programme of five days duration at NERIE, Shillong for the orientation programme.

Background Information about the participants : Need assessment a questionnaire was designed to collect background information about the participants and libraries and sent to the professionals and para-professionals, who were deputed by the SCERTs & DIETs to attend the training programme. The purpose was to assess their needs and plan the programme accordingly.

The responses were analyzed and are tabulated in Table – 1 and Table – 2.

Table – 1 : Qualifications and experience of the respondents

	No. of Librarians	
	Male	*Female*
Academic Qualifications		
Higher Secondary	2	-
UG	10	7
PG	4	5
Professional Qualifications		
B.Lib.	4	5
M.L.I.Sc	2	4
M.Phil in LIS	-	-
NET Qualified	1	-
Experience		
Below 5 years	5	6
Between 6–10 years	7	1
Between 11–15 years	2	2
Between 16–20 years	1	2
Between 21–25 years	1	1

It was found that out of 28 deputed candidates 16 were qualified professionals. However, 12 were from clerical staff / teaching staff and were assigned to work as Incharge Librarians. While designing the training programme, it was kept in view that fundamentals of the subjects were also explained for the benefit of para-professionals.

Table – 2 : Background information about the Libraries

A. Resources in Libraries

S. No.	Type of Materials	Below 200	201 to 1000	1001 to 5000	Above 5000
1	Books	3	7	12	6
2	Current Journals	7	5	-	-

B. Budget sanctioned to Libraries

Annual Budget	Number of Libraries
NIL	20
Below 1 Lakh	3
Above 1 Lakh	5

C. Infrastructure and Usage of Computers in Libraries.

S.No.		Yes	No
1	Computer	4	24
2	Printer	4	24
3	Software	2	24

Out of the total 28 libraries only 6 libraries were having collection above 5000 and none of these libraries were subscribing to learned periodicals. Most of the libraries were not receiving the fund from the parent organization for purchase of books and periodicals. Only 4 libraries had computers and only 2 had software. They had no hands-on-experience on computer before joining the training programme.

After the registration of the participants and inaugural function each participant was requested to provide detailed information about their libraries. It was found that most of the libraries were having single staff with the single room and poor collection that too not organised scientifically. Even the libraries with the minimum resources were not utilized fully by the users. Shortage of manpower and lack of resources, infrastructure and technical expertise were the main causes of poor development of libraries in the North Eastern region.

METHODOLOGY

- Lectures by experts
- Presentation by participants
- Discussions
- Practical exercises / assignments to participants
- Interactive and Participatory activities
- Hands-on-experience on computers to develop computer skills

COURSE CONTENTS

The experts were requested to prepare training modules on important topics for the training programme. They were requested to teach standard techniques also.

During the training the following topics were discussed:

Theory

- Knowledge Representation in Library Classification Schemes;
- Library Collection Development, Organisation and Maintenance;
- Framing of Library Rules;

- Library Classification DDC 22nd ed.;
- EDUSAT e-course Digital Library;
- The Shape of the 21st Century Library;
- Core Competencies for Library Staff;
- Library in Education;
- Library in Automation;
- Library Cataloguing;
- Professional Ethics for Library Staff in the Context of Library Services; and
- Library User Services in the Digital Era.

Practical

- Library Classification Practical
- Library Cataloguing Practical

Computer Skills

- Developing a Bibliographic Database Using WINSIS
- Hands on WINSIS

Visit

- Visit to RDIC, North Eastern Council Library

28 Library Professionals and para-professionals of SCERTs, SIEs and DIETs of North Eastern Region attended the five days training programme. During the training programme the topics covered were Library Rules, Collection Development, Processing of Books, Maintenance and Binding of Periodicals, Organisation of knowledge, such as classification, cataloguing, indexing, abstracting, and metadata. The participants were introduced to computer applications to Libraries. Theory and practical exposure were given on classification and cataloguing and participants also developed a bibliographic database using WINSIS. Each

participant was provided with a software copy of WINSIS so that the participants when they return to their institutes are able to start creating standard catalogue records. Visit to RDIC, North Eastern Council Library were also arranged. The methodology followed for the training programme was lectures by experts in field, Presentation by participants, Group work, and Interactive and participatory activities. A package consisting of 12 papers on the subjects covered in the training was given to each participant as instructional material.

END OF COURSE FEEDBACK

The participants were requested to fill up the feedback questionnaire. The objective was to improve the future training programmes.

1. What do you think about the structure and organisation of the training programme to meet the objectives ?

Very well Structured	Well Structured	Somewhat Unstructured	Very Unstructured
11%	86%	3%	Nil

2. How useful this training will be to you immediately in your organisation ?

Very Useful	Quite Useful	Of Limited Use	Not at all Useful
43%	43%	14%	Nil

3. How useful this training is likely to be for the future jobs you may handle ?

Very Useful	Quite Useful	Of Limited Use	Not at all Useful
71%	18%	11%	Nil

4. Practical orientation of the training programme.

Highly Practical Oriented	Practically Oriented to a Great Extent	Practically oriented to a Limited extent	Not at all practically oriented
14%	43%	43%	Nil

5. How far have you been benefited from interaction with the fellow participants during the training programme?

Substantially	Considerably	Fairly	Not at all
18%	36%	46%	Nil

The quality and relevance of Training materials used for the training programme.

Majority of the participants responded that they found training materials relevant and easy to implement in their Libraries.

Sessions or activities that the participants found most interesting and / or useful

Some of the participants felt that some of the routine practices explained by the resource persons would help them to organise their libraries. A few also mentioned that they had good experience of developing a bibliographic database using WINSIS.

Training methods used for the training were helpful to impart knowledge and develop skills for implementation of ICT

Majority of the participants felt that more hands-on-experience on computer would have been helpful to develop computer skills

Ways in which the training programme could have been improved

More training modules on different topics should be developed for imparting training. Computer Lab, where they could learn more practically, was needed. A few of the respondents stated that if the training were conducted in the institute, where a well organised library exists, the participants would have been able to avail library facilities also.

Other topics that the participants would like to be addressed in future training programmes

The following topics should be covered during the future training programmes :

1. Base development in fundamentals of computers, Windows, MS Office
2. Capacity Building of Library Professionals by using ICTs (Part 1 & 2)
3. Library Automation
4. Use of Open-Source ILS (Koha)
5. Capacity Building in Digital Age
6. Information Retrieval
7. Advanced Level Techniques

The participants evinced keen interest in the Library and Information management techniques and took active part in practical exercises in Library classification and cataloguing. They were very much interested in learning the computer basics and library software for creating standard catalogue records for the books. They felt confident and better equipped to manage libraries and provide better services to the users. They evaluated the programme as highly useful.

IMPACT OF TRAINING PROGRAMME

The Librarians / Incharge Librarians of SCERTs, SIEs, DIETs of North Eastern Region were expected to utilize the knowledge and experiences acquired through providing new services and enhancing the existing serviced using IT. Librarians has an added responsibility of introducing the students to the world of books and inculcating in them the love for books and habit of life long reading which is so vital for the overall development of the personality of students.

The training imparted to the participants will definitely help them to plan and improve library services. Better library resources and services will definitely have impact on the quality of school education.

EVALUATION

Evaluation was done through monitoring of the services planned out by the respective libraries through questionnaire. Correspondence/visit by the DLDI staff to selected libraries was made to get the feedback on the extent of development and modernization of their libraries.

Orientation Programme For Key Resource Personnels From Libraries Of SCERTs, SIEs, DIETs of North Eastern Region (2009-2010)

The participants of 2006-07 requested that similar training programmes should be organised by NCERT in future also. NCERT approved one orientation programme for North- Eastern Region for 5 days duration for 30 **key resource personnels** from Libraries of SCERTs, SIEs, DIETs of North Eastern Region in 2009-2010. The training methodology will be participative and interactive with active involvement of participants in group works, individual assignments etc. The training material, developed by DLDI will be provided to the participants for reference. Experts would provide to the participants inputs on the latest development in the field. "Hands on experience" will be provided on IT.

It is proposed that training programme will be conducted during 16-20 November, 2009 at NERIE, Shillong.

DEVELOPING THE TRAINING MODULES

The programme is proposed to be organised in two levels. In the first level a training manual will be prepared based on the needs and requirements of Teacher Training Institutes Libraries to modernize and improve its functions and services.

As a first activity, a two days meeting was organised at DLDI, NCERT on 27th – 28th March, 2008 for the preparation of the training manual for use in the subsequent training programmes.

The training modules on the following topics were prepared by the experts for the training programme:

Role and Functions of Libraries of SCERTs, SIEs and DIETs in India.

- Background
- Objectives
- Administrative Structure
- Infrastructural Facilities
- Services

Knowledge Representation in Library Classification Schemes

- Classifications Systems

- Dewey Decimal Classification: New Features in 22nd Edition
- Colon classification (CC)
- Universal Decimal Classification (UDC)

User Education Programmes

- Aims of User Education and Orientation
- User Education Planning
- Forms of User Education
- Instructional Methods
- Library skills
- Information skills

Collection Management in Libraries

- Purpose of collection development
- Collection management policy
- Guiding principles
- Collection development- Techniques and procedures
- Problems in collection development

Library Maintenance

- Concepts
- Process/ Functions Of Library Maintenance
- Stock Verification
- Withdrawal And Weeding

Library Consortia with special reference to NCERT

- What is a library consortium?
- Definition of library consortium
- Need of library consortium
- Benefits of library consortium

- Objectives of Library Consortium
- Ideal features of Consortium
- Issues related to library consortium
- Major Consortia in the India
- Types of Library Consortium
- Consortium models
- Proposed model of NCERT Consortium

Library Automation

- Concepts
- Processes and implementation strategy

Library Services in Changing Scenario

- Reference Service
- Book Lending Service
- Inter Library Loan Service
- New Arrival Service
- Current Awareness Service (CAS)
- Selective Dissemination of Information (SDI) Service
- Indexing Service
- Abstracting Service
- Bibliographic Service
- Internet Services
- OPAC
- Reprographic service

Planning and Organization of DIET Library

- Objectives
- Planning of Library Building
- Library Furniture And Equipment

- Library Committee
- Library Rules
- Library Records And Statistics

NEW ROLES / RESPONSIBILITIES OF LIS PROFESSIONALS

The future training programmes for SCERTs, SIEs, DIETs should try to develop the following skills needed for the 21st Century Librarians to succeed in this knowledge environment :

i) Librarianship Skills

ii) Twenty Technology Skills Every Librarian Should Have

1. Word Processing Skills
2. Spreadsheets Skills
3. Database Skills
4. Electronic Presentation Skills
5. Web Navigation Skills
6. Web Site Design Skills
7. E-Mail Management Skills
8. Digital Cameras
9. Computer Network Knowledge Applicable to your School System
10. File Management & Windows Explorer Skills
11. Downloading Software From the Web (Knowledge including eBooks)
12. Installing Computer Software onto a Computer System
13. WebCT or Blackboard Teaching Skills
14. Videoconferencing skills
15. Computer-Related Storage Devices (Knowledge:

disks, CDs, USB drives, zip disks, DVDs, etc.)

16. Scanner Knowledge
17. Knowledge of PDAs
18. Deep Web Knowledge
19. Educational Copyright Knowledge
20. Computer Security Knowledge

iii) Managerial Skills

iv) Leadership Skills

v) Information Skills

vi) Communication Skills

Technologies will come and go. Change is inevitable. But if librarians can adapt to and embrace change, can easily learn technologies, can keep up with changes in the profession, can plan for new services and evaluate old services, can develop services that meet the needs of all users, can evaluate technologies and can sell their ideas and market services they will be better able to meet the challenges of changing user populations and changing technologies.

REFERENCES

1. Babu B. Ramesh, Vinayagamoorthy P. and Gopalakrishnan S., ICT Skills among Librarians in Engineering Educational Institutions in Tamil Nadu, *DESIDOC Bull. Inf. Technol.*, 2007, 27(6), pp 55-63.
2. Kannappanavar, B.U. & Kumbargoudar, Praveen Kumar. Management skills of library professionals in agricultural science universities in India: An evaluation. *University News*, 2005, **43**(46), 5-9.
3. Kumaresan, S.C. Quality training and information professionals. *University News*, 2002, **40**(23), 1-4.
4. Mestri, M; Kumbargoudar, P; and Gobbur, DS; Design of training programmes for LIS professionals in emerging ICT environment, 2006. In H. Chandra (Ed.), Initiatives in Libraries and Information Centers in the Digital Era. Proceedings of the National Conference

Papers, Coimbatore: SALIS 8-10, Jul , pp230-237.

5. NCERT, Agenda for the 42nd Meeting of Programme Advisory Committee (2006-07) of NCERT

6. NCERT, Agenda for the 45th Meeting of Programme Advisory Committee (2009-10) of NCERT

7. Pitroda, S; National Knowledge Commission – Report to the Nation 2006. New Delhi: National Knowledge Commission, Government of India, 2006

8. Rajalakshmi, P.M. Role of librarians/information professionals in 21st Century. *In* SIS 2004 on Digital Information Exchange: Pathways to Build Global Information Society, 22-23 January 2005, Central Library, IIT Chennai, pp. 425-30.

10

Capacity Building of Library Professionals: A Case Study of Sir Dorabji Tata Memorial Library

Prabhu B.Gaddimani
Mr. Ravi Pothare
Muttayya Koganuramath

INTRODUCTION

In the 21st century, information revolution has dominated every aspect of our lives. Like natural resources, information has rightly been recognized as an important vital resource for growth and development of society.

Human society has undergone sea change due to phenomenal growth of information and application of information technologies in the form of high degree of computerization and transmission of electronic information telecommunication network in all walks of life. The new technology combines both continuity and fundamental change. Characteristics of present information society reflects in (i) use of computers and telecommunication technologies in handling information (ii) Growth of infrastructural backbone for IT application (iii) Shift of occupation from manufacturing to information based activities (iv) Information as capital resource base (v) Rapid and convenient delivery of information (1) This impact of ICT forced librarians towards the digitization of documents and information services.

SIR DORABJI TATA MEMORIAL LIBRARY (SDTML): AN OVERVIEW

The SDTML library came into existence in the year 1936, when the TATA INSTITUTE OF SOCIAL SCIENCES was established. The library is well equipped with good number of books, journals, E books and E journals in the field of social sciences and also with modern and latest technology to cope up growing need of information seeking in multidisciplinary subjects.

In the global information scenario, the main objective of the library is to support teaching and social research in the social science with the view to provide upto date knowledge to professional persons in social science and applied research. The library started with 5000 books and 30 periodicals in 1936, the collection as on data, shows the growth of library.

Library Collection Profile

Books	=	1,09,000 (Includes Bound Volumes)
Current Periodicals	=	290
Indian	=	133
Foreign	=	157

Periodical Holding	=	1100
E-Journals	=	7500+
Online Databases	=	15
CD-ROM Databases	=	5
E-Books	=	53 (started this year)
Audio-Visual Materials	=	1600
Theses & Dissertations	=	2450
Total area of the library	=	43,800 Sq.ft.
Total area constructed	=	20,800 Sq.ft.

CAPACITY BUILDING: CONCEPTUAL ANALYSIS

Capacity building is defined as the "process of developing and strengthening the skills, instincts, abilities, processes and resources that organizations and communities need to survive, adapt, and thrive in the fast-changing world." (Ann Philbin, Capacity Building in Social Justice Organizations).

As far as library and information services is concerned, the term capacity building is identifying the strength, weakness, opportunities and threats to the profession in present interdisciplinary dynamic world. In this regard the following important responsibilities needs to be adopted by library community as team leaders.

- To design and implement the capacity building for the staff's and any other member of the institute in terms of user oriented services;
- To set standards and ensure those standards are maintained at all the levels of library and information resources;

- To develop databases of resources available in the library (Internal and External);
- Develop innovative tools and methods to enhance training and teaching process;
- To systematic assessment of needs of the particular user. (2)

Digitization: A Concept

Digital library is common word now. Every library professionals know and understand the term. Let us have a look at some of the experts in the library and information science field, who have defined this term. According to Dr. M.T.D. Gandhi "The actual meaning of the digital library means remote access from any point of the work at library content and services, combining bibliographic news, electronic texts, image banks and all kinds of information by means of computer network".(3)

Digitization means acquiring, converting, storing and retrieving the standardized and organized manners, with the help of modern technological gadgets.(4) Three most fundamental obstacles impending the transformation and modernization of information services in developing countries like India are mainly: the volume of materials published, its limited publishing in local language, its unlimited publication in print and electronic form, and various barriers to come out.

All such barriers are leading libraries and information professionals to build up professional capabilities of manpower from unskillful to skilled and skilled to multiskill, information literacy, development of infrastructure and networking of libraries and information centres. Among all barriers information literacy is the most dominant element in capacity building. Martin has rightly been pointed out clearly that, "Information literacy is the interest, attitude and ability of individual to appropriately use digital technology and communication tools to access, manage, integrate and evaluate information, construct new knowledge and communicate with others in order to participate effectively in information society" (5)

SDTML INITIATIVES IN CAPACITY BUILDING

The present case study basically describes how TISS has applied various tools and techniques to develop a modern skilled and capable Library and Information Science Professionals in the digital environment.

The University Grants Commission (UGC) has identified the Tata Institute of Social Sciences (TISS) as a centre of excellence to conduct Refresher courses in Library and Information Science. SDTML TISS has conducted two refresher courses for developing capacity building for Librarians and Information Professionals.

- UGC sponsored Refresher course on "New Challenges in Information Management: Issues and opportunities for Librarianship" TISS, Mumbai, from 1-21 September, 2003.
- UGC sponsored Refresher course on "IT for Librarians", Sir Dorabji Tata Memorial Library, TISS, Mumbai, September 6-26, 2004.
- BOSLA/TISS organized one day seminar on "Resource Management" on 8th Nov. 2003. This seminar guided imparting knowledge to prove that the age old notion of ownership has transferred into an era of access to information by all irrespective of location, distance, time and also economic status.
- Two days workshop on " Information, Communication

Technologies for Librarians" was held from 15- 16 Oct. 2004 to empower library and information professionals to update the importance of ICT , which play a vital role in striking a balance between IT related role modern technologies and the traditional one. ICT provides one –stop-shop for all kinds of information, be it a catalogue, various databases, electronic journals, and e-books etc.

- TISS/ICSSR workshop: ICSSR sponsored training workshop on "Exploring Social Science Information in Digital environment on 27-30 May, 2002. The workshop examines the information resources and enormous advantage of digital technology.
- Special lecture on "Future of Librarianship: the road ahead". Jointly organized by BOSLA and TISS on 10th May, 2008.
- Two day workshop on "Creating Digital Libraries, using Dspace" Jointly organized by BOSLA and TISS on 11-12 Aug, 2007.
- International workshop on "Democratization of information with focus on Libraries" TISS, Mumbai on 18th Jan, 2004.
- International conference on "Knowledge for all: role of Libraries and information centers" held on 12- 15 Nov. 2008, in collaboration with TISS and ILA.

After conducting these seminars, workshops, training and user awareness programmes, all library professionals have developed the skill and capability to take-up the digitization projects in the TISS library.

DIGITIZATION OF THESES AND DISSERTATIONS (DSPACE PORTAL)

SDTM Library has set up a DSpace archiving facility for the TISS research community, using the DSpace open source software developed by the MIT libraries & Hewlett-Packard. This service enables the Institute community to archive their reprints, post prints and other scholarly publications. In keeping with the objectives of the open access movement, TISS expects this service to facilitate the institute researchers in self archiving and long-term preservation of their scholarly publications. To provide easy access to these publications world wide and improve impact of their research, dspace@tiss can be accessed by anybody after submission of documents to this archive. This service is limited to the TISS research community and the faculty members.

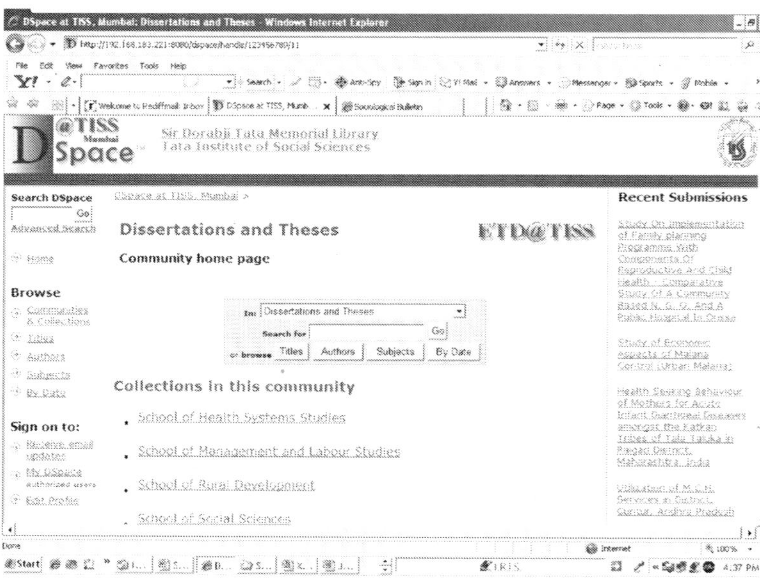

Electronic Thesis and Dissertations (ETDs)

UGC INFONET: E-SERVICES

TISS library professionsals have developed the Cyber library to provide one point information services to the users.

UGC-Infonet E-journals Consortium has established a seamless link between the UGC and the universities. It's a major step towards the establishment of network of all Indian universities and is brought under one roof. A MoU has been signed by the UGC, *INFLIBET*, *ERNET India*, and the host University. Under this initiative UGC is modernizing the University Campuses with State-of-the-art campus wide networks and setting up its own nationwide communication network.

TISS Library is one of the first institute to implement the *UGC-Infonet* programme with 4 mbps high bandwidth Internet connectivity in the campus. Access to the following full- text e-journals databases has been provided through the campus intranet.

Project Muse, JSTOR, Wiley Interscience, Springer link, Cambridge Journals Online, Oxford University Press, Taylor and Francis Journals, ISID Online and JCCC@GUC-Infonet.

Sage Journals online, Emerald Management Extra, India Business Insight Database, ABI/INFORM Dateline, ABI/INFORM Global, ABI/INFORM Trade & Industry, Indiastat.com, and World Bank Databases.

E-Books

The library acquired "GVRL e-Books to e-resources collection. Gale Virtual reference library is a database of encyclopedias and specialized reference sources for multidisciplinary research. These reference materials once were accessible only from the library. But now can access them online from the library intranet website. There are 53 e-books available in the library. Access to e-Books can be from: http//192.168.10.11

Cyber Library 24x7

A Cyber library is set up(SDTML) with the financial assistance from the Sir Dorabji Tata Trust to facilitate students, faculty members to access knowledge resources in world wide web, and in libraries of partner universities and institutions. Some databases like Project Muse, Springer link, JSTOR, Blackwell provide access to full text journals through UGC-Infonet E-Journals consortia, 24X7 On-line journals and resources of partner libraries, self operated laser printing and Xeroxing facilities, reading and computing facilities are also available at this library.

SDTM Cyber Library

M. K. TATA MEMORIAL LEARNING CENTRE FOR THE VISUALLY CHALLENGED STUDENTS

M. K. Tata Memorial Learning Centre has been setup at Sir Dorabji Tata Memorial Library, TISS in 2008 to provide innovative teaching techniques and philosophy that continues to have far-reaching effects on the lives of visually challenged, and taking them to new heights of independence. M. K. Tata Trust, Mumbai has funded the project. Ms. Piloo Tata, Chairperson, M. K. Tata Trust has inaugurated the centre on 7th May, 2008, during the Institute Convocation function. The Centre has acquired latest technologies to assist visually challenged students and faculty members. For the first time, partially sighted people can now read for long periods of time without tiredness. It is an unique computer reading facility for visually challenged impaired members with a congenial classroom environment. The Centre is aimed to provide, barrier free access and independent reading room to library resources. The Centre believes that, with proper training and opportunity, visually challenged people can compete on terms of equality with their sighted peers.

M.K. Tata Memorial Learning Centre for Visually Challenged

Air conditioned lab with 20 HP computers loaded with many software's like JAWS Pro 9.0, Kurzwell, Magic Magnification Software Pro, OBR Braille software, Teachers Talking Pro, Pen Friend word prediction software, Spell Well etc. The centre also equipped with Prisma, Zoom-Ex and Sara text reading systems which enhance significantly the reading experience for users who are partially sighted.

InfoMail

'InfoMail' is one of the much appreciated services provided by the Library. This service is provided by means of email to inform the students, research scholars and faculty members of the Institute. The content of this informative 'InfoMail' service is categorized into three parts viz, Events/ Announcemets, Information Sources, and Informative Website.

In the Events/Announcements part, the professional events such as seminars, workshops, conferences, MDPs, training programmes, call for papers, and fellowships/ scholarships at national and international levels are included, the second part, 'Information Sources is to cover the reading/ reference materials received as gratis such as working papers, discussion papers, technical/trend reports, magazines, journal issues, booklets, etc. and third part I-Site to mention about the useful and informative website of their interest.

E-CAS

The library brings out current additions containing bibliographic entries pertaining to the document added to the library. It includes books, conference proceedings, reports and other documents added to the library. It is a monthly publication. The entries are arranged subject wise.

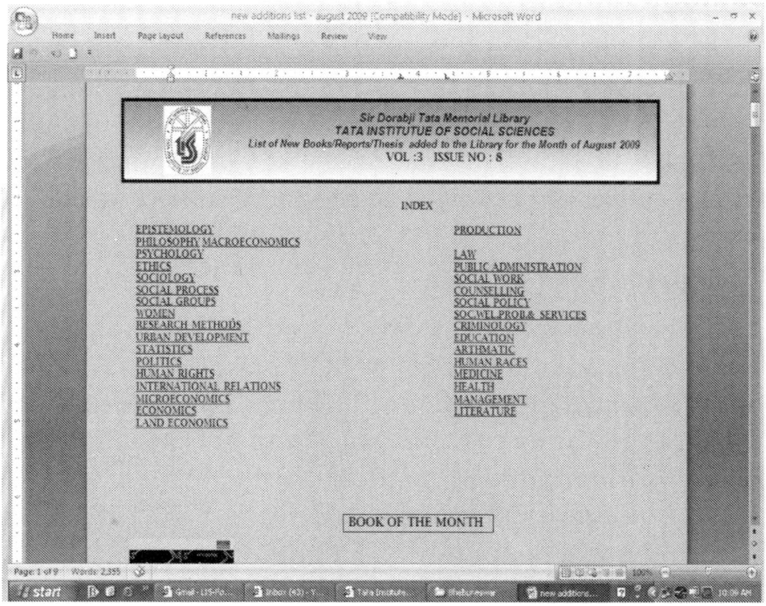

E-CAS

E-SDI

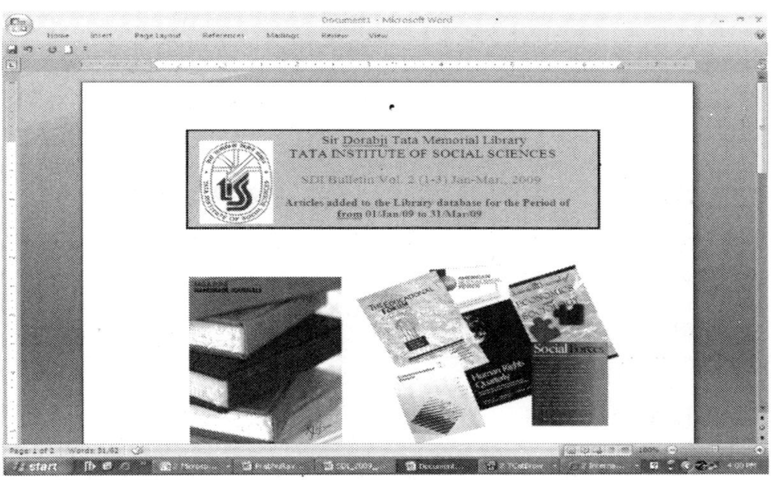

E-SDI

This service gives the record of articles published quarterly in the journals. Selection of the article is done from the journal subscribed by the library. Subject coverage is according to the needs of research scholars and faculty user profile. This includes journal article, annual reports. All the articles entries are arranged according to subject wise.

RESOURCE SHARING

The library maintains excellent relations with a number of institutions and libraries, including American Resource Centre Mumbai, British Council Library, Indian institute of Technology, Indira Gandhi Institute for Development Research, International Institute for Population Studies, Nirmala Niketan, College of Social Work, SNDT Women's University, Mumbai and Developing Libraries Network (DELNET).

Borrowing and lending requests in 2002 to 2008

Year	Total Number of loan requested received	Total Number of loan requested satisfied of which	%
2002-03	88	64	72.72
2003-04	168	148	88.09
2004-05	190	160	84.21
2005-06	120	99	82.50
2006-07	214	184	85.98
2007-08	170	155	91.17

FUTURE PLANS

SDTM library is ever trying hard to cater to the needs of its user community. It is aspiring to accomplish the below mentioned plans in near future:

- VPN Library has a future plan for providing Virtual Private Network (VPN) for accessing E-Resources from anywhere.
- Integrating information from the primary level, secondary and university level.
- E-modules preparation of E-Books for distance learning.
- Projecting the electronic resources, through the institutional archives.

CONCLUSION

SDTML (TISS) library has developed expertise for building the capacities of library and information professionals from semiprofessional assistants to the level of University librarian. The entire activities of the library have been revamped as part of restructuring exercise, keeping in mind the importance of ICT and its relevance to the present century.

By conducting various programmes in TISS and participation in seminars/workshops/conference at national and international levels has strengthened the knowledge of library professionals.

To create new generation of professionals with the infusion of ICT application, TISS is starting new Post Graduate Diploma in Digital Library management. This will be benchmark in 21st century library management education with focus on the user, particularly new generation of library and information students existing professionals.

REFERENCES

1. Saha- Saha, K. Towards the new information society: trends in the Indian Scenario. In "Towards the new information society of tomorrow: information, challenges and impact. New Delhi: FID Insdoc, 1998.
2. Source: http:/216/119.85.211/artmanz/publish/ Indian_jobs/ articles_15675.shim1
3. Gandhi, R.T.D. Ramesh: Role of librarian in Digital libraries, 5th international conference CALIBER 2007, Punjabi University, Chandigarh, 08-09, February, 2007.
4. Sharma, S.: Knowledge management in digital era: a challenge to library professionals" In "ILA bulletin 2006, 42 (2), 10-13 Pg.
5. Martin, A. and Madigan, D." Digital literacies for learnig" London, facet publishing, 2006.
6. TISS Annual Report 2009.

11

Skill Enhancement Programme for Library and Information Science Professionals and Role of CRL, Kolkata in Professional Development with Special Reference to Assam

Nirmal Ranjan Mazumadar

INTRODUCTION

The libraries are facing new challenges, new competitors, new demands, new expectations and a variety of information services from user community. To satisfy the users' demand, the libraries should have two pre-requisites i.e. a huge diverse collection of documents and a group of trained professionals. As the Library and Information Centers are basically manpower oriented organization, the image of such institute is directly dependent on the quality of the personnel engaged there.

DEVELOPMENT OF THE LIBRARY AND INFORMATION PROFESSIONALS

The advanced application of information communication technology, the library is changing its traditional concept rapidly. Library and information centers are now turn over to the global information hub, available and accessible to the users at any distance with a single mouse click on the computer monitor. In such changing situation, the library and information professionals have to play an active and important role in organizing and managing the information and in providing them to the respective users in most convenient way. The basic objective of the entire library & information centre is to become the right place to the right users for getting right information in the right form at the right time in a right way. As the Library and Information Centers are manpower oriented organisation, the success of such institute is directly dependent on the skill of the professionals. A skilled person can face the challenges occurs in a particular profession and can cope up with the ever-changing Information & Communication Technology (ICT) based library environment.

For the development of a profession and to keep the professionals up-to- date with the latest trends, besides the regular fulltime course content, different short term programmes are also very necessary to make the professionals professionally 'true professional'. In the Library and Information Science profession also, short term programmes like seminars, workshops, lectures, discussions etc are now arranged by different bodies.

In India, besides the Department of Library & Information Science (DLISc) of different universities and institutions, a number of professional bodies and other organizations are there for the library and information science profession & professionals at different level; these bodies are now given proper emphasis on the development of the same. Recently different workshops, seminars and conferences etc, are arranged at National and International level in different areas of India along with the North Eastern Region. Central Reference Library, Kolkata is such an Institution of National importance which is taking continuous activities for the continuous development of the professionals.

THE CENTRAL REFERENCE LIBRARY, KOLKATA

The Central Reference Library (CRL), Kolkata is a subordinate office of the Ministry of Culture, Government of India. It is one of the pioneer institutions in India in the field of compilation of bibliographies. Since 1958 Central Reference Library has been publishing the Indian National Bibliography in Roman Script, which is a comprehensive record of Indian publications. Apart from this it also compiles the respective language bibliographies, which are being published by State Governments. The INB is presently published monthly with yearly cumulative volume in 14 Indian languages. The CRL is presently preparing the bibliography with the help of software like LibSys and GIST. The National Library, India located at Kolkata is receiving the publications under the Delivery of Books (Public Libraries) Act of 1954 and these are forwarded to the CRL for inclusion in the INB.

The CRL, Kolkata, in associated with different LIS Schools and Libraries of the NE India has been taking number of professional measures for the development of profession. Here, in this paper some recent activities of this Library in North Eastern Region have been highlighted.

RECENT ACTIVITIES OF CRL, KOLKATA FOR SKILL ENHANCEMENT OF LIBRARY AND INFORMATION SCIENCE PROFESSIONALS IN ASSAM AND NE INDIA: A STUDY

On the direction and encouragement of the Department Culture the Central Reference Library, Kolkata is actively participating in the development of the North Eastern Region. As part of this activity the CRL regularly organizes skill enhancement training programmes for Library professionals of the North Eastern region on the *Compilation of Bibliographies* in their respective languages. This is a continuing scheme.

In 2007, a National Seminar on 'Problems and Prospects of Rural Libraries with reference to North East India' was jointly organized by DLISc, Gauhati University, Assam and CRL, Kolkata. This seminar stressed on the study on the present status of the rural library services & systems of this region. Here special importance was given on the participation of the rural librarians from the different parts of this region. A proceeding with a collection of presented research papers of various LIS professionals from different part of India as well as abroad is published in book formed.

'Training cum Workshop on Compilation of Bibliographies on North Eastern Indian Languages' was held from February 4-8, 2008, which was jointly organized by

CRL, Kolkata and Center of Library & Information

Science Studies (CLISS), Dibrugarh University, Dibrugarh.

An International Conference on 'Role of Library and Library Professionals in Knowledge Society' was held at NEHU, Shillong, Meghalaya, organized by DLISc, NEHU and CRL, Kolkata on 17-19 March, 2008, where a number of participants from Assam was there along the professionals from other part of the country and abroad.

In the beginning of this year 2009 a National Seminar on 'Digitization and Networking of Library and Information Centers in NE India' was held in Gauhati University. This two day seminar held on 9-10 January was the joint venture of DLISc, Gauhati University and CRL, Kolkata. This Seminar gives special stress on the need and importance of networking facility linking the library and information centres of this region. Here a proposal is also raised on the establishment of the NEILIBNET. A proceeding of this seminar has been just published in book formed which is edited by Library and Information Scientist Prof Narendra Lahkar assisted by Dr S.K. Singh.

Manipur University has jointly organized a National Seminar with CRL, Kolkata on 'Preservation and Conservation of Information Resources in Knowledge Society: Issues, Challenges and Trends' in Manipur University on last 3-4 March, 2009. This Seminar aims to initiate the Library and Information Professionals of NE India with the areas of preservation methods and techniques in the changing areas of ICT.

From last few years, CRL, Kolkata has been organizing an Apprenticeship programme for the library and information science students. In this one-month duration training programme a group of LIS students, each batch generally consisting five students representing from different

Indian universities, are practically trained to work in a real library environment and to use software packages i.e. LIBSYS, GIST etc. This type of 'earn & learn' training is very beneficial both for the students and the Library & Information Science profession as well. In the year 2008, three students from DLISc, Gauhati University has successfully completed this programme.

These practical-oriented skill enhancement programmes are very necessary and prolific for the library staffs, which can introduce them with advanced technology and refresh and retrained them with various technological skills.

CONCLUSION

The skilled library professionals can provide instructions and support to the end-users in using different information sources. The skill enhancement programmes arranging for the library and information professionals may become fruitful if they spontaneously participate in such programmes. CRL, Kolkata is in a leading position in North Eastern part for arranging and organizing different skill development programmes in collaboration with teaching department LIS of various universities of North East India. The University Libraries and other Professional Organisations should come forward and take the opportunity from CRL, Kolkata in getting support for organizing such programmes. Apprenticeship and Internship programmes are also very fruitful approach in enhancing skills among library and information science professionals. DLISc, Gauhati University, Assam starts Internship Programme for 2nd and 4th semester students from this session. This is a very practical step in developing the LIS students to cope up with the practical working environment.

REFERENCES

1. CORRALL, Sheila.1995, 'Academic libraries in the information society'. *New Library World*. Vol. 96, no. 1120, pp. 35–42
2. JOSHI, S.C. & MEHTA, S.N.2005. *National information system: planning and management*. Global Vision Publication, New Delhi.
3. JYOTHI, P. & VENKATESH, D.N. 2007, *Human resource management,* Oxford, New York.
4. MAZUMDAR, Nirmal Ranjan. 2007, 'Skills for library and information professionals working in borderless library'. *Library as a global information hub: perspectives and challenges, proceeding of PLANNER -2007,* INFLIBNET Center, Ahmedabad, pp 421-429.
5. RAJYALAKSHMI, D. 2004, 'Information professionals' knowledge and skills for information management'. *ILA Bulletin*. Vol. 40, no.3, pp. 5-12.
6. RAMAMURTHY, C.R.2004, 'Globalisation *and library information networking*'. Author Press, Delhi.
7. RAWATANI, M.R. & YUSUF, Mohammad. 2002, 'Professional manpower needs for libraries with special reference to skills'. *ILA Bulletin*. Vol.38, no.3, pp.81-83.
8. SEETHARAMAN, S & VENKATESWARA PRASAD, B. 2007, *Human Resource Management,. Scitech Publication, Chennai.*
9. SINGH, Rajesh and SINGH, Rajesh Kumar. 2003, 'Competencies and skills for university library and information professionals in 21st century'. *Herald of Library Science*. Vol. 42, no.3-4, pp. 185-191.
10. SMITH, Iia. 2003, 'Continuing professional development and workplace learning 5: human resource development - a strategic imperative'. *Library Management*. Vol. 24, no 8-9, pp. 443-445.

12
Capacity Building through e-Dissertation Repository at DLIS Gauhati University

Dipen Deka
Apurba Jyoti Majumdar

INTRODUCTION

When we talk about capacity building we mean developing the resources, the resources may be human or the collection. Here we are concentrating on developing the resources of the Department of Library and Information Science, Gauhati University. We the human resources in the department are forced to increase the resources to cope up with the current environment.

DEPARTMENT OF LIBRARY & INFORMATION SCIENCE, GAUHATI UNIVERSITY

In Gauhati University, the Department of library and information science (DLISc) started its activities long back in 1966 when it started the BLIS course in evening shift under the headship of Mr. Jogeswar Sharma. He was the Librarian of Gauhati University at that time and only Master degree holder in this subject. In the same year i.e. 1966 Mr. R L Mittal and Ms Alaka Buragohain joined the department as teachers. In 1976 and 1979, Ms Alaka Buragohain and Mr. Bhadra Borah (teachers of the department) got masters degree respectively from Delhi University. As a result, the department introduced master level LIS education (M Lib Sc) in 1979. In 1983 the department got independent status by the university by separation from the library. In that year the department renamed as department of Library and information science and the courses also renames as BLISc and MLISc respectively. [2]

DIGITAL REPOSITORY

Digital repository has evolved as a result of creation of e-resources in various forms. These are journal articles, conference papers, ETD, lecture notes, question papers, etc. Again the OSS movement has intensified the creation of digital repositories in the Universities and in different organizations. DR can be created with limited fund and resources for the members of a particular category or for all types of users i.e. open for anyone.

The creation of digital repository is the result of Open Access (OA). OA is the free online availability of digital content. OA has become increasingly important and potentially divisive issue in recent years, as journal inflation rates have increased. For many librarians and scholars, journal price inflation is itself the central problem and open access is the solution. OA holds promise to remove both price and permission barriers. In fact, OA is a step ahead of Free Access which removes just the price barriers by providing free access to end users.[1]

DIGITAL REPOSITORY OF E-DISSERTATION

E- dissertation forms an important component of the e-resources of the DLIS as every year 25 dissertations are added to the dissertation collection. These are primary sources of information on various areas of LIS. The student of MLISc 4th semester has to submit one dissertation on a topic as a part of curriculum each year. That is how the e-dissertation forms an important collection of DLIS, GU. The importance of the dissertations is that they are the research work done on important aspects of LIS in different areas of Assam. No other source of information can give us so much information compared to the dissertations.

PLANNING

In planning stage it has to be decided whether all the dissertations will be included or not. Which software we are going to use, what are the hardware we need, whether the DR will be open to all users over web or only for the users of DLS,GU.

At first we need the dissertation in electronic format. Earlier the dissertations were submitted in printed format only and from the year 2007 the students have to submit the one electronic copy (in CD) of the dissertation along with the printed format also. So, we can now utilize the dissertations in electronic format in establishing a digital repository of e-dissertation.

SELECTING SOFTWARE

A number of Software solutions are currently available for building Institutional Repository System that can support different document types including electronic thesis and dissertation. Several Open Source Software (OSS) and OAI-

Table: OSS Software with their features

Features	GSDL	Eprint	DSpace	Fedora
Open source	Yes	Yes	Yes	Yes
Operating system	Linux and	Linux Windows	Linux and Windows	Linux and Windows
Web server	Apache	Apache 1.3	Apache 1.3/2.0 and Jakarta Tomcat	Tomcat 2.4
Language	Perl	Mod-perl 1.0	Java 1.3, JSP	J2SDK v.1.4
Database	Its own	MySQL	PostgreSQL 7.3	MCKoi v. 0.94 (default) MySQL/Oracle 9i (optional)
Resource Identifier	No	OAI Identifiers	CNRI Handles	Uses own Persistent Identifiers (PID)
Metadata Standard	Dublin Core	Dublin Core	Qualified Dublin Core	Dublin Core
METS	No	No	Yes	Yes
OAI-PMH v2.0	Yes	Yes	Yes	Yes
Supported file formats	MS-Word, PDF, HTML,PostScript, JPEG, GIF	MS-Word, PDF, HTML, JPEG, GIF	MS-Word, PDF, HTML,PPTs, JPEG, GIF	MS-Word, PDF, HTML, PostScript, JPEG

complaint allow its users to build an open-standards compliant interoperable Institutional repository. Few of them are: [3]

From the above four OSS, the authors suggest to use DSpace for its following features

- It has a good web interface
- Ability to manage various file formats
- Flexibility to organize repository collections according to the University's faculty/departmental structure
- Relies on a qualified version of the Dublin Core schema
- Uses free text searching
- It has inbuilt OAI protocol

So, we have selected DSpace software for building the repository.

We have decided that the dissertations, which are in ms word format, will be converted to pdf format first and then it will be uploaded in the repository for the users. For this purpose we need software, which can convert the word, files into pdf format.

- 123PDFConverter
- Docsmartz PDF Converter Pro 6.1
- Quick pdf converter 3.0
- Quick All to pdf 3.0
- Quick 1-2-3 All to pdf
- Word2Pdf

From the above we have selected Word2Pdf software which is freely available.

IMPLEMENTATION

In this stage we have to define the community, collection and the metadata to be used. At present we have created only one community, i.e. MLISc E-Dissertation. Under this community we have collections as follows

- Academic Libraries
- Public Libraries
- Library Management
- Application of ICT in libraries
- Library Technical Operations
- Library Legislation
- Library Building
- Library Association
- Library resource sharing and networking
- Collection Development
- Digital Library

Under each collection we will start uploading the dissertation from the year 2009. It is obvious that the more collections will be added as and when required.

Another important area of establishing the digital repository is selection of metadata. We have planned to upload the dissertation chapter wise. While uploading the dissertation we have to assign metadata to each chapter.

We have selected Title, Creator, Subject, Date, Format, and Language metadata elements of Dublin Core.

Table 1. Metadata elements selected for the E-dissertation repository

Sl. No.	Elements
1	Title: the name given to the resource by which the resource is formally known
2	Creator: An entity primarily responsible for making the content of the resource
3	Subject: Subject will be expressed as keywords or key phrases or classification codes that describe the topic of the resource.
4	Date: Date of creation (yyyy-mm-dd)
5	Format: the file format in which it is available
6	Language: Language of the object

CONCLUSION

The digital repository of e-dissertation of the MLISc of the Department of Library & Information Science, Gauhati University is at the initial stage. So, there will be lots of modification on the policy and technology in near future. The repository will be opened at first to the users of the Department of Library & Information Science, Gauhati University only for pilot study. According to the response received, we will try to modify it. After that it will be opened for the web users.

REFERENCES

1. Deka, Dipen (2006). The role of Open Source Software in building Institutional Repository. In K. Manoj Kumar, RAth. Pravakar, Chand, P et.al (Eds.), Digital preservation and access to information in the twenty first century, Proceedings of PLANNER 2006, (pp. 121-127). INFLIBNET: Ahmedabad.
2. Lahkar, Narendra (2004). Twenty five years of MLISc dissertations of Gauhati University: a study. *Journal of Library and Information*

Science Gauhati University, 1(1), 7-28.

3. Pathak , Deepshikha & Deka , Dipen (2009). Gauhati University Repository: A model, In Lahkar, Narendra& Singh, S K.(Eds.), Proceedings of National Seminar on Digitization and Networking of Library and Information Centres in NE India, (pp. , 474-490). Guwahati: Department of Library & Informaton Science, Gauhati University.

13
Improving Library Capacity by Automation: The Case of Academic Libraries in Orissa

Priya Ranjan Mahalik

INTRODUCTION

Library automation is the order of the day. Application of information technology in libraries has become a reality and urgent necessity. Recent years have witnessed an unprecedented growth in the availability of both bibliographic and on-line databases of all kinds. There has been a tremendous and enormous quantity of publications in different forms, such as books, journals, reports, theses, dissertations, patents, standards, CD-ROM databases. It is difficult on the part of the library to provide services through manual methods up to the entire satisfaction of the users. In the present situation most of the end users are computer literate and they expect various types of computerized library services and on-line information available in the library premises. The situation has alarmed that all library professional staff should be familiar with computerized library services. Hence, it is the need of the hour that all academic libraries in Orissa require automation of its collection and services.

The paper is intended to reflect the need for library automation in academic libraries of Orissa and the problems associated with it and the future prospects required.

LIBRARY AUTOMATION

It is the first and foremost important thing for a modern library is its automation of information activities. This era is the era of speed. No one wants to misuse his or her time. It is, therefore, necessary to automate all the functions of the library. It's preferable to have computerized catalogue instead of card catalogue; it's preferable to have computerized issue and return system instead of manual one; it's preferable to have electronically printed membership card than manual card. In an automated atmosphere, the library can provide all these facilities. In other words, we can consider a library as a modern library only when the total operations of the library are automated.

The libraries primarily provide services on following three heads such as,

1) Acquisition of information
2) Organization of information
3) Dissemination of information

The acquisition of information refers to the procurement of different types of documents from different vendors or publishers. The organization of information refers to technical processing of documents for further use of end users and the dissemination of information refers to different types of services and products provided by the libraries. All these above jobs involve different types of activities like classification, cataloguing, serial control, circulation, reference services, and documentation activities. The traditional libraries usually provide manual services but library computerization entails automation of all the above activities of the library through computer systems. In order to computerize the library operations the pre-requisite elements are

a) hardware components
b) software packages
c) networking
d) trained manpower/library staff

The success of library computerization depends upon a definite plan of action of a team headed by a librarian. The team determines the library needs and objectives and identifies the priority areas of computerization in the light of available and limited resources. These include the procurement of hardware equipments, installation of software packages, networking with national level networks, development of data inputs procedures.

The first and foremost requirement is selection of hardware components. The team must select a suitable hardware components and purchase from the branded computer manufactures or suppliers. The second is the selection of appropriate software package. There are certain national level standardized software packages developed by government bodies and non-government organizations. A library must choose popular software which are given by a government organization. SOUL is a software developed by INFLIBNET for automation of libraries which is provided at low cost. Although Libsys is good software, due to high cost no college library is able to purchase the same software. All college libraries in Orissa should form a consortia and develop networking so that a common platform for network is developed using common software for library automation. The Govt. of Orissa should make a policy on which a particular standardized national level software is procured and utilized for all the college libraries in Orissa.

Most of the college libraries in Orissa are manned by professional staff without having adequate exposure to library computerization. The government may take a decision to make them trained and send to a training school imparting automation of library activities. Once the college library starts its automated operations such colleges need user education programme to educate the users to make them computer savvy.

BACKGROUND OF INFORMATION TECHNOLOGY APPLICATION IN LIBRARIES IN ORISSA

With the rapid use of IT, libraries in Orissa face a period of transition. Every organization, big or small, try to adopt a computer system in their work set up and in libraries. But, only such organizations/libraries which can effectively manage to computerize their library and information activities seem to have properly adopted IT. One can find that there is negligible application of IT in true sense of the term in libraries of Orissa. Although, this needs a survey, one can hypothise that the application of IT in libraries in the state is at the minimal stage. The adoption of IT in Orissa can be attributed to four factors:

i) Attitude and interest of the Library Authority;
ii) Availability of trained professional in libraries;
iii) Adequate funding provision for library automation; and

iv) Evolving a policy on library automation.

For the purpose of library automation, the libraries in Orissa can be grouped into three heads, which are: 1) college libraries under State Governments: 2) Libraries in Govt. aided colleges and 3) University Libraries. One may ask the distinction between two types of libraries at different government level in terms of application of information technology. Here it may be mentioned that college libraries in state govt. and Govt. aided colleges have clear a distinction on the above four attributes. The Govt. college libraries have certain funding provision for procurement of computer peripherals, and for providing training for their professionals, where as, the aided colleges do not have sufficient fund and interest for the application of IT in their libraries.

Libraries are primarily built upon the contribution and dedication of library professionals. Hence professional manpower requirements is a basic need in which real growth and development of library occurs. In respect of library professionals having adequate training in IT, there is no scope and opportunity for such professionals to work in the state govt. libraries. The library authorities in the state do not evolve any policy, considering the importance of the technical know-how and technical manpower development. They are neither sponsoring their library staff for training in IT nor creating an environment of developing a school of IT at the government and university level for imparting training.

PROBLEMS OF LIBRARY AUTOMATION IN ORISSA

The academic library environment in Orissa is far from satisfaction in every aspect. The college library is neither adequately funded nor resource allocation is sufficient. While the budget for purchase of books and periodicals is insufficient in relation to users needs most the librarian question the development a computerized library. In such a situation the library authority of the college is not interested for library automation. The faculty and students community are more habituated to use of traditional library operation. They have never complained for automation of library activities and use of computer in library operations. While the trained man power for library automation is pre-requisite, the library authorities are no more interested to make the library personnel educated in library automation and networking operations. As observed the selection of local software is more preferred than a standardized popular package made nationally available.

The libraries in Orissa experience following problems in terms of information technology and its application.

a) Lack of definite and clear goal by the parent organizations puts the libraries in a fix; as a result the real purpose of IT application is being defeated.

b) Absence of adequate enthusiasm and attitude of library authority makes the situation difficult to automate the library in the right direction.

c) Inadequate fund provision for computerization of libraries is the main cause responsible for under-employment of IT.

d) Library professionals do not enjoy freedom to work as a result they are not encouraged to undertake modernization of libraries.

e) Lack of adequate training facilities and absence of IT education in the state for the library professionals is one of the reasons that reflect such a poor state of IT application in libraries.

f) Lack of appropriate user education programmes dissociates the potential users from the library to use the users.

g) Absence of right and appropriate technology and equipments for modernization of library suffers from the setback of IT application in libraries in Orissa. (Mahaptra, Padhi, 2002)

ATTITUDE TOWARDS LIBRARY AUTOMATION

In order to develop a good library system and modernization of libraries the concept of attitude is highly essential. The library authority must have a positive attitude and take sincere steps in developing a good library system. It is an acknowledged fact that library in colleges of Orissa are not developed up to a national standard. Most of the libraries do not have a computer system in library premises. The Principal/head of the college must take immense interest of computerization of library activities. The Professor-in-Charge/ the Chairman of library committee must develop positive attitudes towards implementation of library automation. The librarian and the library staff of the college should be enthusiastic in library computerization activities of the whole library. They should propose to automate their libraries and expedite the process and see how library computerization is implemented so that users get substantial benefit. Unless the authorities and different functionaries in the academic environment do not develop immense interest in library automation nothing would happen. Hence, positive attitude towards library automation is an essential factor for success of library automation.

SUGGESTIONS

Library automation and networking has been a

common practice in all over the world. Orissa may not stay back in this respect. The following suggestions appear to be appropriate in terms of IT application in libraries.

- The Govt. of Orissa may formulate a policy for library automation and networking among academic libraries in Orissa.
- Standardized hardware components for all college libraries may be provided by the government so that it would easier for college authority to implement the library automation.
- National level standardized software may be procured for all college libraries so that a common platform may be developed for networking of academic libraries in Orissa.
- Library professionals in college and universities may be given adequate training so that they feel proficient in managing in library automation activities.
- User education programme may be imparted for the teaching faculties in college and universities so that the user groups are made themselves aware and educated about the benefits of the library automation.
- Leading colleges and universities in Orissa may organize training workshops, seminars, symposium and other short-term training programmes on library automation and networking so that, the library professionals may benefited out of such activities.
- The working library professionals need to accept the changes with the latest developments of IT application in libraries.
- The library authority without any discrimination and delay should accept the adoption of IT in their libraries.
- Efforts should be taken up by library for retro-

conversion of the existing documents into digital form.

CONCLUSION

Library automation is the essential input for modernization of libraries in present day digital environment. While, most of the academic libraries in India have adopted already library automation and networking facilities, Orissa is the only exception in this regard. The libraries in Orissa are not up to the mark in respect of computerization and networking. In order to develop proper library automation and networking the initiative from the government is considered vital. The library authorities in college and universities must develop positive attitude and immense interest in computerization of library activities and networking. The library professionals must feel themselves competent and show their interest in implementing library computerization programmes. Proper education in computer networking be given to library professionals for their professional development. Once the libraries are automated, a new working environment will be developed and the scenario for modernization is visible.

REFERENCES

1. VERMA (I.B). Modernization of Academic Libraries. Vistas of Information Management. New Delhi, 2002
2. Mahapatra,R.K. and Padhi,P. Application of Information Technology in Orissa: Problems and Prospects. IASLIC Bulletin 40(4) Dec 2004.

14
Capacity Building of College Libraries in Orissa

Arjuna Jena
Rabindra K. Mahapatra

INTRODUCTION

College library plays an important role in all the educational activities of the parent institution. An educational institution without a library is like a body without soul. A well equipped and well managed library is the foundation of the academic institution in which it serves. One cannot think of a college without a well equipped and well managed library. Libraries in colleges are the living force and are the centre of all educational activities of the institution. If one considers a college as a living being, the teachers and scholars are the head, students and readers are the body, the library is regarded as the heart. Now-a-days library has become an indispensable part and parcel of all academic activities and a vital component to fulfill all educational activities. College libraries in Orissa are functioning far behind satisfaction and needs capacity building in every sphere of activities for all round development and excellence of academic system.

MEANING AND DEFINITION

The term capacity building denotes the amount that some thing can hold, the ability or power to achieve it. Capacity - the word derived from the Latin word capacitas which means capacity for something. The power of containing a certain quality exactly; the power of receiving ideas or knowledge, active power, ability as man with the capacity of judging in a moral or legal sense, maximum output or production.

Building means to make something for a particular way or for a particular purpose, to use as the basis from which to develop to base hopes, to depend on some thing, a structure with walls and a roof, such as house for shelter.

Thus, capacity building means to build or establish a base in such a way which has competence, ability or quality of power to hold or dependable or to achieve the goal.

Capacity building focuses on a series of actions directed at helping in the development process to increase the knowledge, skills and understandings and to develop the attitudes needed to bring about the desired development change. It is the process of equipping individuals with understanding skills and access to information, knowledge and training that enables them to perform.

STATE OF LIBRARIES IN ORISSA

In Orissa there are 11 Universities, 24 Post Graduate College, 1470 Degree college, 1382 Junior college, 886 non aided college, 143 Sanskrit college, 44 Law college 143

Professional college, 07 Medical college, 65 Engineering college, 16 Pharmacy college, 47 M.C.A. Institute, 44 M B A college, 231 Vocational college, 14 B. Ed college, 10 Teachers training college, 02 IASE, 01 GTTC, 66 Secondary training college, 13 DIET, 24 Navodaya Vidyalayas. Each Educational Institution has library of its own. A list of libraries attached to academic Institutions of Orissa are given in table-1.

Table – 1

Sl No.	Academic Institutions	Govt.	Aided	NonAided	Total
1.	Universities/ Deemed Universities	09	-	02	11
2.	Post Graduate college	24	-	-	24
3.	Degree College	44	257	-	301
4.	Junior College	48	488	725	1261
5.	Sanskrit Colleges	03	22	128	153
6.	Law College	04	30	10	44
7.	Medical College	03	-	04	07
8.	Engineering College	05	-	60	65
9.	Pharmacy	01	-	15	16
10.	M.C.A Institute	13	-	34	47
11.	M.B.A College	8	-	36	44
12.	Vocational (Govt. Non-Govt.)	57	—	204	231
13.	B.Ed. College	14	-	-	14
14.	Secondary Training College	65	01	-	66
15.	Navodaya Vidyalaya	24	-	-	24
	Total				2048

Table 1 shows the present scenario of academic libraries of Orissa. As per the overall estimate there are almost 4000 library professionals working in different educational institutions in Orissa.

The libraries attached to educational institution of Orissa are characterized by inadequacy of funds, poor infrastructure, insufficient services to the users, and inadequate salary structure of the library professionals and ill management of library system etc. in Orissa. While all these negative aspects predominate the academic library scenario it is high time that the capacity building approach to develop the library system for academic upliftment and attainment of highest academic excellence is the need of the hour.

The paper is designed to depict the existing plight of college libraries that need the resultant approach for improvement of the *status quo.*

STAFFING AND MAN POWER DEVELOPMENT

MC Farland is of the opinion that "staffing is the function by which managers build an organization through the recruitment, selection and development of individuals as capable employees".

An organization for its efficient working is totally dependent upon proper staffing and recruitment policies. The staff employed should have special aptitudes and capabilities for performing a particular kind of job. A librarian should be a competent person to serve as a public relation officer i.e. to serve as a liaison officer between the reader and the book.

The state of libraries in Orissa is far from satisfaction because college libraries in Orissa are running without professionally qualified librarians. More than 30 years back in the year 1977 Government prescribed the yard stick (staff pattern) for recruitment of library staff for college libraries.

At that time trained library professionals are not available due to lack of library science training institutions in the state. At present the situation is quite different. Now library science education in bachelor's degree and master's degree level are available in different universities and colleges of Orissa. M Phil and Ph D degree courses are also available in most of the leading universities of Orissa. Although trained library professionals are available in plenty in the state and most of them are remaining idle without any employment. Government of Orissa have been still appointing simple graduates and non-graduates as different category of librarian in colleges. There is no provision for the appointment of qualified librarians in colleges if the roll strength of a college does not exceed 1500. Most of the college libraries in Orissa are managed by untrained professionals like simple Graduates and non-Graduates due to lack of roll strength.

At present, about 5% of the colleges in Orissa have roll strength 1500 or more. So the post of trained graduate librarian has not yet been created in 95% of colleges in the state. College authorities do not regard their libraries as prestigious establishment and do not offer them special consideration. The position and status availed by the college librarians is just like mere clerks. It is clearly understood from the table-2.

The information is based on the Yardstick fixed by the Government vide G.O. no. 23905/EYS, dated 08.07.19977 Statement – I.

Table – 2

Sl. No.	Admissibility of post	Name of the post	Revised pay w. e. f 01.01.2006
1.	Roll strength up to 500	Non-Graduate Librarian (Intermediate Pass)	5200-20200 + G P 2000
2.	Roll strength exceeds 750	Graduate Librarian (Simple Graduate)	9300-34800 + G P 4200
3.	Roll strength exceeds 1500	Graduate Librarian (Graduate with Dip. in Lib. Sc.)	9300-34800 + G P 4200

In the state of Orissa most of the college libraries are poorly staffed. As per the yardstick fixed by the Govt. for college libraries there is no provision for the appointment of adequate number of staff as per the work load. The yard stick (staff pattern) fixed by the Govt. is not based on scientific method. Due consideration has not been given on the factors like appointment of professionally qualified persons as librarian, increasing work load, roll strength, job chart, qualification of library professionals, status etc.

QUALIFICATION

Every profession needs professional education to handle all the activities and services evolved around it. For the librarianship it is essential to recruit a person having professional training and expertise. A librarian without professional training is a store keeper of books and other reading materials.

Library management, now a days is a specialized job and it needs proper training and expertise. It has a scientific character. Scientific management is the application of the principles and methodology of modern science and technique. Library is an organization needs scientific management. A person appointed as Librarian should have requisite qualification and proper recruitment policy should be followed to attract and retain talent in college education.

To attract and retain talent in Higher Education the UGC has fixed high academic qualification for the librarians with status and pay scale at per with the teachers where as the state government of Orissa is still appointing simple graduates and non- Graduates as librarians in college libraries of Orissa which is beyond expectation. It is clearly understood from the table given below.

Table –3 : Qualification fixed by the Government for College Librarians in Orissa.

Sl No.	Name of the Post	Qualification
1.	Non Graduate Librarian / Junior Librarian	Intermediate Pass/ Matric with diploma in library science
2.	Graduate Librarian / Assistant Librarian	Simple Graduate/ Intermediate with diploma in library science
3.	Librarian	Graduate with Diploma. in Lib. Sc.
4.	Senior Librarian	Graduate with degree in Lib. Sc.

The Education commission under the Chairmanship of Dr. S. Radhakrishana has recommended:

"The Library should have adequate and well qualified staff. At the top there will be a man of caliber, who has specialized in some aspect of library science after having done a full degree course and who has capacity for administration and management."

The qualification fixed by the government of Orissa is more peculiar in comparison to their counter part posts in other states in India. The qualification fixed as per the yardstick at the initial stage of opening a college is simple Intermediate in Arts/ Science/ Commerce up to roll strength 500. If the roll strength does not exceed 750 there is no question of any change in the designation, pay scale, required qualification for the post.

The Minimum Qualification fixed by the UGC for the college librarians to attract and retain talent in higher education and to maintain standard in higher education is as the following:

i) Qualifying in the national level test conducted for the purpose by the UGC or any other agency approved by the UGC.

ii) Master's degree in Library Science / Information Science / documentation or an equivalent professional degree with at least 55% of the marks or its equivalent grade of 'B' in the UGC seven point scale plus a consistently good academic record, computerization of Library.

There is no proper rules, regulations and guidelines for the library professionals in Orissa. They have been working without any job satisfaction. They are working just like the store keeper of books or library clerks. The salary structure of college librarians is very measurable in comparison to other state governments in India which reveals the height of frustration among the librarians. For the same, most of the library professionals those were in library service do not like their children to take library science education as a career even for the future generations. Such type of attitude of the library professionals is the reflection of a sense of dissatisfaction with the prevailing condition in the library profession. Librarians in Orissa are still not clear as to why the authorities don't accord due status and recognized their services as a profession. That is the pity with college education in Orissa.

In this connection, it may be stated that the state Government of Orissa should think it proper to revise the prevailing yard stick (staff pattern) and necessary provision may be made in the revise yard stick for appointment of trained personal as librarian and qualification may be fixed as stipulated by the UGC from time to time irrespective of the size and roll strength of the colleges in Orissa.

SCOPE FOR PROFESSIONAL DEVELOPMENT/ ACTIVITIES

The National Policy on Education recommends that in view of challenging and dynamic situation in the profession, the Indian library and information professional must be given every facility to update & utilize his/her expertise, so as to keep abreast of latest development knowledge by organizing continuing education programmes in the field.

In case of Orissa there is no scope for the librarians to improve their professional qualification. There are several barriers and obstacles at the Government as well as college authority level. There is no study leave facilities for the library professionals to under go training to acquire and improve their professional expertise. They are not allowed to attend seminars, conferences, work-shops, refresher courses and orientation courses organized by professional Associations, Universities, Colleges, and the UGC. There is an instant occasion that the refresher course organized by Sambalpur University department of Library Science sponsored by the UGC was postponed due to lack of adequate number of participants. To enhance professional qualification of librarians is totally ceased by the Government. As per the defective staffing pattern non professionals like simple graduates and non graduates are entering to Library profession. They have no scope to acquire professional qualification. There is no financial and leave protection support neither from government nor from the college authority side to enhance their qualification. In many institutions the authorities are not taking any interest and encourage their librarians to take part in professional activities.

STATUS OF LIBRARIANS

In this direction, it may be stated that Government of Rajastan have gone much more ahead as compared to other states in India in improving status of Librarians working in colleges and Universities. At the Annual Conference of college Principals in 1965, it decided that the librarians be recognized a member of teaching staff. It also accepted by the then Director, Dr. V. V. John and in this connection, at the suggestion of the Director, it was agreed that for all academic purposes, Librarians should be reckoned as members of the teaching staff of the college irrespective of the classification made for administrative purpose by the government.

The Librarians working in College Libraries in Andhra Pradesh, they have been designated as lecture in Library Science and treated at par with the teachers in colleges and they are availing teacher status. In respect of their pay scale they are enjoying UGC pay scale and grade at par with the teachers. When the pay scale of teachers in colleges are revised at the same time to pay scale of college librarians are also automatically revised. There is no difference in pay scale and status in between the librarians and teachers in Andhra Pradesh.

In West Bengal, Calcutta University after a prolonged persuasion by the Association (West Bengal College Librarians Association) at last the syndicate has approved the teacher status to the librarians on 12.3.1991 as per recommendation of the committee appointed by the syndicate in its meeting held on 21.6.1988.

The minutes of the meeting of Calcutta University Syndicates dated 26.3.1991 resolved as the following:

"................ Librarians of Non- Government affiliated college be given the status of teachers "Status" being defined as a position in the hierarchic structure of an organization .... in recognition of different nature and condition of work of Librarians from that of teachers, they may be declared as non-vocational staff". Similarly, in almost all the state in India, librarians are availing UGC pay scales and status at par with the academic staff except in Orissa.

Regarding position and status of college librarians, the state Government of Orissa is three steps back in comparison to other states in India. The librarians in Orissa are far behind availing UGC stipulated pay scales. Orissa is the only state delinked from the national mainstream. The position and status availed by the librarians in college Libraries of Orissa is beyond expectation. They are working just like the store keeper of books or library clerks. They have been working without job satisfaction.

While some other state Governments have declared librarians academic staff, the state Government of Orissa have categorically refused to accept the same status to librarians in the state.

It is noteworthy to mention here one of the recommendations of the UGC committee on the University/ College Libraries under the chairmanship of Dr. S.R. Ranganathan that:

"the high academic and professional qualifications the combination of academic and administrative responsibilities the library staff should be same as that of the teaching and research staff."

Realizing the composite nature of work of the professionally qualified librarians in higher strata and education in our country, Dr. Rangnathan's epoch making recommendation was accepted by the UGC and implemented in 1961. Since then librarians in colleges over the country are availing status and position at par with the academic staff. If we compare there is a hell and heaven difference in between the librarians working in the state of Orissa with the counter part posts in other states in India.

SALARY STRUCTURE

The salary structure of college librarians is very miserable in comparison to their counterpart posts in other state governments in India which reveals the height of frustration among the librarians. It is very difficult to attract and retain talent in higher education due to low emoluments. Although library profession is a noble profession the qualified young men and women of ability (capacity) are not prefer to enter library profession. In this situation it is difficult to expect better library services in the state of Orissa. Most of the library professionals do not like their children to take library science as a career even if for their future generations. Such type of attitude of library professionals is the reflection of sense of dissatisfaction with prevailing condition in the library profession of Orissa. When almost all the states in India, librarians are getting UGC pay scales, whereas, it is a distant dream for the college Librarians in Orissa.

Table - 4 : Schedule of Block Grant 100% block grant as on 01.01.2004

Sl No	Name of the Post	Scale of pay	Basic Pay & increment		Total	DA @ 41	Grand Total per month
1	2	3	4	5	6	7	8
1.	Lecturer	6500-200-10500	6500	1400	7900	3239	11139
2.	Demonstrator	5000-150-8000	5000	1050	6050	2481	8531
3.	P.E.T.	4500-125-7000	4500	875	5375	2204	7579
4.	Store Keeper	4000-100-6000	4000	700	4700	1927	6627
5.	Librarian/Asst Librarian	3200-85-4900	3200	595	3795	1556	5351
6.	Junior Clerk	3050-75-4590	3050	525	3573	1466	5041
7.	Library/Laboratory Attendant	2650-65-4000	2650	455	3105	1273	4378
8.	Peon and other Class-IV employees	2550-55-2660-60-3200			2550	410	2960
12144174							

The Table 4 states that librarians working in college libraries of Orissa are now getting their total monthly salary in serial No. 5 column No. 8.of the table which is less than Demonstrators, PETs, Store-Keepers. The status and position of librarians in the hierarchy structure of college education is clearly understood from the schedule of block grant as fixed per month by the Government w.e.f. 01.01.2004. 'Block Grant' means Government has decided to grant a fixed amount to the employees of an aided educational Institution without any hike in their pay in future. There is no increment, no D.A., no revised pay for them is earmarked. The state Government is now introducing Block Grant for the librarians working in college libraries in Orissa. There are also other modes of payment of salary for the college librarians such as full aided, contractual, management paid etc. This is the pity in librarianship in Orissa.

The UGC recommended pay scales effects from 01.01.1996 are as the following:

Table - 5

Sl No.	Name of the post	Scale of pay w. e. f. 01.01.1996
1.	College Librarian	Rs. 8000 – 13500/-*(At par with the lecturers)*
2.	College Librarian*Senior Scale*	RS. 10000 – 15300/-*(at par with the lecturer Senior Scale)*
3.	College Librarian*Selection Grade*	Rs. 12000 – 16400/-*(at par with the Lecturer Selection Grade)*

PROMOTION PROSPECTUS

A person appointed as Librarian retires as such without any promotional prospectus, any carrier advancement or time bound advancement pay scale. There is no promotional avenue for the librarians. There are some instances that a person joined as non graduate librarian in the scale of pay of Rs.5200-20200 grade pay Rs. 2000 (now revised) retires in the same scale of pay without any change in his position, grade, pay scale etc.

FUNDS

The National Policy on Education recommended that adequate financial support for the development of Libraries and information system will be made available by the Government of India and the state Government. The national as well as state Government should provide for an expenditure of 6-10% of their education budgets for the Libraries. All educational institutions should similarly provide for their Libraries 6-10% of their total budget.

No organization can function properly without adequate funds. The libraries in Orissa have been given almost the lowest priority in the matter of allocation of funds. The libraries, as has been observed, are handicapped in their acquisition policy and services due to lack of funds. There is no budgetary provision for college libraries in Orissa for purchase of books, Journals etc. In case of Govt. college there is provision for financial support in some extent but it is not sufficient to solve the increasing need of the students and staff members. In case Non-Govt. aided colleges there is no provision of funds of any kind from the Government side for the development of libraries. All the aided college libraries of Orissa mostly depend on collection of fees from the students. It is not enough for the proper management, collection development etc. Some times the UGC used to give financial assistance for purchase of books. It is not adequate. Although, 90% of the students are getting their education in Non-Government aided colleges in Orissa, the state

Government have not been taken any positive steps for improvement of library services.

INFRASTRUCTURE

Most of the college libraries are housed adjacent to classrooms and have no separate planned model library building. Now-a-days library automation and networking is a prerequisite for the collage libraries. Most of the collage libraries have no computers. Some libraries have computers without proper software and the librarians have no knowledge about to computer operation. Again, it is a matter of surprise that when Govt. of Orissa recruiting simple graduates and non-graduates as librarian it is a dream to think about capacity building in collage libraries or to enter in the Information Communication Technology sector in digital era.

COLLECTION DEVELOPMENT

The process of collection development in college libraries in Orissa are beyond satisfaction. Most of the collage librarians are totally ignored in the process. Their suggestions and recommendations are not at all taken into account. The departmental teachers are entrusted by the principal to procure books for the library according to their own choice. In the classroom they prescribe students to refer such books whereas they totally forgot at the time of purchase these titles to procure for the library. It is too difficult on the part of the librarian to satisfy the increasing demands of the students and users. It is essential to introduce proper procedure for the same to make the library collection sound in all aspects.

LIBRARY MANAGEMENT

Librarians working in college libraries are not given adequate professional freedom to manage the library. In Orissa, academic libraries are generally functioning under the guidance of Prof.-in-Charge of the library. It is essential to formulate library Committee in colleges where the librarian is the member secretary and the Principal of the college is the Chairman of the Committee and other members selected by the Principal from the faculties as per the UGC norms and a single man as professor in charge should be discontinued. The responsibility of the library should be given to the librarian independently to manage the library under the supervision of the library committee. The librarian should be directly responsible to the principal in all the library matters.

NEED BASED CAPACITY BUILDING

To enhance usage and readership of the library, Librarian should on a continuous basis take up the work of research into the needs and interest of the users. Need based collection becomes meaningful and hence leads to more usage and participation. The librarian should resist attempts to determine library materials are to be or not to be, available to the users of the library.

The selection of books for libraries is not a form of censorship. It presumes the right of the readers to read books widely and to form his own judgment, and it is designed to achieve this.

The librarian has a greater responsibility to keep open the channels of communication at his disposal so that he may discover and serve the needs and interest of the users. Librarians should educate the users about what they can do to help them for better access to information. Librarian can not merely act as informer but naturally is an educator as well.

To utilize the library collection fully, the librarian should know about his users and their need, library users are unique in nature, so the library professionals should try to know who are the users of the library, what types of services they like in what purpose they need such services and does the library collection fulfill their needs etc.

SUGGESTIONS

In view of the above situation, it is essential to improve the working conditions of libraries in Orissa in the sense of capacity building and to yield output up optimum level. Hence it is suggested that:

- The appointment of simple graduates and non-Graduates as librarian may be discontinued and the prevailing yardstick for both Government and non-Government college library may be revised accordingly and necessary provision may be made in the yardstick giving opportunities for the trained personnel to enter into the library profession and the knowledge of computer application is to be fixes as desirable qualification.
- Due to provision in the yardstick some untrained person are entering in the library profession without library science qualification. They may be given chance to acquire professional qualification with consequential service benefits.
- Government of Orissa should come forward to extend UGC stipulated pay scales and status at par with their counter part posts in other state in India to work the

librarians in a healthy environment.

- Due to advancement of information communication technology it is essential to upgrade professional activities of the library professionals for the same. The state Government may consider organising and sponsor library professionals to acquire knowledge on latest trends and developments in the field of library and information services.
- Necessary budgetary provision may be made at the Government level for the all-round development and better functioning of college libraries in Orissa.
- The responsibility of the library may be entrusted to the librarian to manage the library independently under the supervision of library committee instead of a non professional as library in charge.
- A State level Library Advisory Committee may be constituted to fix the work load, job chart, library automation and networking and other pros & cons of the library by which the service condition of college libraries shall be improved.

CONCLUSION

Libraries are store house of knowledge and librarianship is a revered job. Libraries in Orissa are not improved in terms of collection, organization and services. It is due to the fact that the decisions for the libraries are taken by the head of the organization without the consultation of the library professionals. Librarians do not take part in the decision making process for the library development. The authority in the higher echelon does not consider the library as an essential component of the system. The main focus is the appointment of qualified librarians. But the Government has prescribed the qualification criteria in such a manner that qualified persons are not given weightage in the job. The libraries do not have adequate infrastructure to provide the required services to the user groups. The application of information technology in libraries is a matter of concern for the library authority, since most of the libraries do not have the computer.

Librarianship appears to be an interesting and exciting profession. Because the job involves managing information and knowledge for education of the people from different streams. In order to make the library system effective and successful the status of the librarians should be improved. In case of the state of libraries and librarianship in Orissa the situation is very grim and needs serious introspection. Librarians are not given their desired position, status and salary. The library staffs are ignored in all respects which hinders the growth and development of libraries.

Non implementation of UGC pay scale by the Government of Orissa is a major setback to the library profession. Once the UGC scale is implemented all the problems of librarians in academic institution will be solved. They will get their status and positions equivalent to faculty in colleges and universities. What to say of UGC pay scale the librarians working in small colleges are getting less salary than clerks. Their work environment is not at all encouraging. There is no promotional avenue for the Librarians in their whole career. If libraries are to be developed, the primary job of the government is to improve the status and position of the library staff so that the real capacity building of the academic libraries will be realized in concrete form.

15
Biomedical Health Information Services in RMRC Library & Information Centre, Bhubaneswar

Banamber Sahoo

BACKGROUND

Regional Medical Research Centre, Bhubaneswar was established in March 1981 with Research focus on lymphatic filariasis and other diseases of regional importance. Regional Medical Research Centre Library came in to existence in the year 1983 with very few collections of Books and some foreign journals. Till 1989 the library was managed to grow by the scientists without any professional librarian. During last part of 1989 i.e. September 1989, the library got its professional staff in the form of Asst. librarian to house the library. After ICMR's library modernization programme the Centre's library has been categorized as Category- II library as per the review committee report of Govt. of India. The library houses nearly 10,000 volumes of Books, Monographs, Annual Reviews and Reports. Besides that nearly 100 print journals subscribed by RMRC Library in addition to more than 1500 online journals subscribed through ICMR and NML consortium.

INTRODUCTION

The main aim of the Library & information centre is to provide relevant and latest biomedical information in the shortest possible time, to the researchers and biomedical scientists of the insitute. Few years back information needs of the users were catered from *MEDLINE* CDROM (Off-line database) . Now that trend has completely changed by providing online literature search through Internet and Online journals either through open access source or Journal consortia through ICMR/ NML. It provides both library and Information services not only to the scientists and researchers of this Centre but also to the researchers, doctors and academicians of this state. The foreign journal collection of this library is unique in Orissa in the field of medical sciences. For the calendar year 2007 the library subscribes 48 foreign journals and 40 in various fields of medical sciences and public health. The library possesses LAN printer- cum -digital Copier,in order to provide library, Information and reprographic support to its users. The library is computerized with Libsys-IV . Library and Information Centre provides Local Area Networking (LAN) to the Institue scientists.Dedicated LAN server and Antivirus server has been installed in the library for ICMR library networking of the country. In publication activities, the library publishes Bi- Annually Library News Letter and RMRC News Bulletin. Besides that, the library works as publication cell of the Centre which publishes periodically IEC materials on various diseases, Posters and pamplets on research findings and Institute's Annual report.

BIOMEDICAL INFORMATION SEVICES AT RMRC LIBRARY

ICMR e-Consortia

Through ICMR e -Journal consortia, all 26 ICMR Institutions of the country are able to access following six high impact weekly journals of the world where all latest research findings come out.

Journal	Web site
Science	*http://www.sciencemag.org*
NEJM	*http://content.nejm.org*
BMJ	*http://www.bmj.com*
Lancet	*http://www.sciencedirect.com*
Nature	*http://www.nature.com*

ICMR-NML- ERMED CONSORTIA

In this consortium total 1515 Medical journals are accessible. www.nmlermed.in.

The participating libraries are National Medical Library (NML), all 26 ICMR libraries, AIIMS library, JIPMER library and other DGHS libraries.

INTERNET

Internet plays vital role in library and information services. The traditional reprint request for scientists through card has been shifted to on-line reprint request. After installation of LAN system in the library and BSNL Broadband network in RMRC library, on-line reprint requests are being done for the scientists and researchers through Internet. The library is also sending our reprints to the requester through e-mail by scanning the articles of our scientists. Internet facility is available for all ICMR scientists for searching various on-line databases, full text journal articles, and abstracts and subject searches for scientists for presenting papers and preparing scientific talks and seminars. E- mail facility is open for all scientific staff of the centre.

RESOURCE SHARING

All ICMR librarians have formulated an ICMR Librarians group mail (*icmrlibrarians@yahoogroups.com*) for resource sharing. Any article available in any ICMR library can be obtained and delivered to scientists through this group mail services. This service is being provided to all ICMR scientists as resource sharing among ICMR libraries of the country.

Off- Line MEDLARS

Library possess MEDLINE-CD ROM database for the period 1966-2002. This facility is extended to all library users as off-line MEDLARS services. The researchers and scientists and doctors from various medical colleges are making use of this facility. This facility is provided free of cost to all users. This MEDLINE database carries abstracts of more than 6000 Biomedical journals covered in Index Medicus.

LAN Printing /Photocopying

LAN Printing and Photocopy facility is available for scientists and researchers of ICMR free of cost.A digital copier cum - LAN printer is installed in library for better reprographic services.

PUBLICATION CELL

The library & Information Centre is doing publication activities of the Institute. RMRC News Bulletin and Library News Letter are being published from this division. IEC materials on various diseases are also made on local languages for distribution to the public. Besides, the division looks after the publication of Centre's Annual Report.

The following are the publications from RMRC being published from library division.

1. RMRC News Bulletin
2. Library News Letter
3. IEC Materials on various diseases on Malaria, Filariasis, Sickle cell diseases, IDD, in regional language.
4. Posters on recent advances in Fiariasis, Malaria, Sickle cell diseases, and diarrhoea for children.

JCCC@ICMR

J-Gate Custom Content for Consortia (JCCC) : A customized gateway and search tool developed for the users of the Member libraries of ICMR (JCCC@ICMR) by Informatics India Ltd., Bangalore.

- Indexes and updates every week, articles published in all journals subscribed by all ICMR Libraries and open access journals .
- A Web Interface for browsing TOC (Table of Contents) of journals searching by author, title, keywords, and abstract

- Getting full-text of the Articles online/requesting photocopies of articles from any ICMR Libraries.
- Creating Alerts through MY TOC service.
- Promotes sharing journal literature within ICMR Libraries
- Provides a common searchable database for around 478 subscribed journals and 215 open access journals — print or electronic.
- Facilitates obtaining photocopies of articles quickly from any ICMR Library as an integral part of searching.

THE COCHRANE LIBRARY

(New health information resource now available across India)

Indian Council of Medical Research (*www.icmr.nic.in*) is sponsoring the Internationally renowned Cocrane Library, the free online data base for all Indian Internet users to this online health Information resources. The Cochrane Library is a collection of regularly updated evidence based healthcare databases, including gold-standard Cochrane Systematic Reviews, that can help clinicians and consumers make decisions about what treatments are best for them and their patients. This information is produced and assembled by the Cochrane Collaboration (www.cochrane.org), a UK registered international charity, which is considered to be one among the leaders in the field. "This is an important step in making high-quality health information available to professionals, researchers and the general public," said Professor N.K. Ganguly, Director General of ICMR. "Anyone in India with access to the Internet will now be able to use what is regarded as the world's best single source of evidence on the effects of different forms of health care".

The Cochrane Library is available at *www.thecochrane library.com*

MedIND (Biomedical Journals from India)

medIND the product of NIC_ICMR Biomedical Information System provides Online access to full-text of Indian biomedical periodicals to the users. There are some Indian journals that are available full-text over the Internet, but medIND make them available Online from one point. There are other journals of which just the contents, with or without abstracts are available over the Internet. Hence, a need is there for one such central resource that would make available full-text of the Indian biomedical journals.

The Indian MEDLARS Centre (IMC) has already developed a bibliographic database of 75 biomedical journals. This database, IndMED, is accessible from IMCs webpage (http://indmed.nic.in) to the medical professionals, free of cost. The database aims at covering peer-reviewed journals from 1985 onwards. With very few Indian journals, available full-text on the Net, the Indian MEDLARS Centre, took up the challenge to develop a database of full-text of Indian biomedical journals. This medIND database is accessible free of cost to the medical community in India as well those outside the country.

CONCLUSION

The RMRC Library and Information Centre is unique in the field of biomedical information system in eastern region. Its journal collection and services have been rendered to researchers, scientists, academicians and doctors of the Orissa and neighboring states. A proposal for creating e-library in RMRC has been approved by ICMR and it will be completed in 11th plan period.

16
Applying Innovations in Systems and Services of Libraries and Information Centres

Dillip K. Swain
Kamal Lochan Jena
Priya Ranjan Mahalik

"Difference is not always better but better is always different" (Luce, 2003)

INTRODUCTION

Innovation policy, although fashionable is often misunderstood; it is an appendix to science and technology policy, as often presented. Innovation-the application of knowledge of all types to achieve desired social and economic outcomes-is broader than science and technology, often combining technical, organizational, and other sorts of changes (**World Bank**, 2007).The innovation system plays an important role in acquiring, creating, adopting, and disseminating knowledge, which is crucial for success in the knowledge economy. The innovation system in any country consists of the network of institutions, rules, and procedures that differ how the county acquires, creates, disseminates, and uses knowledge (**Dahlman and Utz**, 2005, p.75). Librarians are now actively engaged in developing digital libraries, which will extend and enhance the common notion of a library. In so doing they will help extend the limits of electronic imaging, data transmission, automatic indexing, natural language processing, and numerous other related technologies. If history is any guide, librarians will uncover the problems, help to define the solutions and be among the earliest adopters of those solutions (**Malinconico**, 1997).Contextually, the philosophy of innovations is applied to the organizational and operational excellence of libraries and information centres all across the world.

CHANGE AND INNOVATION

The terms change and innovation are often used interchangeably. An innovation, or a change, is traditionally defined as any idea, practice or object, which is seen to be new by the individual or the organization either adopting or rejecting it. Even though the idea has been around for a while and is known to other organizations, it is still considered an innovation or a change if it is new to the organization considering it (**Pungitore**, 1995, p.8). Therefore, change or innovation in libraries and information centres has become imperative due to the technological revolution and prolific growth of electronic information of late.

WHY LIBRARY INNOVATION?

Due to dramatic changes in the information environment and the ICT sector, library managers have interest not only to adapt to these sweeping changes, but, more importantly to trigger innovative ideas from their personnel with a view to remain at the frontiers of knowledge rather than mere passive observers. Technology can be used creatively in service delivery by means of the mobile phone, for instance. Some libraries have adopted this tool to send overdue reminders to patrons for the late return of library materials whereas others use this for current awareness. While technology is definitely part of the solution, there is no reason to over-glorify technology and overlook the human resource behind the technological revolution (**Ramjaun, 2008).** Librarians have, in recent years, by introducing OPACs, CD-ROM databases and Internet access into their libraries, convincingly demonstrated their ability to master, manage and use advanced technologies. Thus, it has become fashionable to speak of a new librarianship and of a new image of librarians. The perception may be new, and recognition gratifying, however, in reality librarians have long been pioneering users of new technologies. Contrary to popular notions, librarians have always been among the first to adapt ad use the latest information handling and communication technologies (**Malinconico**, 1997).

The range and complexity of challenges facing libraries and librarians today are unprecedented. Certainly the proliferation of information technologies has made a significant impact on libraries in the way they deliver their services and content as well as the format of that very content as most libraries move towards digital collections or at the very least hybrid print and digital collections. In this environment there is also growing expectations of users for quality, accuracy and immediate responsiveness to their needs (**Sidorko**, 2007).**Ramjaun** (2008) **remarks that Innovation in libraries is inevitable due to the following reasons:**

- The discovery of unmet user needs.
- The introduction of new services or the retooling of traditional services resulting in a better user experience.
- Creative collaboration among libraries or between libraries and other institutions explorations of the future of libraries.
- Implementing new technologies to improve and extend library services to meet user needs.
- Redefining processes that encourage finding new and better ways to make library collections and facilities more useful.
- Incorporating best practices from foreign libraries wherever possible.

In order to survive major changes in the environment, libraries have to become more innovative. Innovation exploits change and provides libraries with the means to deal with the unstructured problems arising out of changing environments (**Bryson**, 1996). In a nutshell, it is evident that due to flood of electronic information harmonizing with the advent of modern ICT devices, the information professionals desperately seek to revamp and re-engineer their methods of delivering services to the users' community by switching over traditional practices to electronic information systems and services through an innovative approach.

SUCCESS FACTORS FOR INNOVATION

Roberts and Fusfeld (1981) have rightly identified five key factors that are responsible for the success of innovation namely, idea-generating, chompioning, project leading, gate-keeping, and sponsoring or coaching. Their ideas on the critical functions in the innovation process may be illustrated in fig 1

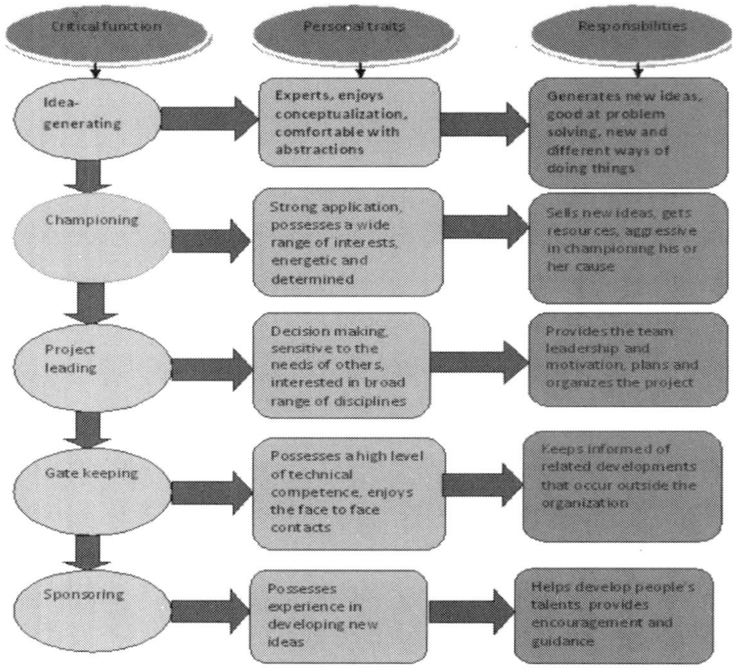

Fig. 1. Critical functions in the Innovation Process

Source: Roberts and Fusfeld (1981); authors

POLICY INSTRUMENTS FOR LIBRARY INNOVATION

The successful implementation of the scheme of Innovations in libraries largely depend upon various policy instruments depending upon the library ambiance, administrative lookout, readership,the size of the libraries, technological infrastructure, investment capacity and such other factors. Accordingly, objectives of innovations vary from libraries to libraries depending upon their technological set-up. Table I depicts the policy instruments applicable to different types of libraries with regard to their innovation objectives:

Types of libraries	Innovation objectives	Policy instruments
Library with low-technology	Build awareness of scope and benefits of innovation	• Management and skills development • Innovation awareness and understanding • Productivity enhancing services • Innovation identification and match making
Library with modest technology	Introduce basic innovation skills, encourage adoption and application of new ideas	• Product diversification and quality improvement • Management and skills development • Internet-based information services • Technology awareness and marketing • Support for technology adoption • Consultancy and technical assistance support
Technically competent library	Build in-house innovation capabilities	• Internet-based information services • Innovation and technology support • Linkages with academic researchers

Source: Adopted from World Bank, 2007

IMPORTANT TRENDS IN LIBRARY INNOVATION

Savenje (1999) remarks that currently libraries find themselves confronted with a second computerization wave. The first wave took place during the seventies and turned manual back-room activities such as acquiring, distribution, and cataloguing into computer-controlled activities. Commercial enterprises began marketing and selling products designed for computerizing the library's distribution cataloguing and acquisition systems. Essential in the computerization wave of the 90s in the deployment of computer networks, campus wide networks at universities as well as national and international networks. These networks provide access to remote electronic information by means of library information systems. Furthermore, available electronic information is no longer limited to so called secondary information (catalogues, bibliographic databases). Also primary information has now become electronically available. Presently, we can refer to the electronic full-text versions of scientific journals. Electronic text books and readers enable us to consult information outside the library i.e, at the professional and private worksite of the library's traditional customer within the context of innovation. **Savenije (1999)** points out the following three fundamental trends:

- The library is shifting its focus from concentrating on supply towards centring on what is asked for by its customers. In correspondence with this trend, information reference is becoming more and more significant. The library acquires a gateway function, referring to information, irrespective of the location where it has been physically stored. Growing importance will be put on navigation. By and large, users will prefer to find their own way across the large amount of available information. To an increasing extent, services will be offered from a distance: the users will choose to consult their sources sitting at their own desk, at their own computer. This in turn, implies that the library needs to increase the accessible electronic collection, which is accomplished by disclosing sources elsewhere, but also by electronically providing material that has already been available on paper.

- As a result of growing internet, the library services are blending with the teaching process. A similar trend can be observed in the process of research. Here, the fundamental stages are the identification of sources, the exchange of information with colleagues, the interpretations and analysis of data and the dissemination of findings. In this case, the boundaries between the provision of information and the various stages in the research process are fading as well. Comparable tendencies are becoming apparent in other primary processes they are serving. This implies that we should no longer consider the library task as some sort of overhead services. On the contrary, they are developing into a directly productive force.
- A third trend is related to the so called information chain. The role of the library is often described as a link in this information chain. At the moment, we can notice various problems connected to this chain. Traditionally, the various stages have been strictly distinguished in terms of chains main functions, i.e, subsequently in the production, distribution, acquisition, and consumption of information. However, this chain is exploding due to technological developments and information transfer and the system is starting to shrink due to the pressure exerted by the environment.

Comprehending the above trends, the traditional practice of librarianship is rapidly adapting to innovations in the form of novel strategies coupled with creativity and new technological adoptions.

TECHNOLOGICAL TRENDS

It should not be inferred that technology alone will solve the library's operational problems. There is a great need to understand more fully the fundamentals of library service and the nature of user needs. Librarians will have to become more knowledgeable about consumer demand, the uses of information and the value of information to the user(**Drake and Olsen,** 1979).Technological innovations have the potential to alter the nature of any industry. The information industry seems particularly subject to the effects of technology and currently is adapting to the introduction of a number of technological advances that are associated with the general availability of networked electronic information resources. The advent of systems that allow documents to be created electronically, stored and maintained in computers, and easily found and read using high-speed communications networks may produce dramatic changes in the information industry. It is certainly not clear whether documents prepared, distributed, and used through this new technology will replace or augment information resources published using more traditional media, but it seems likely that this new technology will bring about some changes in the structure of information industry(**Allen, B.1995**),

Technological change provides a case in point. Based on their knowledge of what is possible in today's high technology world and their awareness of successful technological applications in other libraries, professional librarians may have a vision of where the library should be heading with regard to the provision of information in electronic or digital form (**Pungitore, 1995, p.13**).The rapid pace of technology innovation requires librarians to look for simple ways to monitor new trends that may affect library services. Podcasts, RSS readers and messaging networks like Twitter each represent low-threshold tools that can serve as resources for breaking news, reviews, and technology journalism. Many libraries have enthusiastically courted innovation by adopting collaborative Web 2.0 technologies, designing content for mobile devices, and incorporating video into their next-generation library websites, in an effort to improve services for patrons and collaboration among staff and colleagues. While the academic community can always rely on technology-oriented journals and newsletters produced by their peers to place innovation in context and document new implementations over time, the breakneck pace of web, technology, and gadget innovation requires us to look for simple ways to stay current on a daily basis (**Wilson**, 2008).

PODCASTS

Podcasts are audio or video programs posted online in standard formats such MP3 and MP4 and distributed by subscription via RSS syndication. Since the ability to record and upload content is now within reach of just about anyone with a laptop, a portable headset, and a free blogging account, the range of topics and perspectives available is truly staggering(Ibid).

RSS FEED READERS

RSS feed readers aggregate news headlines, blog posts, articles, and other dynamic content from across the web, all in a single convenient preview and reading environment. Also known as news readers, these applications provide a convenient way for users to subscribe to their favorite web sites and to monitor each new item posted, without ever having to visit the site itself. Virtually every website, blog, online newspaper, or social networking site now incorporates either RSS or ATOM coding, two XML-based syndication standards that make subscription to the latest news an effortless process. Feed readers can be web-based applications, standalone clients, or elements incorporated into the web browsers and email clients we already use on a daily basis (Ibid).

WEB-BASED RSS READERS

Web-based RSS readers like Google Reader, Bloglines and Shyftr offer free, flexible platforms for users to follow as many websites as they like. Web-based readers are similar to popular webmail services like Hotmail and Yahoo Mail in that they allow users to create personal accounts and log in from anywhere in the world, while retaining personal settings and content. Google Reader can be accessed directly at URL http://reader.google.com. Users who already have a Google account associated with Gmail, Google Calendar, or Google Documents may log in with their usual credentials. New users can "Create a New Account" and then immediately start building a personal news page (Ibid).

TWITTER

Although podcasts and RSS readers provide fast, efficient tools for monitoring technology news, information professionals should also consider adopting Twitter (http://twitter.com), the popular Web 2.0 messaging service, as a connection to breaking news and insights as they first stream out across the web. Twitter is an online social networking service that allows users to create a personal account and leave brief public messages of 140 characters or less. Many libraries have already started experimenting with library Twitter accounts as an outreach tool to share news, events, and links with their patrons. However, Twitter can also be viewed as extremely powerful, customizable news feed (Ibid).

WEB PUBLISHING

Wordpress started out as a quick, free, **open-source solution blogging solution** just a few years ago; today it is a perfect alternative to building a web site from scratch. In addition to being free to use (and easy to install), the Wordpress community has exploded, with thousands of users and programmers creating custom themes and plug-ins to completely change the way the software looks and operates. The most important aspect of the software is it's easy-to-use interface and content management system. With it's visual rich editor, anyone can publish text and photos to the web site. Other options include multiple authors (with separate log-ins), built in RSS (Real Simple Syndication) technology to keep subscribers updated, and a comment system that allows readers to interact with the sites content. A fantastic way to communicate with patrons, staff, etc **(Hebert, 2006).**

Drupal is another open source web publishing option that some libraries may want to consider using. One of the most important aspects of any library is its community, and that's where the technology behind Drupal might come in to play a little better. Many have used the software to **build rich community based web sites** where many different users can control a large amount of content. Some examples include web portals, discussion sites, corporate web sites, and intranet (internal) web applications. Just like Wordpress, Drupal as an ever growing community of users developing add-ons to make the software work better in addition to providing technical support online to answer any of your installation or maintenance difficulties **(Hebert, 2006).**

MediaWiki is the original software that powered the famous Wikipedia, which basically allows users to create and edit information from a very simple to use text interface. Another open source wiki platform is *TWiki*, a flexible and powerful enterprise wiki that is perfect for project management. These wiki solutions can be used as alternatives to the web publishing methods used above, but can better be used as the library's place to **keep maintenance and training information available** that can constantly be updated as library operations change and develop. Imagine keeping the employee and support community of your library up-to-date with the inner workings through a community wiki, where they can go to troubleshoot any problems that may have been already solved once before in the past(**Hebert, 2006).**

Synthesite.com is one of the free web publishing sites. Librarians should make their website free of cost on this site and also can publish their documents easily (**Biswas and Paul**, 2009).

THE DEVELOPMENT OF SOFT ENVIRONMENT FOR INNOVATION

The development of soft environment mainly consists of four aspects (**Sheng and Sun**, 2007):

- The first is to set up the vision of knowledge innovation in libraries.
- The second is to foster the spirit of consciousness of daring to run risk and do innovation. If there is not the atmosphere of encouraging staffs doing innovation actively, and staffs are only demanded to satisfy with status quo and drift along, staffs naturally do not engage in any innovative activities, let alone failure.

- The third is to set up incentive mechanisms to encourage staffs to participate in knowledge exchange, sharing, and creation.
- The fourth is to create a kind of atmosphere allowing failure. As there always exist a great variety of risks for innovation, not every innovation dooms to be success.

INDIAN SCENARIO

The National Knowledge Commission (NKC) was set up by the Prime Minister of India to guide and advice for the proper utilization of the vast knowledge base of India towards building an equitable knowledge society. Library and Information system and services (LIS) is one of the major issues of concern in the prime focus area of Access to knowledge. The NKC therefore took it up as one of its first initiatives to review the present LIS scenario of India and prepare a roadmap for more relevant and need based Library service. There is a need to formulate and create mechanisms and institutions which will bring about a paradigm shift in the LIS scenario, to bridge the gap between the information poor and the information rich **(Das Gupta,** 2007).With the mandate of NKC, different types of libraries have been networked through relevant ICT applications. Libraries of IITs and IIMs have taken up right kind of initiatives in digitizing resources, creating institutional repositories, and developing websites. All university libraries of the country have started to revamp and re-engineer their services through electronic media by e-subscriptions, e-journal consortiums, and priced online databases. Above all, the urge for innovations of libraries and information centres in India is quite conspicuous.

CONCLUSION

A lot of strategies can be adopted to develop knowledge innovation culture of libraries, which consists of establishing the environment beneficial to knowledge innovation, creating a learning culture, shaping knowledge-based team organization, improving trust and cooperation, enhancing human resource development and cultivating knowledge innovation talents (**Sheng and Sun**, 2007). The tools and resources that we present in this paper are just a glimpse of advanced technology innovations. There are numerous other modern technologies developed of late. Therefore, it is high time for the policy makers, planners, and library administrators to properly look at how they encourage innovations in libraries for ensuring effective channelization of information resources. Moreover, the information professionals are supposed to keep track of the revelations of technology innovations so that their practical applications in libraries and information systems can be effectively implemented for promoting up-to-date and value based information services to the users of innovative techno generation.

REFERENCES

1. Wilson, D. W.(2008), "Monitoring technology trends with podcasts, RSS and Twitter", Library *Hi Tech News,* Vol.25 No. 10, pp.8-12.Availabe at: *http://www.emeraldinsight.com/Insight/ViewContentServlet?contentType=Article&Filename=Published/EmeraldFullTextArticle/Articles/2390251003.html,* accessed 5 September, 2009.
2. World Bank.(2007), "Innovation policies in Latin America II" Office of the Chief Economist, Latin America and the Caribbean Region, Washington, DC.
3. Dahlman, C. and Utz,A.(2005), "India and the knowledge Economy : leveraging strength and opportunities", The World Bank, Washington, DC.

4. Roberts, E. B. and Fusfed, A. R. (1981), "Staffing the innovation technology based organization", *Sloan Management Review*, Spring, pp. 19-32.

5. Ramjaun, I.(2008), "Creativity and innovation in Libraries", available at: *http://liamofmauritius.wordpress.com/2009/03/21/creativity-and-innovation-in-libraries/*

6. Sheng, X. and Sun, L.(2007)"Developing knowledge innovation culture of libraries", *Library Management*, Vol.28 No ½, pp. 36-52, available at: *http://www.emeraldinsight.com/Insight/ViewContentServlet?contentType=Article&Filename=Published/EmeraldFullTextArticle/Articles/0150280104.html*, accessed 9 September, 2009.

7. Malinconico, S. M.(1997), "Librarians and Innovation : An American view point", *Program*, Vol.31 No.1, pp.47-58, available at: *http://www.emeraldinsight.com/Insight/ViewContentServlet?contentType=Article&Filename=Published/EmeraldAbstractOnlyArticle/Articles/2800310104.html*, accessed 4 September, 2009.

8. Allen, B.(1995), "Academic information services: A library management perspective", *Library Trends*, Vol. 43 No.4, pp.645-62, available at: *https://www.ideals.uiuc.edu/bitstream/handle/2142/7987/librarytrendsv43i4j_opt.pdf?sequence=1*, accessed 4 September, 2009.

9. Bryon, J.(1996), Effective library and information centre management, Jaico: Bombay.

10. Savenije, B.(1999), "Organising library innovation", available at: *http://www.library.uu.nl/staff/savenije/publicaties/ticer99.htm*, accessed 9 September, 2009.

11. Drake, M. A. and Olsen, H. A.(1979), "The economics of Library Innovation", *Library Trends*,Vol.28, No.1, pp.89-106, available at: *http://www.ideals.uiuc.edu/bitstream/handle/2142/7064/librarytrendsv28i1h_opt.pdf?sequence=1*, accessed 12 September, 2009.

12. Pungitore, V. L.(1995), Innovation and the library : the adoption of new ideas in public libraries, Greenwood press; West port, available at : *http://books.google.co.in/books?hl=en&lr=&id=ofSKdqu7XlgC& oi=fnd&pg=PP13&dq=%22library+innovation%22&ots=e2BM6mhMVc&sig=sZi2-evu3DnRe5yaDb8EU_LB26g#v=onepage&q=&f=false*, accessed 12 September, 2009.

13. Das Gupta, K.(2007), "The Knowledge Commision and Libraries : A vision for the future", Delhi Library Association Networking Professionals, Dr. Ranganathan Lecture Series, Fifth lecture, available at: *http://www.dlaindia.org/srr7.htm* , accessed 12 September, 2009.

14. Sidorko, P. E.(2007), "Fostering innovation in library management and leadership", *Library Management*, Vol.28 No.1/2 , pp.5-16, available at:*http://www.emeraldinsight.com/Insight/ViewContentServlet?contentType=Article&Filename=Published/EmeraldFullTextArticle/Articles/0150280101.html*, accessed 13 September,2009.

15. Hebert, E.(2006), "How Open Source Software Can Improve Our Library", available at: *http://www.degreetutor.com/library/managing-expenses/open-source-library*, accessed 15 September, 2009.

16. Biswas, G. and Paul, D.(2009), "Open source resource for library and information centre for their service", In Kumar, S, Ed. Library & Information Technology : Driving Management Education, New Delhi, Vayu Education of India

17

Corporate Planning for Academic Development: Role of Capacity Building

Kailash C. Das

INTRODUCTION

The iconographic power of a library expresses a purpose not just to collect, but also to organize, preserve, and make knowledge accessible. Today on the campus of virtually every higher education institution, the library occupies a central position. In its placement and prominence, the academic library conveys its integral role in supporting higher education's core missions of research and education.

Academic libraries are changing in response to changes in the learning and research environment and changes in the behavior of library users. The changes are evolutionary. Libraries are adding new, digital resources and services while maintaining most of the old, traditional resources and services. Finding and funding the appropriate balance of digital and traditional initiatives challenges strategic and financial planners. Library administrators feel pressured to respond to the transforming needs and expectations of users (Troll, 2002).

COPING WITH CHANGE IN LIBRARIES

Academic and research libraries have been early adopters of digital technologies and have provided leadership and training to help remake the academic enterprise. And yet, libraries and the librarians who lead them now find themselves asking a series of fundamental questions:

To what extent, and in what ways, are academic libraries likely to change?

- What new roles will librarians come to have in the changing information environment?
- What aspects of the academic library will prove the most resistant or impervious to change?
- Will technology finally spur a recasting of how colleges and universities produce and disseminate knowledge?

To answer these questions is to realize that the years ahead constitute an age of transformation for academic and research libraries. At the outset of the twenty-first century, these institutions confront the need to reconceive and reconstruct the means by which they support faculty and students in research and education. The business of libraries can now be understood as one component of a rapidly evolving, almost wholly transformed environment in which information is proliferating at heretofore unimagined rates. The ability of academic libraries to deliver authenticated and reliable information is continuously challenged by new technologies. To cope up with these problems librarian has to act as facilitator between users-library staff-administrator and plan accordingly like at corporate level to face the emerging change in libraries.

LIBRARIAN AS FACILITATOR

What should be the role of librarians and libraries in the new information age? The following are some samples of the types of changes that are commonly anticipated or hoped for. In the new information age the functions and role of librarians will be as outlined by Church (1996) as

1. Consultant
2. Analyst
3. Facilitator/Trainer
4. Intranet Content Manager
5. Product Planner and Marketer
6. Corporate Knowledge Manager

The role of a facilitator is to guide people in discovering new approaches to problems. According to Keith Coriell (2001), the key characteristics of a good facilitator are:

- asking others for their opinions rather than advancing their own;
- compromising rather than dictating;
- building relationships rather than being task-oriented;
- adapting to changing situations;
- maintaining objectivity;
- effectively using skills to invoke participation and creativity;
- being knowledgeable about client issues;
- understanding and dealing with group dynamics.

All facilitators need to possess these characteristics. However, it is equally important to know who the appropriate facilitator in a given situation is. The basic requirement is that the facilitator must have some sort of relationship or familiarity with the client and their issues. This enables the client to feel comfortable enough to provide adequate feedback and honest responses to questions. Who will be better facilitator than the librarian in capacity building for staff, users and authority in a library?

Some libraries are making this transition and doing it well. However, it appears that many libraries either have not yet begun to make needed reforms. Many diverse issues, such as personnel, budget, equipment, skill level, enthusiasm, knowledge, and organizational culture, contribute to the difficulty of making this transition. How to plan a strategically coordinated and comprehensive change process that is not only successful for the library, but also increases the value of the library to the whole organisation. This will be possible through an effective strategic planning. Strategic planning can also help to cultivate an organizational culture that understands and uses information as a business tool.

WHAT IS STRATEGIC PLANNING?

Strategic planning is an organisation's process of defining its strategy or direction, and making decisions on allocating its resources to pursue this strategy, including its capital and people. Strategic planning is the formal consideration of an organization's future course. All strategic planning deals with at least one of three key questions:

1. "What do we do?"
2. "For whom do we do it?"
3. "How do we excel?"(Wikipedia).

According to Schulz (1998), there are a number of potential benefits which can arise from greater involvement in strategic planning. These include:

- gaining a better sense of the library's and individuals' roles in the organisation
- appreciating the interdependence of different areas of library and university
- realising a shared sense of vision
- improving organisational communication and develop strategies for networking.

STRATEGIC PLANNING IN ACADEMIC LIBRARIES

There are a number of similarities between strategic planning and organizational development. Both approaches are used by administrators to manage change in a systematic fashion. *Strategic planning* emphasizes environmental scanning and goal setting, whereas *organizational development* relies on intervention techniques, such as benchmarking and team building. Strategic planning for academic libraries has greater impact when administrators understand the political nature of the decentralized academic system and particularly how decisions are made in their institutions. Consequently, organizational development becomes an "accretion of hundreds of largely autonomous actions taken for different reasons, at different times, under different conditions, by different people."(Cohen and March, 1974).

Although librarians have become adept at strategic planning methodologies, and may become campus leaders in designing and implementing this process, libraries are typically given scant mention in the strategic plan of the institution. How can academic libraries best conduct strategic planning? There are three main strategies for maximizing planning outcomes. These are to build upon the diversity of stakeholder interests, to form alliances and coalitions for the advancement of the library's own interests, and to market a persuasive planning document.

Patricia Senn Breivik (1993) poses three questions that campus planners need to ask about their libraries and computing services,

- "How can information resources and technologies best support institutional priorities?"
- "How can we best organize our information resources and technologies to make the strongest contribution to the identified priorities?"
- "How can we best deploy our limited human and fiscal information technology resources so that all graduates are information literate?"

Strategic planning in academic libraries can reach its full potential when the university community addresses such questions and then integrates solutions into institution wide planning. Three general strategies may be useful. **First,** acknowledge that plans, programs, and policies are politically rational only when they can be accepted by affected constituencies. This requires the kind of library leader who understands that multiple interests exist among various stakeholders and who is committed to developing processes for resolving important issues of conflict. **Second,** form alliances and coalitions among key library stakeholders. **Finally,** create persuasive and attractive planning documents that can be widely distributed to external constituencies.

CAPACITY BUILDING AND LIBRARY

Capacity building is the elements that give fluidity, flexibility and functionality of a program/organization to adapt to changing needs of the population that is served. (Wikipedia).Capacity building is defined as the "process of developing and strengthening the skills, instincts, abilities, processes and resources that organizations and communities need to survive, adapt, and thrive in the fast-changing world." (Ann Philbin, Capacity Building in Social Justice Organizations Ford Foundation, 1996)

The principal objective of capacity building is:

- to improve the quality of decision making,
- programme eficiency, and
- managerial performance in the planning and implementation of the organisation's mission.

REASONS FOR CAPACITY BUILDING?

- a major change in the external environment;
- a lack of internal ability to address a critical organisational challenge;
- pursuing an alliance with another organisation;
- governance issues;
- leadership transition or support;
- desire to undertake organisational planning

Capacity Building is much more than training and includes the following: Human resource development, the process of equipping individuals with the understanding, skills and access to information, knowledge and training that enables them to perform effectively. Organizational development, the elaboration of management structures, processes and procedures, not only within organizations but also the management of relationships between the different organizations and sectors (public, private and community).Institutional and legal framework development, making legal and regulatory changes to enable organizations, institutions and agencies at all levels and in all sectors to enhance their capacities (*citation: Urban Capacity Building Network*).

For organizations, capacity building may relate to almost any aspect of its work: improved governance, leadership, mission and strategy, administration (including human resources, financial management, and legal matters), program development and implementation, fundraising and income generation, diversity, partnerships and collaboration, evaluation, advocacy and policy change, marketing, positioning, planning, etc. For individuals, capacity building may relate to leadership development, advocacy skills, training/speaking abilities, technical skills, organizing skills, and other areas of personal and professional development. (*Evaluation of Capacity Building: Lessons from the Field* by Deborah Linnell, published by the Alliance for Nonprofit Management).

The most effective librarians will be those who forge connections between strategic planning, organizational development and technological change, as a measure of capacity building. A number of librarians mentioned particular areas of their institution's strategic plan which they felt the library had a significant contribution to make. These included:

- Teaching and learning: especially in relation to e-learning, ICT, accessibility, working with academic departments
- Research
- Effective use of ICT and e-learning, the development of electronic library services
- Widening participation: off-campus access, involvement in summer schools
- Student experience

- Regional agenda e.g. partnerships with outside libraries
- Staff development
- Knowledge transfer e.g. providing information to 'incubator companies'
- Resource planning
- Quality issues
- Overseas links: e-learning and electronic resource provision.

CORPORATE PLANNING

Corporate planning represents a formal, structured approach to achieve objectives and to implement the corporate strategy of an organization. It has traditionally been seen as the responsibility of senior management. The use of the term became predominant during the 1960s, but has now been largely superseded by the concept of strategic management.

Organizational development activities such as team building events are an effective way to strengthen the organization relationship. Such corporate events can come in the form of corporate parties, company picnics or other group of activities. Team building events are held to strengthen the organization, providing opportunities for members of the organization to find ways of working as a cohesive team. Critical areas for improvement of organization run by these development activities include communication, motivation of employees and skills (Greg, 2009).

Corporate planning approach is potentially useful for libraries to:

- Improve services for users;

- Articulate the importance of and need for their services and resources to a variety of stakeholders including funders, institutional managers, library staff, other university staff, students and the wider academic community;
- Determine how effectively the libraries aims and objectives are being met and feed into library planning and strategy;
- Align library aims and objectives more closely with institutional outcomes;
- Contribute effectively to the setting of institutional outcomes.

Libraries have also to plan such type of organizational activities to motivate the staff and build a strong team to work in a team to serve its users.

CUSTOMER CARE AND SERVICE PHILOSOPHY

Let us look at customer service in the corporate setting. What is the corporate philosophy of customer service, and how is it provided? How the concept of customer service can translate to a library setting, is arranged in three sections:

i) a discussion of the current state of customer-service orientation in the library;

ii) an examination of top-ranked service providers in the corporate world and their philosophy of customer service; and

iii) the viability of adapting a service mentality to the library setting.

CURRENT STATE OF CUSTOMER SERVICE IN THE LIBRARY

McDonalds and MasterCard share similar philosophies. They are both examples of a new type of organization- the service organization. "Service organizations are becoming more important in our daily lives as the United States changes from manufacturing to a more service-oriented society (Whitlatch, 1990).This change have also affected the way customers are treated. Service organizations are beginning to focus on serving the customer, or "customer service."

This new generation of pampered customers has a certain set of expectations. They expect to be served by employees who are not only knowledgeable about their products, but who are courteous at all times to all customers.

The customer takes these service expectations to the library as well. Today, when patrons walk into a library, they expect to be warmly greeted by a courteous librarian. When they ask a question, they expect a prompt, correct answer. They also expect to be treated with courtesy and full attention, regardless of their own behaviour. Instead of pointing out where a book is located, employees are encouraged to walk with the customer to the correct section of the store, find the correct book, and place that book in the customer's hands (Strickler,1992).Weekly seminars for employees in corporate sectors are conducted to make them acquainted about their products and services.

In nutshell, Good customer service includes these elements:

1) Employees need to treat the customer as a valued person, not an interruption;

2) Employees need to have some type of investment in the company, so they feel a part of the organization;
3) Employees need to know as much as they can about each product they sell; and
4) Make sure customers have what they want when they leave.

Librarians can do the same thing. Reference librarians are often told that they need to ask "is this what you're looking for?" or "do you need more information?" This question-asking can't be stressed enough as a primary form of customer service. A librarian needs to listen and ask probing questions in order to find the best information before sending the person to the stacks. Questioning at this point also helps clarify the need if the patron's questions are unclear. A librarian can check with the patron on his satisfaction with the library's service. If possible, check on patrons to see if they are finding what they need. A librarian can also walk the floors of the library and randomly ask patrons how their search is progressing. This shows patrons that the library really cares about their needs. Always make sure that the patron knows he's welcome to come back to the reference desk, if he needs further information. Also, a survey of patron satisfaction might help steer the library in the right direction. If librarians adapt a customer-service orientation within the library, it will continue to attract curious patrons. These patrons, if treated like welcome customers, will continue to support the library, rather than take their information needs somewhere else (King, 1996).

PLANNING FOR CUSTOMER-FOCUSED LIBRARY SERVICES

This begins with looking at these services from the customer's viewpoint. With this focus as a guide, the preparation of goals and objectives needs to be a corporate response to a re-examination of the library's business, the library's customers, and what those customers consider to be of value (Catt, 1995).

Planning for customer-focused library services, concepts such as the following need to be thoughtfully considered and implemented if the pursuit of the good or quality service is to be perceived as an acceptable corporate value:

Attitude : Both the individual and collective attitudes of the library administration, managers, staff, and trustees toward providing quality customer focused service need to be perpetually monitored and challenged. Are library staffs indeed listening and performing as customers want?

Internalization : Participants need to have the library mission become second nature to them. Posting the mission statement in several conspicuous places is a good way to constantly reinforce the agreed-to course of action.

Process : Development of a means of successfully achieving all tasks in the planning process is critical to success. The process provides the road maps which all have agreed will take the organization forward.

Data Collection : Collection of information about what the customers perceive as value needs to become a continuous process.

The following represents additional training or planning tips which will be useful in the pursuit of offering quality services:

Respect the simplicity of planning basics : Keep the process and application of the basics simple. Avoid complexities.

Examine personal philosophy regarding success : Is it more important for the library as an organization to succeed than for a single individual or group to succeed? *Become focused or intentional about a single mission.* Keep the mission and supporting goals and objectives before all participants and customers continuously.

Generating a score of ideas can be stimulating: Determining whether these same ideas need to be translated into real services is a more difficult task. Often the later step is omitted. It is a common pattern to go directly from idea to implementation. Each part must fit the whole.

Resources can impose limits on what it is practical to offer : It is important to be realistic.

Develop a mutually agreed upon direction for each part of the process : Document the chosen process.

Determine whether customer focus is a concept the library can exclusively adopt : The result of this acceptance will be providing what customers want rather than what the leaders of the library may want.

Determine what could stand in the way of being successful and how potential deterrents will be managed to achieve quality service.

Train and retrain staff to be able to successfully offer what customers want : Remember to spend time with new participants to help them see and buy into the course that the library is presently pursuing.

Use talents available to the library creatively and wisely : Get outside help. Put a team together which brings a variety of strengths? Volunteers can be valuable and valued friends. Match volunteer talents carefully to tasks. An outsider can be a tremendous asset if appropriately assigned.

Compromise is not a sign of weakness but one of strength : Bringing a host of ideas together and developing them into a focused plan can be challenging but ultimately rewarding.

Actively solicit frequent customer input: Determine how to use this information to make adjustments to services. *Respect tradition but question it.* Ask if the traditional services are still working or merely comfortable and easiest to offer?

Value each customer like a friend : Monitor customer losses and determine what can be done to avoid future loss.

Review progress toward the achievement of goals and objectives regularly at both board and staff meetings. Ask the customers about progress too.

THE CHALLENGE

Studies of individuals and organizations who achieve success demonstrate that planning and preparation are fundamental to the realization of that success. It sounds so easy, especially since the fundamentals of planning are readily understandable. However, it is the daily translation of these fundamentals into a successful program that provides the challenge. Librarians need to start thinking of marketing not as selling, but as another form of customer service. This approach is more familiar to librarians, who are generally customer-oriented. As a start, the corporate mission statement can be used as a guide (Brown, 1997). Using the corporate mission statement keeps the library mission meaningful within the organization's overall goals. Brown (1997) also suggests that the library mission statement:

- be stated in one sentence
- express the purpose of the information center
- acknowledge the people using the services
- support the enterprise's overall mission statement

With a mission statement as a guideline, the library staff should be able to organize their efforts towards supporting the overall organizational goals. The mission of the library thus sets the parameters of any marketing decisions (Olson & Moseman, 1997).

THE COMMITMENT

A key to success, in a library, is that application of basic planning fundamentals. There is, however, a critical pre-requisite to this step. *The first step must be commitment to a well-conceived and simple course of action.* That commitment might be defined as acquiring, keeping, and *satisfying library customers* by providing services and programs that a majority of customers have expressed an interest in receiving. It will mean defining mission statement, roles, goals, and objectives from the customers' point of view rather than operating from the library's historic or even current perspective.

Coincidently this happens to be the basic premise of the marketing concept. Whenever customers investigate the services offered by a library, they instinctively ask themselves two questions, "What's in it for me?" and "How much will it cost me?" These are the price/value questions. Library customers weigh the trade-off between what they will gain and what they will pay. Customers usually pay with commodities like time, convenience, and energy in addition to tuition, taxes, or fees.

When library administrators adopt this modern marketing concept, they are buying into the idea that the existence of the library is justified through the satisfaction of what customers need and want (Crompton & Lamb, 1986, p. 3).

LIBRARY AS SERVICE ORGANISATION

What do service-oriented organizations do differently from other organizations which are not perceived as being service-oriented by their customers?

In 1980, Citibank compiled the results of a study conducted with 18 highly service-oriented companies. Specifically, the Citibank (survey) companies do the following:

1. promote from within;
2. continually monitor service levels via service audits;
3. make sure senior management is actively, visibly committed to service excellence;
4. regularly recognize and reward outstanding service by employees;
5. invest heavily in formal, ongoing training;
6. practice teamwork and open communications;
7. measure service performance against explicit standards;
8. actively seek customer feedback on service and use it in decision making;
9. use employee attitude surveys to continuously assess the organization's internal health; and
10. have a strong sense of employee accountability ("Each of us is the company"). (Disend, 1991, pp. 15-16).

Staffs need to be well trained to be able to provide

responsive customer service. This is a financial investment in quality service which is required to ensure that staff is current in relevant areas of professional expertise as well as the provision of quality library service. A plan for training each employee should be established in every library. Because the world both inside and outside libraries is changing so rapidly, focused staff training programs will help to keep the library responsive to the resulting changes in customer requirements and desires as well as the library's abilities to meet those needs.

CONCLUSION

Corporate planning approach is potentially useful for libraries to:

- Improve services for users
- Articulate the importance of and need for their services and resources to a variety of stakeholders including funders, institutional managers, library staff, other university staff, students and the wider academic community
- Determine how effectively the libraries aims and objectives are being met and feed into library planning and strategy
- Align library aims and objectives more closely with institutional outcomes
- Contribute effectively to the setting of institutional outcomes.

Perhaps libraries of all sizes, shapes, and types are at a crossroads in determining their future. Terms like "re-engineering" and "re-inventing" are becoming common in the discussion of what organizations, both profit and nonprofit, will need to face in order to flourish. The way things have always been done is no longer adequate. The basic rules remain the same, but the interpretation is changing. The focus must shift from inward to outward. The customers' needs and perceptions are relevant. Service is giving something of value in exchange for something else of value. Where is the plan taking the library? Is it a worthwhile and value-adding journey?

Expect this journey to be different than any one previously taken. Expect the pursuit of providing quality library services to be worthwhile but perpetually challenging. Expect difficulties. Expect to re-invent the library in the context of what the customers think is important. Expect to be realistic about available resources. Expect success!

REFERENCES

1. Brown, Suzan A. "Marketing the Corporate Information Center for Success." *Online*. July-Aug. 1997. *Trade & Industry Database*. Online. InSite Pro. 17 July 1997.
2. Coriell, Keith J. (2001). *Facilitator-A Definition. Southwest Facilitators Network*.http://www.southwestfacilitatorsnetwork.org/_disc5/00000006.htm
3. Crompton, J. L., & Lamb, C. W., Jr. (1986). Marketing government and social services. p. 3
4. Dave Strickler, "What I learned in a bookstore," Library Journal 117 (June 1992): 48.
5. Disend, J. E. (1991). How to provide excellent service in any organization. Radnor,
6. Jo Bell Whitlatch, "Reference service effectiveness," RQ 30 (Winter 1990: 205
7. King, David (1996). Transferring corporate service philosophy to a library setting. LIBRES: Library and Information Science Electronic Journal, June, 1996 Vol 6 (1/2).
8. Michael D. Cohen and James G. March, *Leadership and Ambiguity: The American College President* (New York: McGraw-Hill, 1974), 104.

9. Olson, Christine A. and Suzanne Stewart Moseman. "Overworked? Understaffed? Don't Stop Marketing!" *Information Outlook*. Mar. 1997. *Trade & Industry Database*. Online. InSite Pro. 17 July 1997.

10. Patricia Senn Breivik, "Investing Wisely in Information Technology: Asking the Right Questions," *Educational Record* 74 (summer 1993): 47–52.

11. Schulz, Lisa (1998), "Strategic Planning in a University Library", *Marketing LibrarServices* 12(5)

12. Troll D .A. (2002) *portal: Libraries and the Academy*, Vol. 2, No. 1 (2002), pp. 99– 123. Copyright © 2002 by The Johns Hopkins University Press, Baltimore, MD 21218.

18
Leveraging of Corporate Culture in Library Management

Puspanjali Jena
Dipak Kumar Khuntia

INTRODUCTION

Culture is made up of the values, beliefs, underlying assumptions, attitudes, and behaviors shared by a group of employees in the organization. Culture is the behavior that results when a group of employees arrives at a set of, generally unspoken and unwritten, rules for working together. An organization's culture is made up of all of the life experiences each employee brings to the organization. Culture is especially influenced by the organization's founder, executives, and other managerial staff because of their role in decision making and strategic decision. Culture is the environment that surrounds one at work all the time. Culture is a powerful element that shapes one's work enjoyment, work relationships, and work processes. But, culture is something that one cannot actually see, except through its physical manifestations in one work place.

In many ways, culture is like personality. In a person, the personality is made up of the values, beliefs, underlying assumptions, interests, experiences, upbringing, and habits that create a person's behavior. Culture is represented in a group's language, decision making, symbols, stories and legends, daily work practices.

DEFINITION OF TERM "CULTURE"

The term "culture" originally coines from social anthropology. Late nineteenth and early twentieth-century studies of "prim-itive" societies: Eskimo, South Sea, African, and native Ameri-can revealed ways of life that were not only different from the more technologically advanced parts of America and Europe but were often very different among them. The concept of culture was thus coined to represent, in a very broad and holistic sense, the qualities of any specific human group that were are passed from one generation to the next. The ***American Heritage Dic-tionary*** defines "culture" more formally, as "the totality of so-cially transmitted behavior patterns, arts, beliefs, institutions, and all other products of human work and thought characteris-tics of a community or population. Organizational culture has two levels, which differ in terms of their visibility and their resistance to change. At the deeper and less visible level, culture refers to values that are shared by the people in a group and that tend to persist over time even when group membership changes. These notions about what is important in life can vary greatly in different companies; in some settings people care deeply about money, in others about technological innovation or employee well-being. At this level culture can extremely be difficult to change, because group members are often unaware of many of the values that bind them together. At the more visible level, culture represents the behavior patterns or style of an organization that new employees are automatically encouraged to follow. We say, for example, that people in one group have for years been "hard workers", those in another are "very friendly" to strangers, and those in a third always wear very conservative clothes. Culture, in this sense, is still tough to change, but not nearly as difficult as at the level of basic values.

CONCEPTUAL ANALYSIS OF THE TERM "CULTURE"

Following four pints are different characteristics of culture.

Culture is behavior : Culture is a word used to describe the behaviors that represents the general operating norms in environment for people at work. Culture is not usually defined as good or bad, although aspects of one culture are likely to support one progress and success, and other aspects impede one progress. A norm of accountability will help make one organization successful. Tolerating poor performance or exhibiting a lack of discipline to maintain established processes and systems will impede success.

Culture is learned : People learn to perform certain behaviors through either rewards or negative consequences that follow their behavior. When a behavior is rewarded, it is repeated and the association eventually becomes part of the culture. A simple thank you from an executive for work performed in a particular manner, moulds the culture.

Culture is learned through interaction : Employees learn culture by interacting with other employees. Most behaviors and rewards in organizations involve other employees. An applicant experiences a sense of one's culture, and his or her fit within the culture, during the interview process. An initial opinion of one's culture can be formed as early as the first phone call from the Human Resources department.

Sub-cultures formed through rewards : Employees have many different wants and needs. Sometimes employees value rewards that are not associated with the behaviors desired by managers for the overall organization. This is often how subcultures are formed, as people get social rewards form coworkers or have their most important needs met in their departments or project teams.

DIFFERENCE BETWEEN ORGANIZATIONAL CULTURE AND CORPORATE CULTURE

Organizational culture is an idea in the field of organizational studies and management which describes the psychology, attitudes, experiences, beliefs and values (personal and cultural values) of an organization. It has been defined as the specific collection of values and norms that are shared by people and groups in an organization and that controls the way they interact with each other and with stakeholders outside the organization. This definition continues to explain organizational values beliefs and ideas about what kinds of goals members of an organization should pursue, and ideas about the appropriate kinds or standards of behavior the organizational members should use to achieve these goals. The organizational values develop organizational norms, guidelines or expectations that prescribe appropriate kinds of behavior by employees in particular situations, and control the behavior of organizational members towards one another.

Organizational culture is not the same as corporate culture. It is a wider and deeper concept, something that an organization 'is' rather than what it 'has' Corporate culture. The total sum of the values, customs, traditions and meanings that make a company unique. Corporate culture is often called "the character of an organization" since it embodies the vision of the company's founders. The values of a corporate culture influence the ethical standards within a corporation, as well as managerial behavior.

SCOPE OF THE PAPER

There are several factors that bear a significant influence in shaping the management style of an organization. These, include leadership style, organizational factors, motivational methods and tools, as well as communication styles and methods. There are however many organizations who view their corporate culture only as a recruitment tool and an element in employee motivation and communications. The focus is now shifting, and organizations are realizing that an effective corporate culture engages employees at a fundamental level, and translates that engagement into high performance. An effective culture also aligns with the organization strategy to ensure the organization meet its long-term goals. So, the present paper focuses the fundamental needs of the corporate culture of the library organization to meet the present demands of the users. Library managers live within the corporate culture. They must understand it as a basis for diagnosing and solving problems and for developing new policies or procedures. They may be involved in managing the culture at the time of change or during crises.

OBJECTIVES OF THE PAPER

This paper is a critical analysis of managing the library's corporate culture to enhance organizational efficiency, productivity, and efficient service system. It seeks to sensitize the library managers through divergent views and opinions on how they can manage the corporate culture of their organizations, and to apply the basic principles of corporate culture management to library management. In response to the emergence of Information and Communication Technologies (ICT) that have brought changes to libraries, the paper explores the management of change in library's corporate culture, especially in this era of ICT.

LITERATURE REVIEW

The current interest in corporate culture began in the 1980s with the work of writers such as ***Alien and Kraft (1982), Deal and Kennedy (1982),*** and above all ***Peters and Waterman (1982).*** Academics had drawn attention to its importance much earlier. Indeed, ***Allaire and Firsirotu (1984)*** showed that, more than twenty years before the work of Peters and Waterman, there was already substantial academic literature on organizational culture. ***Blake and Mouton (1969),*** for example, were already arguing that there was a link between culture and excellence in the late 1960s.

Turner (1990) traced the "culture craze" of the 1980s to the decline of standards in manufacturing quality in the USA and the challenge to its economic pre-eminence by Japan. He comments that the concept of culture holds out a new way of understanding organizations, and has been offered by many writers as an explanation for the spectacular success of Japanese companies. ***Bowles (1989),*** among others, observes that there is absence of a cohesive culture in advanced economies in the West, and that the potential for creating systems of beliefs and myth within organizations provides the opportunity for promoting both social and organizational cohesion. The case for culture was best summed up by ***Deal and Kennedy (1983),*** who argued that culture rather than structure, strategy, or politics is the prime mover in organizations.

Culture, as ***Elridge and Crombie (1974)*** state, refers to the unique configuration of norms, values, beliefs, ways of behaving and so on, that characterize the manner in which groups and individuals combine to get things done. Culture defines how those in the organization should behave in a given set of circumstances. It affects all, from the most senior manager to the humblest clerk. They and others judge their actions in relation to expected modes of behaviour. Culture legitimizes certain forms of action and prescribes other forms. This view is supported by ***Turner (1990),*** who observes that cultural systems contains elements of "ought" which prescribes forms of behavior or allow behaviour to be judged acceptable or not. Culture is not static. As the external and internal factors that influence culture change, so culture will change. However, cultural change will be slow, unless there is some major shock to the organization (Burnes, 1991). This in itself may not be a problem, if other factors also change slowly. In addition, like ***Handy (1986), Allaire and Firsirotu (1984)*** argue that, to operate effectively and efficiently, an organization's culture needs to match or be appropriate to its structure. As ***Handy (1986)*** commented "experience suggests that a strong culture makes a strong organization, but does it matter what sort of culture is involved? Yes, it does. Not all cultures suit all purposes or people. Cultures are founded and built over the years by the dominant groups in an organization, what suits them and the organization at one stage is not necessarily appropriate for ever - strong though that culture may be. For a variety of reasons, organizations may find that their existing culture is inappropriate or even detrimental to their needs. In such a situation, many organizations have decided to change their culture. Many writers advocating culture change, including ***Peters and Waterman (1982)*** with their seven steps to excellence, take a very prescriptive line. Others appear to underestimate the difficulty involved in changing culture. There are other writers, however, who while sharing the belief that culture can be changed, take a more considered view. One of the more influential, ***Schein (1985),*** believes that before any attempt is made to change an organization's culture, it is first necessary to understand it. Schein's approach is to treat culture as an adaptive and tangible learning process. His approach emphasizes the way in which an organization communicates its culture to new recruits. It illustrates how assumptions are translated into values and how values influence behaviour. Schein seeks to understand the mechanisms used to propagate culture, and how new values and behaviours are learned. Once these mechanisms are revealed, he argues, they can then form the basis of a strategy to change the organization's culture. The work of ***Schein (1985), Schwartz and Davis (1981), Cummings and Huse (1989) and Dobson (1988)*** provide organizations with the guidelines and methods for evaluating the need for undertaking cultural change. Schein's work shows how an organization's existing culture can be revealed. Schwartz and Davis[1] shows how the need for cultural change can be evaluated and the necessary changes identified. Finally, the work of ***Cummings and Huse (1989) and Dobson (1989)*** shows how cultural change can be and is implemented.

TYPES OF CULTURE

Handy (1986) identifies four types of culture: power, role, task and person. He relates each of these to a particular form of organizational structure.

Power culture is frequently found in small entrepreneurial organizations such as some property, trading, and finance companies. Such a culture is associated with a web structure with one or more powerful figures at the center, wielding power.

Person culture is rare. The individual and his or her wishes are the central focus of this form of culture. It is associated with a minimal structure, the purpose of which is to assist those individuals who choose to work together. A person culture can be characterized as a cluster or galaxy of individual stars.

Role culture is appropriate to bureaucracies, and organizations with mechanistic, rigid structures and narrow jobs. Such cultures stress the importance of procedures and rules, hierarchical position and authority, security and predictability. In essence, role cultures create situations in which those in the organization stick rigidly to their job description (role), and any unforeseen events are referred to the next layer up in the hierarchy.

Task cultures, on the other hand, are job- or project-oriented, with the onus on getting the job at hand (the task) done rather than prescribing how it should be done. Such types of cultures are appropriate to organically-structured organizations where flexibility and teamwork are encouraged. Task cultures create situations in which speed of reaction, integration, and creativity are more important than adherence to particular rules or procedures, and where position and authority are less important than the individual contribution to the task in hand.

IMPORTANCE OF CORPORATE CULTURE IN THE PRESENT ENVIRONMENT

People shape the culture : Personalities and experiences of employees create the culture of an organization. If most of the people in an organization are very outgoing, the culture is likely to be open and sociable. If many artifacts depicting the company's history and values are in evidence throughout the company, people value their history and culture. If doors are open, and few closed door meetings are held, the culture is unguarded.

Culture is negotiated : One person cannot create a culture alone. Employees must try to change the direction, the work environment, the way work is performed, or the manner in which decisions are made within the general norms of the workplace. Culture change is a process of give and take by all members of an organization. Formalizing strategic direction, systems development, and establishing measurements must be owned by the group responsible for them. Otherwise, employees will not own them.

Culture is difficult to change : Culture change requires people to change their behaviors. It is often difficult for people to unlearn their old way of doing things, and to start performing the new behaviors consistently. Persistence, discipline, employee involvement, kindness and understanding, organization development work, and training can assist you to change a culture.

Culture has a vital and measurable impact on the organization's ability to deliver on its strategy.

- It helps to issues such as risk management, customer relationship management, business process outsourcing, change management, growth, or leadership.

- Culture is central for a successful operation and to long-term effectiveness of the organization
- Corporate culture is a key component in the achievement of an organization's mission and strategies, the improvement of organizational effectiveness, and the management of change. Culture is rooted in deeply-held beliefs.
- It reflects what has worked in the past.
- It is a pattern of shared beliefs, attitudes, assumptions and values, which may not have been explicitly articulated.
- Corporate culture shapes the way people act, interact, and strongly influences how things get done. It encompasses the organization's goals, behavioral norms, and dominant ideologies.
- Culture can be expressed through the organization's myths, heroes, legends, stories, jargon, rites, and ritual.
- Corporate culture can work for an organization by creating an environment that is conducive to performance improvement and the management of change.
- It can work against an organization by erecting barriers that prevent the attainment of goals. The impact of culture can include conveying a sense of identity and unity of purpose to members of the organization, facilitating the generation of commitment and shaping behavior by providing guidance on what is expected.
- Culture is manifested in the form of norms, the unwritten rules of behavior and values, that is regarded as important, expressed as beliefs on what is best or

good for the organization and what ought to happen.

ATTRIBUTES OF CORPORATE CULTURE

Corporate culture refers to a system of shared meaning held by members that distinguishes one organization from the other. This is based on some characteristics which, in aggregate, capture the essence of the culture of an organization. Some of the important attributes of corporate culture are as follows (***Robbins, 2004; p. 525***):

Innovation and risk taking : The extent to which employees are encouraged to be innovative and take risks.

Attention to detail : The degree to which employees are expected to exhibit precision, analysis, and attention to detail.

Outcome orientation : The degree to which management focuses on results or outcomes rather than on techniques and processes used to achieve those outcomes.

People orientation : The degree to which management decisions take into consideration the effect of outcomes on people within the organization.

Team orientation : The degree to which work activities are organized around teams rather than individuals.

Aggressiveness : The degree to which people are aggressive and competitive, rather than easy-going; and

Stability : The degrees to which organizational activities emphasize maintaining the status quo in contrast to growth,

LIBRARIES AND CORPORATE CULTURE

Librarianship has strong values which may not always

fit the changing environment. Demands for access and availability may be thwarted by one's desire to preserve and protect materials. Even with interlibrary loan and interlibrary cooperation, there is still a gap in meeting the demands of the library clienteles across the continents, especially in the developing nations of the world. Users are sometimes restricted from accessing some materials because of their sensitive nature and more importantly, the preservation of such materials for future generations.

In the early days of papyrus, clay, and tablet, civilization was at its infancy and there was no need for a global information as the world population was small. But the world is now a global village. Information is vital to the existence of human race and it forms the fulcrum around which the world economy, social, and political activities revolve. The global acceptance of the Internet for shopping, marketing, buying and selling, mailing, charting and communicating, advertising, displaying, campaigning, launching, exhibiting, and so on, shows the crucial role information plays in the existence of human society. There is a higher level of awareness about what information can do. In the present day the difference between a rich man and a poor man is information. One is well informed, and he becomes knowledgeable and therefore powerful and rich. The difference between success and failure, between the winner and the loser, is information. Even the Bible attests to it, saying, "my people perish because of lack of knowledge". Information brings knowledge, and when knowledge is properly utilized, it brings power.

FEATURES OF CORPORATE CULTURE

Corporate culture has a vital and measurable impact on the organization's ability to deliver on its strategy. It has the following beneficial features in the library management

Cooperation : Shared values may enhance goodwill and mutual trust, encouraging cooperation.

Decision making : Shared beliefs and values lead to more efficient decision making since there are fewer disagreements about which premises should prevail.

Control : Strong culture serves as an informal control mechanism.

Communication : Agreement on beliefs and values facilitates communication.

Commitment : Strong cultures foster strong identification and feelings through beliefs and values the employee can share with others.

Perception : Shared beliefs and values pro-vide organization members with shared inter-pretations of their experience.

Justification of behavior : Culture helps organization members make sense of their behavior by providing justification for it.

The following features are advantages for the growth of the organization.

- Corporate culture can have a significant impact, on a firm's long-term economic performance.
- Corporate culture will probably be an even more important factor in determining the success or failure of firms in the-next decade. Performance-degrading cultures have a nega-tive financial impact for a number of reasons, the most sig-nificant being their tendency to inhibit organisation from adopting needed strategic or tactical changes. In a world that is changing at an

increasing rate, one would predict that un-adaptive cultures will have an even larger negative financial impact in the coming decade.

- Corporate cultures that inhibit strong long-term financial performance are not rare; they develop easily, even in firms that are full of reasonable and intelligent people.

NEED OF CORPORATE CULTURE IN INDIAN CONTEXT

Library and Information personnel play a key role in the development of resources and services of university libraries. Because of fluid information environment and rapidly changing work performance requirements, skill and competency gap is often created in employees. "Any large organization today has to survive, grow and prosper in a highly competitive, dynamic, rapidly changing complex environment, where human obsolescence is as common as that of machines and where survival is only of the fittest" ***(Bhatia and Singh, 2000).*** To maintain the competitive level of library professionals, continuing education and need-based training of library staff will be the important requirements. Continuing education and training of staff will not only help to enhance their capacity for work performance and ensure efficiency but also help to quickly adopt and properly adapt with new information handling methods, knowledge management tools and technologies and make effective use of contemporary information systems and services. Keeping in view the ever-expanding operations of libraries and new kind of service demands on one hand and limited financial resource on the other, libraries are developing a corporate culture of management.

Indian libraries also face a great challenge of preparing

and empowering information user communities by imparting need-based information literacy. For decades, India has not been able to make effective use of its manpower because of illiteracy. India will not be able to make most effective use of its literate manpower without imparting information literacy. The libraries are required to launch massive movement and programmes for imparting information literacy to enhance the capacities and competence of information users to make more effective use of information resources and services. The following forces, among other factors, make the corporatization of L & ICs and adoption of corporate culture in libraries imminent:

Orthodox outlook of traditional librarians and their reluctance to adapt changes and to keep pace with the time - a psychological phobia to loose jobs and/or to invite unnecessary work traffic at no extra cost,

Less competence and non-acquaintance of traditional librarians with modern computer and communication technologies and electronic gadgets.

Mushroom growth of computer networks, web resources, Information gateways, OAI, WebOPAC, etc. which have removed the age-old geographical barrier to a great deal.

Availability of a **high percentage of major reference tools** in both CD and Online format coupled with fast communication and contact' facilitated by e-mail system;

The information needs of library customers are not only becoming increasingly complex, but also their **expectations to get** quality and need-based services well in time are becoming sky high.

Traditional reference services are still in the net *of* **conservative and moderate theories,** rather than liberal theory,

Exponential growth of a myriad range of information sources, (hereby making networked-based cooperative approaches (locally, nationally, and internationally) exigent.

The **global economic recession** and at the same time, an abnormal increase in costs of resources, manifold growth in demand, and considerable curtailment in library budget/funding leading to pressure even on dedicated staff in many of the contemporary libraries to reach an unattainable level.

ACTION PLAN FOR CORPORATE PLANNING

The process of organizational culture change will require ongoing commitment and attention to this incremental process that requires time for individuals to learn new ways of working together. The researchers anticipate that it will be useful to reassess the organizational culture during the course of this change to ensure that culture change is indeed becoming embedded in the values and perceptions of the organization and its members. This may be particularly useful to help staff engage in rich conversations about the progress of the Library during this time of change. Assessment of success will also require personal reflection and growth, particularly for leaders and managers in the organization. Creating an organizational culture that fosters staff success begins with understanding the characteristics of the present organizational culture, identifying the desired future culture and what needs to change in that culture to reach desired goals. Staff success can be achieved through both an individual and a collective change process that involves a continuous negotiation between perceptions, values, goals and actions. All of these must be aligned in order lo promote staff They address innovation, future directions and continuous improvement, characteristics of an Adhocracy culture, as well as teamwork, interpersonal relationships and staff development, characteristics of a Clan culture.

In order to manage corporate culture the library must adopt the following ideas.

- Hold idea ***sharing*** events in the workplace and assign responsibility for fostering and ***modeling innovative thinking*** to key individuals in the library, to ensue that ***innovation*** is encouraged and learned at all levels;
- Create cross functional ***taskforces*** that are both problem-solving and idea-generating to develop new or alternate approaches to work, consider divergent viewpoints;
- ***Monitor*** the expectations, preferences and complaints of clients. ***Assign the analysis*** and review of these to a group of staff empowered to make recommendations on actions and future service developments;
- ***Encourage action*** learning amongst staff by first trying out ideas on a pilot work basis and analyzing what is learned from a success or failure.

To manage the future the library should:

- Ask each staff member to ***generate their own vision*** statement consistent with the basic principles and values of the library;
- Identify and ***share events*** which exemplify progress towards the library vision and help make these part of the events that defines success in the library;
- Identify ***priorities*** for work units and individuals and identify achievable actions to these ends.

To manage continuous improvement it is considered important to:

- Make ***continuous improvement as*** a key feature of the vision articulated for each work unit in the library;
- Highlight the importance of ***assessment*** and provide ***training for staff*** to understand the process and value of assessment and improvement;
- Help the staff understands the basic elements of ***reflective practice*** and encourage them to use this as a personal and group tool for reviewing and improving activities;
- Actively seek out ***improvement ideas*** from the staff and emphasize trends in improvement, as well as big ideas.

To manage teams we should:

- Provide ***team building and communication training*** and expertise, teaching the staff to behave in teams for maximum benefit;
- Ensure that teams as much as possible include representation from a variety of subcultures and groupings to ensure that all perspectives are heard and staff engagement is at its peak;
- Encourage ***interdisciplinary and cross functional teams*** for service development and problem solving;
- Keep teams ***issues-centered, and future-centered*** and help teams seek alternative and creative solutions.

In managing interpersonal relationships we will;

- Be clear about the expectations of staff performance and be ***consistent in interpersonal interactions***;

- Create an environment where ***opinions are valued, considered and respected*** by all;
- Try to succeed by ***organizational transformation;***
- Ensure that team leaders are ***accessible to the staff*** to deal with concerns, problems and successes;

To manage the development of staff we should:

- Establish goals for the staff that are specific, measurable, aligned to the library's mission, reachable but still a stretch and time-bound;
- Encourage and support the staff in taking risks, cultivating excitement in trying something that may result in improvements and ensuring that learning occurs from mistakes and failures;
- Provide opportunities for the staff to learn new tasks, enrich and expand their jobs by adding responsibilities that require the learning of new skills and abilities;
- Recognize and expand the existing the staff expertise and talents;
- Encourage staff to take responsibility for activities and provide coaching and support for this increased autonomy.

Through these key actions a culture change will occur that reflects the goals of most librarians of the organization resulting in a strong foundation to support ongoing change.

MAJOR WORK VALUES OF CORPORATE CULTURE IN LIBRARIES

The following should be the desirable work values of a library adopting corporate culture:

- service-bent of mind;

- zeal to learn;
- accountability;
- adaptability to changes;
- strong commitment;
- courtesy and respect to customers;
- continuous quality control;
- autonomy to staff;
- effective and excellent communication;
- flexible procedure;
- dedicated, innovative, and good morale;
- recognition and reward for excellence;
- honest, and productive mind;
- service orientation, training, inter-section;
- transfer at given intervals;
- scholarships and awards; and
- feedback and treatment.

IMPACT OF FIVE LAWS ON LIBRARY CULTURE

Ethics of librarianship denotes the conduct and behavior of those who adopt the profession. A library professional owes certain obligations to the library's clientele, society, its resources, and the library professional organization and to himself. The five laws of library science propounded by Dr S.R. Ranganathan are the cardinal principles to be observed by a library professional in all his activities. The five laws - books are for use, every reader his/ her book, every book, its reader, save the time of the readers, and a library is a growing organism - provide essential guidelines for librarians with the potential for planning and providing patron services in all types of libraries. These are elemental laws and are meant to endure. These are also pertinent to the present era of information technology, where electronic, communication and processing technologies are influencing every walk of life, including libraries and information management to a great deal.

The ***first law*** emphasizes on the use and service which is also reflected in the development and refinement of techniques and methods of library and information work: from the "library economy" of the late nineteenth century to the "library science" and "information science" of the present times. The ***second law*** emphasizes that the business of the library personnel is to know the reader, to know the book, and to actively help in finding by every person of his or her books. The ***third law*** emphasizes that every book in a library should find an appropriate reader. It is stated that "not to be touched is a sin for a book" and investment on unused book is a dead investment. In terms of S.R. Ranganathan, books are mute and inert and cannot express their desire. It is the job of the library staff (unlike the role of a salesman) to find a suitable reader for each and every book acquired in a library. Library personnel play a vital role of a "match maker", who matches a book with its appropriate reader. According to the ***fourth law,*** a library must examine every aspect of its policies, Corporate rules, procedures, and systems with the one simple criterion that saving the time of the reader is vital to the library's mission and culture. Saving valuable time of the users means providing efficient, quick and thorough access to its resources. The ***fifth law*** tells us about the vital and lasting characteristics of the library as an institution and enjoins the need for a constant adjustment of our outlook in dealing with it. It enunciates a fundamental principle that governs the planning and organization of libraries. If the library staff do not adapt a culture compatible to time and acceptable to all, it would be difficult for them to serve the library customers better in a growing organization like, library.

So, the five laws of Dr Ranganathan have formidable influence on the culture and class of a library which itself conserves and transmits culture; underpins education, both individual and formal in a wide spectrum of subjects.

CONCLUSION

The library is an organization that has existed for centuries and has formed its own particular culture, which has not been static. In many cases, a parent institution or organization's objectives determine the library's purpose and functions. The library is an organization where professionals, paraprofessionals, and other specialists work with a common objective, that is, making information available to library patrons. The professional librarians are the key actors in creating library culture, and they have principles, rules, and guidelines for service, while being guided by professional ethics.

Cooperation among staff is a vital ingredient for a healthy corporate culture. Cordial and cooperative interaction among staff enhances service. Gone are the days when librarians hide behind counters, wearing long faces and snubbing the innocent patron who is in desperate need of information. Librarians need the charisma of a good public relations officer. Public relations revolves around image making. A good corporate culture will present a good image for the library as an organization where the information needs of its internal and external public are always met.

REFERENCES

1. Adeyoyin, Samuel Olu, Managing the Library's Corporate Culture for Organizational Efficiency, Productivity, and Enhanced Service,". *Library Philosophy and Practice, Vol. 8, no. 2 (Spring 2006)*
2. Bhatia, S.K. and Singh, N. (2000). *Principles and Techniques of Personnel Management/Human Resource Management,* 2nd rev. ed., Deep & Deep, New Delhi, p. 91,
3. Allaire, Y. and Firsirotu, M.E. (1984). Theories of oganizational culture. *Organization Studies* 5(3): 193-226.
4. Alien, F.R. and Kraft, C. (1982). The organizational unconscious: how to create the organizational culture you want and need. Englewood Cliffs, IMJ: Prentice-Hall.
5. Armstrong, M. (1991). A handbook of personnel management practice. 4th ed. London: Kogan Page.
6. Barratt, E.S. (1990). Human resource management: organizational culture. *Management Update* 2(l):21-32.
7. Blake, R.R. and Mouton, J.S. (1969). Building a dynamic corporation through grid organization development. Addison-Wesley: Reading.
8. Bowles, M. (1989). Myth, meaning and work organization. *Organization Studies 10(3) :405-423.*
9. Burnes, B. (1991). Managerial competency and new technology: don't shoot the piano player—he's doing his best. *Behaviour and Information Technology* 10(2):91-109.
10. Cummings, T.G. and Huse, E.F. (1989). Organization development and change. West: Minnesota.
11. Deal, T. and Kennedy Deal T. and Kennedy, A. (1982). A Corporate Cultures. Adison-Wesley, Reading.
12. Dobson, P. (1988). Changing culture. *Employment Gazette,* December:657-650.
13. Elridge, J.E.T. and Crombie, A.D. (1974). A sociology of organization. George Alien and Unwin: London.
14. Filby, I. and Willmott (1988). Ideologies and contradictions in a public relations department. *Organization Studies* 9 (3):335-351.
15. Handy, C. (1986). Understanding organizations. Penguin: Harmondsworth.
16. Peters, T.J. and Waterman, R.H. (1982). In search of excellence:

lessons from America's best-run companies. Harper and Row: London.

17. Salaman G. (1979). Work organizations. Longman: London

18. Sathe, V. (1983). Some action implications of corporate culture: a manager's guide to action. *Organizational Dynamics* Autumn:4-23.

19. Schein, E. H. (1984). Coming to a new awareness of corporate culture. *Sloan Management Review,* Winter.13

20. Schein, E. H. (1985) Organizational culture and leadership: a dynamic view. Jossey-Bass: San Francisco.

21. Schwartz, H. and Davis, D. (1981). Matching corporate culture and strategy. Cambridge MA: MAP Concept Paper.

22. Silverman, D. (1970). The theory of organizations. Heinemann: London.

23. Turner, I. (1990). Strategy and organization. *Manager Update* 1(3): 193-206.

24. Uttal, B. (1983). The corporate culture vultures. *Fortune,* Oct. 17

25. Van Maanen J. and Kunda, G. (1989). Real feelings: emotional expression and organizational culture In B. Staw and I. Cummings (eds.): *Research in Organizational Behaviour* 11:43-103.

19
TQM and Capacity Building in Libraries

D.R. Meher

INTRODUCTION

In present knowledge based society/information society, according to A.E.Cawkell, most of the people are engaged in "brain work"... where more attention is paid on information activities and more expenditure is incurred on information (Singh,2008). Information is considered as an important recourse for socio-economic development of society.

Information is used in all spheres of the present-day civilization. At the individual level buyers use information to differentiate and choose from a range of products and services in order to ensure a better standard of living. Organizations use information as an economic resource to introduce innovation and increase their effectiveness and competitive positions.

This scenario has posed major challenges to the information sector, whose prime function is to satisfy the complex and increasing demands for information related products and services (Raina).

So, value-added information services can only provide the conformance to the requirements of the users and their satisfaction. But it is very difficult to give best products and services if there is no precise definition of what is best in terms of library goals.

There is no universally acceptable tool and technique to measure, control and improve the quality of products and services in libraries. Total Quality Management (TQM) is one of such techniques used for the improvement and maintenance of quality or performance of the libraries. Therefore it is necessary for library & information professionals to understand what TQM is (Bavakuty and Majeed, 2005).

WHAT AND WHY TQM

"Total Quality Management (TQM) is a system of continuous improvement employing participative management and centered on the need of customers". The concept of TQM presupposes employees involvement, problem solving team, statistical methods, long term goals and thinking, analysis of problems, and continuous sharpening of quality performance leading to excellence (Rout,1998).

According to Butcher the following factors necessitate TQM in libraries are:

Scarce Resources

Libraries have fewer resources available to them and at the same time facing a demand for more and additional services.

Changing Customer Access and Expectations

Our users want more and they want it at their convenience – by present physically or from distance, that to their expected quality.

Changing Role of Top Management

The role of top management is changing dramatically. We are moving from hierarchical organization to what Peter Senge calls "learning organization".

HRD AND CAPACITY BUILDING

Within the context of Information Polices formulation, major attention must be given to the development of human resource and capacity. HRD programmes, especially education, training, and research and development programmes must be consistent with the current information environment. Learning the skill is to be prime objective.

LIBRARY SCIENCE EDUCATION

At present in India there are 85 universities imparting different level of courses in Library & Information Science, and 50 universities are offering Ph.D Programme. (Agadi, Choukimath and Shoken, 2008). Few universities impart PGDLAN course.

IMPACT ON THE LIS SCHOOLS

In the Information Society/Knowledge society, the discipline Library & Information Science which is concerned with information and knowledge accumulation, organization and dissemination is of great importance to the society.

This discipline is at transitional stage and needs to be

revamped, reinvigorated and strengthened to withstand to the revolutionary changes taking place around, especially in the field of ICT. Imparting quality education by Indian LIS school in the way, so that the products of the schools can comfortably be fit to manage the modern Library & Information Centers (LICs).

ROLE OF INFORMATION MANAGER

- Personal involvement is very essential to manage any Documentation Centre.
- Be clear on subject one is working with.
- Be clear of one's organization's objectives.
- Always give first priority to users.
- Make every system as easy as possible i.e. classification, computerization, shelving, issuing etc.

TRAINING IN THE CONTEXT OF IT ENVIRONMENT

In India most of the libraries lack proper requisites for digital environment. Persons are not conversant with the IT gadgets. The training of library professionals in IT applications is of immense importance for enabling them to functioning libraries effectively. The training programmes include :-

- Practical hands-on training on ICT.
- Continuing education programmes.
- Educational tour.
- Workshop, conference, seminar.
- Refresher course at regular interval.

CAPACITY BUILDING (CB) AND TQM

The word 'capacity' as Chambers dictionary defines is 'an ability or talent'. The phrase 'capacity building' was first coined in 1991 when the United Nations decided to provide assistance to entities / organizations, usually developing countries societies which had a need to develop a certain skill or competence, or for general upgrading of performance ability.

UNDP defined capacity building as "the creation of an enabling environment with appropriate policy...human resource development and strengthening of managerial system". Again recognizes that CB is a long term, continuing process in which all stakeholders participate (Wikipedia). So, CB is much more than training.

TQM, stands for (Kawatra, 2000)

T = Everyone has a role to play (Total people involvement)

Q = Doing right things first time, every time, all the time (Quality)

M = Art of making it happen (Management)

The above acronym reveals almost all the attributes of capacity building defined by UNDP. One's capacity is his property that needs an environment to encash it. TQM provides that environment of Quality Culture / Quality Circle where continuous improvement is the only *mantra*, and the person's capacity is built up not along the organization, rather with the organization.

The principles and techniques of TQM contribute to the capacity of the person who is a part of it. TQM is a blend of four concepts: customer focus, universal responsibility, continuous improvement, and defect prevention (Joseph and Berk, 1995).

An Overview of TQM

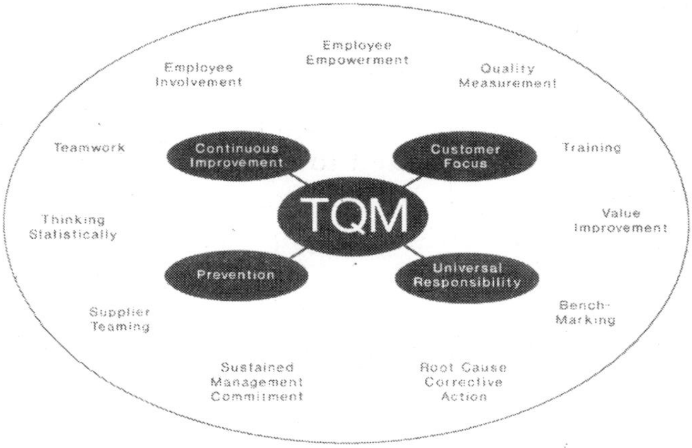

The Elements of Total Quality Management. TQM is centered on the principles of customer focus, continuous improvement, defect prevention rather than detection, and a recognition that responsibility for quality is shared by all of us. Other technologies support these four principles.

Total Quality Management

Customer Focus (Internal & External)

Lee Iacocca once advertised that Charysler has three roles: satisfy the customer, satisfy the customer, and satisfy the customer. That is about summing up the TQM philosophy.

Webster defines a customer as 'one that purchases a commodity or service'. Suppose someone purchases a car, here besides the purchaser his whole family is the customer. In information sector not only who gets and use the information but is affects to whole society.

The concept of internal customer always puts a pressure on the internal seller to improve the later for a zero defect in-house sale, as well as external sale.

Prevention Rather Than Detecting Defects

A popular saying 'an ounce of prevention is worth a pound of cure'. This prompts doing right things first time and all times.

Universal Quality Responsibility

Another basic TQM concept is that the responsibility of quality is not restricted to an organization's quality assurance department, but is instead, a guiding philosophy shared by everyone. Here everyone has to play a role and take responsibility.

Continuous Improvement

TQM espouses a philosophy of continuous improvement in all areas of an organization. With quality measurement this TQM concept focuses on finding shortfalls from administrative to service process that can detract from a quality output, and improving the process to eliminate undesirable output.

Quality Measurement

"If you don't know where you are going, you will probably end up somewhere." A basic TQM concept is that quality is a measurable commodity, and in order to improve, we need to know where we are.

To measure quality of library services SERVQUAL conceptual model is available. Dimensions of SERVQUAL are: tangibility, reliability, responsiveness, assurance and empathy.

A Sustained Management Commitment to Quality

If an organization is serious about implementing TQM, the commitment to do so has to start at the top. If management is willing to let a defective product go out the door or a substandard service is given, then the purpose is failed.

Employees Involvement and Empowerment

Here, every employee is involved is running the organization and play an active role for the organization meeting its goal. Empowerment, here, implies no power in administration; rather, employees are powered with right tools, training and reward. This helps capacity building of an employee.

Team Work (Synergy Team)

TQM proposes a quality circle that comprises most widely publicized 'team approach' to problem solving. It is a technically sophisticated and focused team.

Thinking Statistically

Thinking statistically is another TQM philosophy. For quality improvement it is the ideally suited method.

Benchmarking

It consists of identifying other organizations that perform well and implementing their wisdom into one's own organization. This TQM philosophy consists of defining competitors' best features from both internal and customers perspectives, and than adopting the best practices of their organization to one's own organization.

Value Improvement

The linkage between continuous improvement and value improvement is simultaneously obvious and subtle. This linkage becomes apparent when one considers the definition of quality – "ability to meet or exceed customers' requirement and expectations". The essence of value improvement is ability to meet or exceed customer expectation while removing unnecessary cost. Simply cutting cost, however, will not improve value if customers' requirement and expectations is comprised.

Supplier Teaming

To develop long term relationship with a few high quality suppliers rather selecting those suppliers with the lowest initial cost.

Training

Training is the basic to the TQM process. In order to use these concepts and techniques effectively, people have to be trained in each sphere. Yet another saying comes to mind "if one thinks training is expensive, he should try ignorance."

CONCLUSION

Time has come to think that if a user is getting information on Net why should he come to us .We are to come up to his expectations, by improving ourselves. As Capacity Building is more than training and needs an environment, and principles and techniques of TQM suggest that environment of continuous improvement, the library professionals may think over adopting TQM.

REFERENCE

1. Agadi, K B; Choukinath, P A and Shoken, N .(2008). Kogarnuranth, Kumbhar, B D and Kademani, B D (ed). Prof. C R Karsiddappa Festschrift volume. New Delhi: Allied, p.361

2. Bavakutty, M and Majeed, K C (2005). Methods for measuring quality of libraries. New Delhi: Ess Ess Publications, p.51.

3. Joseph and Berk, S (1995). Total quality management: implementing continuous improvement. 1st ed. New Delhi. Excel Book, p.7-12, 23.

4. Kawatra, P S(2000). Textbook of information science. New Delhi: APH Publishing Corporation, p.68.

5. Rout, R K (1998).*In* Mahapatra, M et al (ed). Information Management in Academic and Research Libraries, Ahmedabad. INFLIBNET Centre.p.127.

6. Singh, S P (2008). Challenges for LIS Professional in Information or Knowledge-Based Society. *In,* Kogarnuranth, Kumbhar, B D and Kademani, B D (ed). Prof. C R Karsiddappa Festschrift volume. New Delhi: Allied, p.361

20
Adapting Service Quality Concepts for the Capacity Building of Libraries

N. K. Dash
J. Sahoo

INTRODUCTION: THE RATIONALE FOR SERVICE QUALITY

The concept of service quality is somewhat elusive and resists easy definition, but essentially it emphasizes customer satisfaction as its primary objective. More traditional measures of academic library quality such as collection size are considered to be of secondary importance

The role, purpose and function of the library are being changed and challenged by its users. Libraries are being called upon to justify their value to its users in a time of budgetary pressure, dwindling financial condition, and growing competition from other public institutions such as hospitals, banks, super malls etc. As more people ask "what are libraries good for?" libraries are subject to increase their responsibilities and accountability. Libraries are being called upon to exhibit their contribution as never before. The service quality model offers a new concept of libraries, by providing a perspective of people as customers.

It is now the period in which libraries should be flourishing, because it is characterized by a growing need for education and information on the part of the general populace. Libraries are declining in popularity while the popularity of books is growing. Huge bookstore, for example, is proving to be the threat to libraries. The Internet itself is a key competitor. Not only can customers purchase books online at outlets such as the Amazon Web site, but also the Internet has become a user's personal library. The user no longer has to go to the conventional library, because he can access information more conveniently from his personal computer.

Faced with such competition, now it is time to market libraries themselves. The situation is analogous to the post office facing the threat from e-mail service and chatting. The way libraries can prosper is by delivering excellent customer service. The situation can be handled well by adapting different marketing concepts. As in marketing, it is time for the Librarians to start thinking themselves as retailers do, and realize that theirs is not just a business but also an interpersonal business, a "people" business. Like companies, libraries must do their best to increase market share. They can do so by enhancing the overall quality of service by that it can attract new customers, do more business with existing customers, and reduce the loss of customers.

The overall quality of service can be improved in several ways. First, by measuring not just the customer's perception of service, but customer's service expectations. Second, by improving service and lowering costs. A third way libraries can enhance service quality is by showing customers respect.

Many of the most common customer complaints regarding service, such as customer disparagement by employees, or being forced to wait for service, could be remedied by basic attitudinal changes by service staff.

The final way that a library can improve the customer experience is by paying greater attention to the overall atmosphere or ambiance. It is popular with customers not just for its outstanding selection of books, but also for its ambiance. Customers love its antique, comfortable feel, and it is the policy of the store to allow customers to sit all day and read if they wish.

Libraries must compete for customers by offering something valuable and then delivering it in a way that creates more value. Libraries must therefore define value and then create it. In an era of Darwinian competition for resources, libraries must compete harder and more passionately if they are to survive. Librarians must ask themselves, "If our library were to disappear from the landscape overnight, would we be missed?"[2]

THE SERVICE QUALITY CONCEPT

The Changing Concept of Quality in library

The concept of quality is not a new phenomenon for library and information science professionals as it is rooted in library principles, practices and activities. Though explicitly not stated, Ranganathan's five laws of library science, particularly the Fourth Law (save the time of reader) implies the importance of quality in library services. The law emphasizes that library administration be simple and efficient to save user's time. Knowledgeable staff provides seamless access to information regardless of format, whether the user is in the library or at a remote location.

Historically, the quality of library has been measured in terms of its collection (size, number of titles and breadth of subject coverage) and various counts of its use, budget and manpower and services. In recent past, this concept has been changed towards the nature of service rendered by the librarians and not merely on the collection and size. However, in the present day context, satisfying the needs of the users is very important and the reliance on the traditional methods might not be sufficient to assess the quality and effectiveness of the library from customer's perspective. Today's academic libraries face competition from alternative, cost-effective information providers. In light of this reality, it is imperative for libraries to seek means to ensure that their services meet and preferably exceed user expectations.

In service marketing literature, service quality is viewed as the comparison of what the customer expected prior to the use of services and the perceived level of services received. Service quality and satisfaction are two significant facets of effective service management. Library and information science researchers have followed the principles of marketing philosophy to focus attention on expectations and an alternative view of quality. Although the concept of quality is not new, measuring service quality as a management technique has gained importance over the last few decades in service industries.

Quality in library and information services can have many aspects. Peter Brophy, starting from the general management literature, has adapted a set of quality attributes to libraries. The following table relies for the most part of Brophy's set and shows the quality criteria with typical examples of their appliance to library & information services.[8]

	Criteria of Library Quality	Example
Performance	A service meets its most basic purpose	Making key information resources available on demand
Features	Secondary characteristics which add to the service but are beyond the essential core	Altering services
Reliability	Consistency of the service's performance in use	No broken web links
Conformance	The service meets the agreed standard	Dublin core
Durability	Sustainability of the service over a period of time	Document delivery within 2 days
Currency	Up-to-datedness of information	Online catalogue
Serviceability	Level of help available to users	Complaint service
Aesthetics	Visual attractiveness	Physical library, Website
Usability / Accessibility	Ease of access and use	Opening hours, website structure
Assurance / competence / Credibility	Good experience with staff's knowledgability	Correct reference answers
Courtesy / Responsiveness / Empathy	Accessibility, flexibility and friendliness of staff	Reference service
Communication	Clear explanation of services and options in language free of jargon	Website, Signposting in the library
Speed	Quick delivery of services	Interlibrary lending
Variety of services offered	May clash with quality, if the resources are not sufficient for maintaining quality in all services	Comprehensive collection, reference service in walk-in, mail and chat form
Perceived quality	The user's view of the service	User satisfaction

THE DETERMINANTS OF QUALITY OF SERVICES IN LIBRARY

In services, it is the customer who defines quality. Therefore, human side of service is key to deliver quality. No doubt many of the determinants for quality of products can be applied to the service but the human side of service is missing to a considerable extent in case of services.

Parsuram A, Zelthaml V.A. and Berry L L, a group of researchers in marketing proposed quality dimensions. Originally their study consisted of 10 dimensions, which are given below, in tabular form. [7]

Quality Dimension	Core Features	Samples of questions to ask
Tangibles	Appearance of physical facilities, equipment, personnel, printed and visual materials	• Are facilities attractive? • Are staffs dressed appropriately? • Does technology adopted look modern?
Reliability	Ability to perform promised service dependably and accurately	• If a response is promised in a certain time, does it happen? •Are exact specifications of user followed? • Are statements or reports free of error? • Is service performed right the first time? • Is level of service same at all times of day and for all members of staff?
Responsiveness	Willingness to help customers to provide prompt service	• When there is a problem, does Library respond to it quickly? • Are Library staffs willing to

		answer users' questions? • Are specific times for service accomplishments given to users? • Are public situations treated with care and seriousness?
Competence	Possession of required skill and knowledge to perform service	• Can library staff provide service without fumbling around? • Are materials provided appropriate and up to date? • Can library staff use the technology quickly and skillfully? • Does staff appear to know what they are doing?
Courtesy	Politeness, respect, consideration and friendliness of contact personnel	• Does staff member have a pleasant demeanor? • Does staff refrain from acting busy or being rude when clients ask questions? • Does staff observe consideration of the property and values of user?
Credibility	Trustworthiness, believability, honesty of the service provider	• Does library have a good reputation? • Do library staff members refrain from pressuring the client? • Are responses given accurate and consistent with other reliable sources? • Does the library guarantee its services?

Security	Freedom from danger, risk, or doubt	• Is it safe to enter the premises and to use the equipment? • Are documents and other information provided for the user held securely? • Are use records of users safe from unauthorized use? • Can user be confident that service provided was done correctly?
Access	Approachability and ease of contact.	• How easy is it to talk to knowledgeable library staff member when user has a problem? • Is it easy to reach the appropriate staff person — In person? — By telephone? — By email? • Are service access points conveniently located?
Communication	Listening to customers and acknowledging their comments; Keeping customers informed in a language they can understand.	• When user contacts service point, will staff person listen to their problem and demonstrate understanding and concern? • Can library staff explain clearly the various options available to a particular query? • Does library staff avoid using technical jargon when speaking with clients?

Understanding the Customer	Making the effort to know customers and their needs.	• Does someone on staff recognize each regular user and address them by name? • Does staff try to determine what users' specific objectives are? • Is level of service and cost of service consistent with what user requires and can afford? • Are service providers flexible enough to accommodate to users' schedule?

Later on these 10 dimensions were pooled into 5 dimensions as given below

10 Dimensions (Original Model)	**5 Dimensions (Later Model)**
Tangibles	Tangibles
Reliability	Reliability
Responsiveness	Responsiveness
Competence	Assurance
Courtesy	
Credibility	
Security	
Access	Empathy
Communication	
Understanding the customer	

The five dimensions of services considered the following issues in library scenario

Dimensions	Definition
Tangibles	The physical appearance of the library: library staff,Facilities and communications materials.
Reliability	The ability of library staff to perform the promised service dependably and accurately.
Responsiveness	The willingness of library staff to help users andProvide prompt service.
Assurance	The knowledge and courtesy of library staff and theirAbility to convey trust and confidence.
Empathy	The caring, individualized attention that library staffProvide to users.

Based on the five SERVQUAL dimensions, the researchers also developed a survey instrument to measure the gap between customers' expectation for excellence and their perception of actual service delivered. From extensive research, Parasuraman, Zethamal & Berry (PZB) concluded that customers ranked the importance of two SERVQUAL dimensions consistently, regardless of service industry. Reliability is the most important contributor to service quality and tangibles is the least important. Within the library setting, similar patterns were found. Preliminary research on the applicability of the SERVQUAL dimensions to measure reference, interlibrary loan, and reserve services in an academic library also support these patterns. PZB's customer-based approach for conceptualizing and measuring service quality offers an alternative for defining the quality of library services. It emphasizes the service nature of libraries, in which the traditional collection-based criteria of quality may be part of, but not the entire component, of excellence. Service quality contributes to value experienced by customers. Value becomes an outcome of excellent service. The SERVQUAL instrument, modified for use in library service settings, provides an outcome measure for managers to gauge their service activities.

GAP THEORY OF SERVICE QUALITY

This model was developed by PZB. The model claims that the consumer evaluates service quality experience as the outcome of the gap between expected and perceived quality. The model emphasizes on the key requirements for a service provider delivering the expected service quality.

The model identifies 5 gaps that can cause unsuccessful service delivery. By learning the flow of this model, it is possible to exercise greater management control over the consumer relationships. The study of this model should lead to an improved realization of the key issues at which the service providers can influence the satisfaction of consumers.

Gap No	What is it?		What causes it?
Gap – 1	Lack of understanding	It is the Gap between consumer expectation and management perception	Management's failure to correctly identify client expectations.
Gap – 2	Lack of development	It is the gap between management perception and service quality specifications	Limited resources, lack of operational tools to bring the client's voice to service specifications; management's indifference andrapid change in market conditions.
Gap – 3	Poor delivery	It is the gap between service quality specification and service delivery	Lack of knowledge about specifications, lack of ability to carry out the specified or lack of commitment by collaborators.

Gap – 4	Unrealistic expectation	It is the gap between service delivery and external communication	Lack of communication and the client does not know what to expect or more is promoted than actually delivered.
Gap – 5	Service gap	It is the gap perceived service and delivered service	A gap or a series of gaps from 1 to 4.

APPLICATION OF SERVICE QUALITY CONCEPT TOWARDS CAPACITY BUILDING

Capacity Building

Capacity building is one of the most fashionable, yet least understood, terms in the nonprofit sector today. It is a process of building capabilities in individuals, groups, institutions, organizations and societies at the local, national and international level to more effectively prepare for and respond to the situation in a sustainable manner. This could be done through value added instruction, training, networking, etc.

In a nutshell capacity building is defined as actions that improve nonprofit effectiveness and enhance a non profit's ability to work toward its mission (Blumenthal, 2003).

Library Capacity Building

Library capacity consists of the people in the library, its culture, attitude, environment and appearance. It requires commitment to training to develop people skills. It requires libraries to identify and take advantage of opportunities and strengths. Capacity requires leadership, long-range thinking and strategic planning; it requires that people who work at the library have the skills and resources to bring about positive change [6]

What are the abilities, talents and skills of people at the library right now? What kind of assistance would library staff be able to offer the community? Noah and Brickman describe capacity building for libraries and offer examples of library capacity-building efforts [5]. The authors identify action steps for librarians who want to develop and implement a plan to build library capacity.

How does one recognize that capacity is being built? The Community Development Handbook [6] identifies factors that confirm capacity is being built. "People are active, interested and participating in what is going on. People may also be questioning, challenging and debating – but they will be debating what should be done, not complaining that nothing will ever change. More people are getting involved, helping to identify key issues, and taking action. Results are becoming obvious and the abilities, esteem and resources of many communities are growing as capacity grows." These factors may also be used to indicate when library capacity is being built.

The SERVQUAL Survey instrument would definitely give the lacunae of the components directly or indirectly associated with the library capacity. And steps could be taken to enhance the capacity of library.

CONCLUSION

Service quality instrument should be framed keeping in view the library environment, it may be adapted. A proper instrument can find the positives and negatives of the library service. This later can be used as boon for capacity building of library, because the components of library capacity are highly associated with the 5 dimensions of Service Quality.

REFERENCES

1. Leonard L. Berry, "Great Service Now: Framework for Action" (paper presented at the annual meeting of the American Library Association, New York, N.Y., July 1996)
2. Danuta A. Nitecki, "Changing the Concept and Measure of Service Quality in Academic Libraries," Journal of Academic Librarianship 22 (May 1996): 181-190.
3. Capacity Building Framework – UNESCO-IICBA, A. Matachi, 2006
4. William H. Newman and HarveyW. Wallender, "Managing Not-For-Profit Enterprises," Journal of Library Administration 1 (Spring 1980): 87-97.
5. Noah, Carolyn and Alan Brickman. "Capacity Building for Libraries." Public Libraries March/April (2004): 102-107. 12 July 2005.
6. Frank, Flo and Anne Smith. The Community Development Handbook. Ottawa: Human Resources Development Canada, 1999. <http:// www1.servicecanada.gc.ca/en/epb/sid/cia/comm_deve/ cdhbooke.pdf>.
7. A. Parasuraman, V.A. Zeithaml, and L.L. Berry, "A conceptual model of service quality and its implications for future research," Journal of Marketing, 49 (1985):41-50.
8. Brophy, P. (2004), The Quality of libraries. In Die effective Bibliothek. Hilgermann, K. and the Borkhorst, P. (eds.) München: K. G. Saur. 30-46.

21 Effective Time Management for Library Managers

Mamata Mishra
Bulu Maharana

"Time is the scarcest resource of the manager; If it is not managed, nothing else can be managed".

– Peter F. Drucker

INTRODUCTION

'Make time your friend, otherwise it will become your enemy'. Everybody, either a professional or a lay man has a relationship with time. Some see it as an enemy, some as a friend. Some people characterized as ***'Th - adrenaline junky'*** **(Singer; 2007), who are** extremeiy busy, always on the go person and never seem to have enough time. However, there are some others manage to get more done in a day than seems humanly possible. Those who are able manage their time effectively are successful both in their personal life and in professional life. The present

development in library technologies has redefined the profession of librarianship. The library managers facing a severe crunch of time in their work due various reasons such as down-sizing of manpower, multi-tasking jobs, increasing number of users and their expectations, time bound academic schedules, handling multiple projects, etc. If the library manager doesn't practice time management, he/she will likely fail to accomplish the tasks to be a successful manager. If a librarian is a poor time manager, he/she will never find the time to develop a vision and a plan for achieving that vision.

WHAT IS TIME MANAGEMENT?

As per Delumeau (2005), Wikipedia, the internet encyclopaedia, defines time management as "a number of techniques that aim to increase the effectiveness of a person in getting the things done that need to be done". It also points out that time management should be called self management, as "time passes without regard to what we do; the only thing we can manage is ourselves." Therefore time management is really about self management, which can be facilitated by a number of different "tools, techniques and attitudes." Time management refers to the development of processes and tools that increase efficiency and productivity.

In her review of time management literature for librarians, Lisa Peterson [1] (*In* Delumeau; 2005) states that working in a library presents unique situations as libraries are service-oriented institutions and their clients mostly "drop in." This creates special time management challenges, whereas in most other professional environments clients are scheduled.

(80/20) THEORY OF TIME MANAGEMENT

Pareto's principle states that, a small number of causes (20%) is responsible for a large part (80%) of the effect. The relationship between the input and output is not balanced as 20% of a person's effort generates 80% of the results. It is vital to focus 80% of one's time on the 20% of his work that really counts. Therefore, it is very important for the library manager to focus on the right 20% of time in the work place. The effective management techniques would be helpful in making the best use of the time in order to produce the desired 80% of result.

Two Extreme Traits

We have all encountered the following type of people, who just can't seem to manage their time effectively:

The adrenaline junky : They are enormously busy, always on the go person has a buzz of activity around them. They are either on the phone or being interrupted by others. Their desks are a mess of unorganized papers and files. They are constantly being pulled off on "urgent" tasks. They tend to work long hours, but ironically, for all their efforts, their projects are always late and off schedule and what they deliver always seem to have problems or involve some type of crises.

The procrastinator : At the opposite extreme, is the personality type that always puts off tasks, hesitates and debates continually and has difficulty making decisions or following up on actions. They never seem to be able to get much done or follow up on what they've agreed to do.

There is a combination of aspects of the above traits in most of us, and we may even swing from one extreme to the other. These are all symptoms of poor time management and recognizing this is the first step toward effective change. The frequently-cited time wasters are often characterised with the following negative attitudes:

- *Too many meetings*
- *Answering e-mail or returning phone calls*
- *Too much socializing*
- *Lack of daily plan and/or self discipline*
- *Attempting to do too much at the same time*
- *Unrealistic time estimations*
- *Poorly organized work space*
- *Unrealistic goals*
- *Inability to say "no"*
- *Inflated ego (thoughts like "no one can do this as well as I can")*
- *Poor communication or lack of information*

QUALITIES OF A GOOD TIME MANAGER AND A BAD TIME MANAGER

Good Time Managers	Bad Time Managers
• Plan for the unplanned.	• Always try hard
• Follow a schedule that can adapt to changes.	• Busy bee • Don't need any help
• Get the important things done.	• Over organizer
• Are productive.	• Perfectionist
• Can juggle several activities.	• Please every body
• Have their short and long term goals in mind.	• Time Nut • Wait to the last minute
• May keep a daily, weekly and monthly schedule	

STRATEGIES AND TECHNIQUES OF TIME MANAGEMENT

Learning time management methods is a skill no different than learning to speak another language or figuring out how to word process. A review of literature shows that, much has been written on time management in general. With regard to techniques of Time Management, Delumeau (2005) in his paper[5] dealt that, Johnson points out two major flaws in commonly recommended techniques for managing time. One is delegating (most of us in library land are not in a position to do this). She suggests this technique should be called "get someone else to do it." The second flaw is having too linear an approach – for example, "first do this, then this" – because life does not usually work this way. A single set of time management techniques may not fit to every one. For time management techniques to succeed, the librarian must fit them into his life style, not the other way around. The following are some of the generalised and well tested techniques of time management.

Planning and Prioritizing

In general, the library manager should draw up a daily list of 'things to do', 'weekly calendar', 'Monthly Goal Calendars', etc. and prioritize them so that he/she can give the greatest time to the truly important tasks. When planning your schedule consider what you know about yourself. Determine what time of day you work best (often in the morning) and do the most difficult tasks then. Do less pleasant tasks before the ones you enjoy - then you "reward" yourself for your earlier hard work. Don't schedule your day to the minute.

Know your Strengths and Weaknesses

The Library manager should be aware about his strengths and weaknesses. *Firstly,* he/she should do more of what he/she is good at and less of what he/she is not good at. If the librarian is an expert in collection development but hate budgets, then he/she should keep the collection development tasks for himself, and assign a staff person who likes working with numbers to put together the first draft of the budget. Then review it with her, and assume the responsibility to complete it, understand it, and present it to management. Secondly, the librarian should know when he/she is most productive and should do most part of the work during that time. Thirdly, like everyone, the librarian should know his/her most effective work style. He/she should use to make the work climate as amenable to his/her style as possible.

Organize Yourself and Work Place

Poorly organized people spend a great deal of their time in hunting for files and important papers. There are several office ware (both hardware and software) tools now available to organize papers, projects, filing systems, desks, and offices. The mode of organizing the things varies from person to person. The librarian should look for a system to organize the office which suits him/her the best. Keeping a picture in the office of what is really important to you - family, pet, place, whatever is your top priority, will remind you of why you are working and why you should work smarter, not harder.

Delegate

Trying to do everything yourself is one of the key symptoms of poor time management. Focus on the tasks you know you can do quickly and effectively, and delegate to others, where possible. Delegating the work does two things: it frees your time for things that only you can do and it builds your staff's abilities and self-esteem. Delegation requires some planning and monitoring to be successful.

- Define the project: its purpose, importance, deadlines, and the scope of the delegate's responsibilities.
- Provide the necessary authority, resources and, support.
- Delegate for results. Let your staff handle projects in their own way. You are after results, not process.
- Review progress and follow-up.

Learn to Say 'No'

Often people are uncomfortable turning down a request for one of several reasons: they don't want to appear confrontational, they don't want to seem to be rejecting the requestor, being asked to do things makes them feel important, they feel that saying "no" will confound their career, or they like being incredibly busy. But this is a bad time management. One should know his limits and should take time to think about the request before saying 'yes' to it. If you feel its unpleasing or hard to say 'No', say 'thanks for asking, but I have prior commitments'.

Avoid Procrastinate

Everyone procrastinates about some things. Determine those unpleasant tasks you'd rather not do, and so put off until they become a crisis. Then, well before they reach a crisis stage:

- Set a deadline
- Do the most unpleasant part first.

- Make a game of it. Turn drudgery into fun.
- Build in a reward

Often procrastination is the result of being overwhelmed by the size of the task. Break big tasks into smaller, more manageable pieces that are easily done in several hours or a day. As you do each one, you will soon realize that, small step by small step, you have almost completed the entire huge task.

Be Proactive

An attitude of "highly successful people," according to Covey, this means you anticipate things and don't wait for them to happen to you. The library managers needed to be proactive in anticipating certain works to be accomplished before the actual need comes.

Decision Making

The library managers need to make informed decisions. Some managers keep on pending making any decision and at a later stage that becomes a crisis. Hence, the library managers should make decision at the right time to avoid the unwanted situations in the management process. The decisions made them should be communicated effectively and clearly.

Managing Interruptions

Interruptions are huge time-wasters. At the very least, they break your train of thought and distract his focus. The library manager should discourage people from dropping in without an appointment to chat except at appointed times. Establish a time when you are available if anyone needs to see you. Phone calls are sometimes more demanding than people. Train yourself to let your phone roll over to voice mail. On your message, remind people to be very specific about why they are calling so that when you return their call. Email can be a time-waster or a tremendous time-saver. Read and respond to emails only at designated times during the day, for example at the beginning of the day, before lunch, and again before you leave work. Chatting online, if not required should be allotted to a scheduled social time. Be polite but direct to say .no' to interruptions.

Maximise 'Fun' Parts

The library manager should enjoy doing his work, and therefore, he/she has to choose the work of his interest. The old proverb, "all work and no play makes Johnny a dull boy," is absolutely true. A well-balanced life includes time for things other than work: for things that are much more important than work; family and friends, health and recreation, spiritual development and volunteerism, among others. So, practicing time management at your job is not merely so you get more work squeezed into an eight-hour day, but mostly so you have time for the important things in life

CONCLUSION

The reason many of us feel stressed in our daily lives is that we have too much to do in a short period of time. Being overwhelmed with activities, assignments and work can lead a person to be "stressed out." Time management is helpful and necessary in our busy lives. In order to balance our schedule we need to be able to organize and utilize our time wisely. Without good time management skills we can easily fall behind in responsibilities and feel like we never have enough time. The libraries of the present time have been passing through great times of change. The library managers are being besieged with work expected from every quarter.

There are many things to be done in a short time. In such a situation, effective time management is important for them to progress with the changing library environment.

REFERENCES

1. Peterson, Lisa C.: *Time Management for Library Professionals.* [Online] http://www.lis.uiuc.edu/review/5/peterson.html. [Retrieved Aug 2005].
2. Effective Time Management. [Online] *http://www.ebay.co/mechantsolutions* [Retrieved 16 Sept 2009]
3. Singer, Warren. 2007. Effective Time Management: Tips and Strategies for managing your time effectively. [Online] *http://www.suite101.com*
4. Patterson, Karen. Time Management. [Online] *http://www.libsci.sc.edu*
5. Delumeau, Andrea. 2005. Time Management for Library professionals. [Online] *http://www.liscareer.com/delumeau_time.htm*
6. Siess, Judith A. Time Management, Planning and Prioritization for librarians. Scarecrow Press; Champaign.
7. Patsula Media. 2001. The Entrepreneur's Guide Book Series. [Online] *http://www.smallbusinesstown.com*

22

Managing Conflicts in Library and Information Centres: Issues and Challenges

Kamal Lochan Jena
Rabindra K. Mahapatra

INTRODUCTION

Libraries are primarily service institutions that cater to information needs of various types of users. Since users, documents and library staff are the components of a library system, the effective functioning of a library depends upon these entities. Again the policy decisions for the development of the library are being formulated by the Library Committee comprising some senior members of the institute. Above all, all the decisions of the library are being approved by the Head of the organization, while all those entities are responsible to library are sidelined the scenario of conflict arises. Despite popular perception, libraries are the organizations that are significantly impacted by conflict. Conflict occurs as a result of disagreement or opposition between / among the individuals or groups within the organization. Conflict can be negative and destructive, but it can also result a positive changes within the organization (*Putnam, 1997*). Conflict is unfortunately existed throughout the World. From the largest affairs of international politics to the everyday matters of work and family life conflicts / disputes between individuals and groups are common and regular. As individuals seek the ways to resolve the dispute, to make the life easier and to find the ways for prospect. As a result, a body of knowledge has developed relating to conflict resolution. Inspite of the neatly organized collection of books in the well furnished building with nicely attired library staff ready to help the users, conflicts are occurring on daily basis. There are many sources of conflict including disputes between the staff and management, between the library and vendors, between the users and staff etc. For this, the library manager is required to follow various methods and styles for resolving the conflict in most effective way. However it depends upon the situation of the conflict. The paper is designed to reflect the emergence of conflicts in libraries and the methods to resolve conflicts.

DEFINING THE CONCEPT OF CONFLICT

According to the Encyclopaedia of Sociology (*1992*) "Conflict theory explains social structure and changes in it by arguing that actors pursue their interests in conflict with others and according to their resources for social organization" (p 288). Conflict can occur from any circumstance when the desires and goals of two persons clash. It can range from small personal interaction to war between sovereign states.

Deutsch (1973) has recognized several factors for conflict. These include the issue control, issue rigidity and issue centrality. The more important an issue is to some one may ultimately decide how severe the conflict will become. The hardest conflicts to solve are those between disputes who have firmly held viewed on issues that are central to their lives.

Though conflict is inevitable, but it acts as a catalyst for change, which in turn leads to the development of an organization or an individual. Within libraries and information centres there are many sources of conflict. These include the structure of organization, technology, communication channels, interpersonal relations and behaviours, personal interests of individuals or groups, physical separations and dependency of one party on another (*Bryson, 1994. p 292*)

CONFLICT IN LIBRARY ENVIRONMENT

Organizational differentiation : Persons serving in libraries perform different kinds of work. As a result different departments have different time horizons, values, goals and management styles. The greater the differentiation between the departments, the greater will be the conflict and greater the need for mechanisms for the integration of the departments. The need for integration is the main source of conflict.

External environment and new technology : The uncertainty and complexity in external environment leads to the internal conflict. In order to accommodate and adapt the new technologies and complexities in the library it requires the human resources to acquire the new technologies, skills and attitudes. A different internal structure is needed to fulfil the corporate goals. Further new technologies leads to the uncertainty over the old ones. In a rapidly changing environment the basic rules and regulations may no longer be relevant for which conflicting options arise and conflict occurs inevitably.

Expansion in size of organization : As the size of libraries or information centres increases, new regulations are evolved to control the behaviour. Further, with the increase in size of the library various departmental activities increases. Always the regulations are not effective to control the organization for which conflict occurs. The expansion of library creates the levels of hierarchy. At this point conflict arises to hold the higher position.

Interdependence : The interdependence and independence of various departments is another source of conflict. Departments or groups who have to share the material resources may be evolved with conflicts. In order to overcome the departments may strive for their independence which further creates conflicts.

Professionalism : Normally the head of the Library & Information Centre and professionals speak the language of their profession or training. Always their language are not recognized or interpreted correctly by the administration for which conflict arises. In other words technical terminologies are used to describe the events with which library professionals are familiar and these are not always extended to other departments either within the library or within the organization.

Policy : Conflict can arise between individuals and groups over policies, practices and plans where the policy goes against their main interests of one or the groups.

Role of library managers : The role expectancies, goals and personal characteristics are the sources of interpersonal conflict between the subordinates and managers. Normally the head of the Library & Information

Centre is working for salary and pay rise whereas subordinates are working to keep their job. Managers have promotion seeking goals and higher order whereas the subordinates are doing the routine jobs which have no promotional benefit.

Budgetary deficiency : Library is a growing organisation. In order to fulfil the needs of the users it needs more budgetary provision. Further the introduction of latest technologies need more funds. But day by day they are facing financial crisis since there is the cutting in the budget. This creates the conflict between the Head of the Library & Information and the administration.

VARIOUS DIMENSIONS OF LIBRARY CONFLICT

For any organization to be effective and efficient in achieving its goal the people in the organization need to have a shared vision of what they are striving to achieve as well as clear objectives for each team / department and individual. You also need ways of recognising and resolving conflict amongst people, so that conflict does not become so serious that co-operation is impossible. All members of any organization need to have ways of keeping conflict to a minimum and of solving problems caused by conflict before conflict become a major obstacle to your work (*http://www.etu.org.za/toolbox/docs/building/conflict.html*). Inspite of these, conflicts arises and is inevitable in organizational structure. The causes or sources of organizational conflict can be many and varied. The most common causes are the followings:

- Scarcity of resources (finance, equipment, facilities etc)
- Different attitudes, values or perceptions;
- Disagreements about needs, goals, priorities and interests;

- Poor communications;
- Poor or inadequate organisational structure;
- Lack of team work;
- Lack of clarity in roles and responsibilities.
  (*http://www.etu.org.za/toolbox/docs/building/conflict.html*)

TYPES OF CONFLICT

The conflict occurs among the persons can be grouped into the following types:

Conflict between individuals : Different persons have different styles of communication, ambitions, nature, works and different cultural backgrounds. In the diverse society the different attitude and nature of individuals leads to conflict between them.

Conflict between groups of people : When the person forms the group, they tried to emphasise the things to make their groups 'better than' or 'different from' than others. This happens when the persons make groups within the organization.

Conflict within a group of people : Even within a organization / team or group conflict can arise among the individuals due to differences in ambitions, desire to obtain power and rivalry between sub-groups.

STAGES OF CONFLICT

In order to handle the conflict the head of the Library & Information should aware about the various stages of the development of conflict. If the leader / head of the Library & Information Centre could be able to identify the main conflict issue and how much it is developed then he could be able to solve the problem before it becomes much serious. According to McNamara (1997) typical stages of conflict include;

Primary conflict : Here the potential for conflict exists i.e. lack of resources and other facilities may lead to the conflict among the persons employed.

Latent conflict : The competition among the persons for various benefits including to hold the higher position.

Open conflict : Some conflicts are in born and could not be avoided and are open in nature.

Aftermath conflict : Sometimes some problems are not solved properly and some potential for conflict exists for revoking the conflict even greater than before.

FUNCTIONS OF CONFLICT

Conflict has a place within Library & Information Centres. It can serve as a unifying function within a group and as a source of feedback. When the conflict occurs the internal differences are overcome within the group which are on some kind of situation. Similarly when the external source of conflict came (may be the threat of closure) all the persons working in the organization became united and do the more productive output. For a healthy growth of organization and smooth management, conflict is needed as it

- helps to raise and address problems;
- energizes work to be on the most appropriate issues;
- helps people "be real" for example, it motivates them to participate;
- helps people to learn how to recognize and benefit from their differences.

Conflict is not the same as discomfort. The conflict is not the problem – it is when conflict is poorly managed that is the problem *(http://managementhelp.org/intrpsnl/basics.htm)*. But conflict is a problem when it

- hampers productivity;
- lowers morale;
- causes more and continued conflicts;
- causes inappropriate behaviours.

(http://managementhelp.org/intrpsnl/basics.htm)

MANAGING CONFLICT

Managing conflict refers to the long term management of stubborn conflicts. It is the label for the variety of ways by which people handle grievances – standing up for what they consider to be right and against what they consider to be wrong. Those ways include such diverse phenomena as gossip, ridicule, lynching, terrorism, warfare, feuding, genocide, law, mediation and avoidance. Which forms of conflict management will be used in any given situation can be somewhat predicted and explained by the social structure – or social geometry – of the case *(Wikipaedia)*. The process of managing conflict is important because sometimes it forces for an organizational change. But for conflict to be effectively managed the organizational goal is to be taken into consideration carefully. In resolving the conflict between management and staff three techniques can be used. These are Win- Lose, Lose – Lose or Win – Win (*Bryson, 1994. p 298*).

In Win — Lose method, the supervisor wins and the employee loses. This method is an authoritarian approach where coercive power is used to bring about the employee's compliance. Here the rule of law overrides the employees demands and may result in employee resentment. It can have negative effects on performance.

In Lose — Lose method, no one is entirely happy. Here the main basis is the compromise where half solution is better than none. Here the strategy is that one party agrees to a solution in exchange for a favour from the other party later.

The Win — Win method provides a solution which is acceptable to all. Here the conflict resolution strategies focus upon ends and goals and identify the sources of conflict and present them to solve participative management technique to gain consensus and commitment to the objectives.

In addition to these the interpersonal conflicts can be managed in following methods. According to *Thomson (1996)* five distinct styles of conflict management exists within the organization including Collaboration, Accommodation, Competition, Compromise and Avoidance.

Avoidance style — Sometimes the head of Library and Information Centre attempts to solve the problems simply by avoiding the conflict. Normally small/minor conflicts need avoidance because involvement to solve conflict may increase it and leads to creation of new conflict.

Smoothing style — The smoothing style refers to the tendency to minimise or suppress the open recognition of real differences in conflict situations. In this process the head of Library and Information Centre acts as if the conflict will pass with time and appeals to the need for cooperation. He tried to reduce the tension by reassuring the parties. This style encourages individuals to cover up and avoid expressions of their feelings.

Forcing style — In forcing style the head of Library and Information Centre used his power to dominate the other party. Differences are suppressed and the parties are forced to adopt the head of Library and Information Centre's position. In this style the losers do not usually accept the final decision and can create more conflict. Normally, this method is adopted when there is an extreme urgency and quick action is needed. It can also be used when an unpopular course of action is necessary for the long term survival of the Library & Information Centre.

Compromise style — The compromise style is used when negotiation is possible. This style is used when both parties recognise that there is the possibility of reaching with the agreement which is more advantageous than if no agreement is made. Early use of compromise results in less diagnosis and exploration of the real nature of the conflict.

Collaborative style — The collaborative style requires the willingness of the head of Library and Information Centre to identify the underlying causes of conflict, openly share the information and search out alternatives considered to be mutually beneficial. Here conflicts are recognised openly and evaluated by all concerned. Sharing, examining and assessing the reasons for conflicts lead to a more through development of alternatives. This method is suitable when there is ample time to find the solution.

CONCLUSION

Library is the centre of knowledge, where the users are coming to collect the data and gain knowledge. So it is expected that the knowledge providers should be knowledgeable in every aspect. Inspite of all expectation the persons employed in the Library and Information Centres are expecting all benefits like any other organization. Although the generation of conflicting situation is a common phenomenon in libraries, it should be restricted to minimum level, so that it will not adversely affect the growth of the Library and Information Centres and services to the users. While managing the library the head of the Library and Information Centre should be very careful because conflict can arise in multiple points. So the head of the Library and Information Centre should also encourage active listening, cooperation, acceptance of differences of the library staff and creative problem solving as all of these skills can help resolve conflict in a manner that may not hinder the growth of the library.

REFERENCES

1. Bryson and Jo . (1996). Effective Library and Information Centre management.. Jayco Publishing House, Bombay.
2. Bargatta, E F and Bargatta, M L (Eds)) (1992). Encyclopaedia of Sociology,. Newyork, NY: Macmillan Publishing Company.
3. Deutsch, M (1973). The resolution of Conflict: Constructive and destructive processes. New Haven, C: Yale Univ Press.
4. McNamara, Carter (1997). Basics of Conflict Management. (*http://managementhelp.org/intrpsnl/basics.htm)accessed on 02.09.09.*
5. Putnam, L. (1997). Productive Conflict: negotiation as implicit coordination in: C DeDreu and E. Van De Vliert (Eds) Using Conflict in Organizations, London: Sage.
6. Thomas, K (1976). Conflict and conflict management, in: M D Dunnette (Ed), Handbook of Industrial and organizational Psychology. Chicago; Rand McNally.
7. (*http://en.wikipedia.org/wiki/conflict_management*).

23
Training LIS Manpower to Work Effectively in A Digital Library Environment

P.N. Mishra

INTRODUCTION

In the context of capacity building of LIS Manpower in a digital environment, this paper intends to put emphasis on development of skills of the LIS manpower working in digital library and information centers, through continued training programs. A blue print has been drawn through comparative study of training programs carried on for library professionals in European and other Western countries including India.

The beginning of this paper reveals the concept of digital format and their use in the libraries along with an exhaustive definition of digital libraries. The work environment of a digital library, improvement of skills of the manpower engaged in it through different training and education programme are the core point of discussion of this paper. The significance of Information Technology and Software Development Education and up-gradation of the technical and managerial skills of the manpower engaged in the digital libraries and information centers to handle On-line information services effectively in the e-world during the current and coming centuries have been vividly discussed.

Moreover, this paper identifies the areas and levels of training and education programme continuing for library professionals by different Universities and Institutions in India and abroad with a special mention of the recommendations of the National Task Force appointed on I.T. and Software Development and the U.G.C.

Suggestions pertaining to the early implementation of the recommendations of the National Task Force and the U.G.C. in all the Universities and Institutions established under the Central and State Jurisdiction in India along with suggestions for adequate funds for the infrastructural development including training of the Library Professionals have been provided with a hope of their quick implementation.

The quantum of research activities on different branches of knowledge in the world and the unprecedented explosion of information there of have compelled the library professionals to accept the most emerging, viable and convenient Digital Format in the libraries to act on-line for information storage and retrieval. The concept of use of digital format in the libraries grows from 1940-50's with the induction of computers. Going through the stages of several experiments and examinations the present format "Digital Library Initiative - II (1998-2002) is now in operation discarding the conventional status of libraries and library manpower.

There was a time when librarianship was considered to acquire knowledge on Library and Information Science along with specialized knowledge on some foreign languages. In addition to this elementary knowledge on Computer Science, Statistics and Management was also desirable.

But during the last two-three decades, it is explicitly the knowledge of computer on more appropriately the knowledge of Information Technology which has gained great significance in the activities of libraries and information centers. In this new digital environment working knowledge and skills of I.T. are essential to prepare library professionals mentally and technically sound to cooperate with the modernization of library services.

WHAT OF DIGITAL LIBRARY

The most effective and exhaustive definition of digital library has been given by BORGMAN. According to him "digital libraries are a set of electronic resources and associated technical capabilities for creating, searching and using information. In this sense they are an extension and enhancement of Information Storage and Retrieval Systems that manipulate digital data in any manner (text, image, sounds, static or dynamic images) and exist in distributed networks. The content of digital libraries includes data, meta-data that describe various aspects of the data and meta-data that consists of links or relationships to other data or meta-data whether internal or external to the digital library.

Digital libraries are constructed, collected and organized by (and for) a community of users and their functional capabilities support the information needs and uses of the community. In this sense they are an extension of a variety of information institutions where resources are selected, collected, organized and accessed in support of a user community.

WHY OF DIGITAL KNOWLEDGE SKILL AND "WILL"

It is expected from the library professionals to possess deep I.T. Knowledge and skill together with "Will" both theoretical and practical to perform their duties in the e-world.

"Skill" is defined as the knowledge and ability that enables one to do something. In other words skill is an acquired ability to perform a work efficiently and effectively. Possession of enough or even excess knowledge makes a person a theoretician without the skill of applying those acquired knowledge in to practice.

"Will" is the important component for making knowledge and skill of a person use in practice. A person may possess enough knowledge and skill but due to lack of will the knowledge and skill acquired by him can not be utilized in practice. Will is that component which motivates a person to perform. Hence knowledge, skill and will are complementary to each other and these three qualities of library professionals can achieve better service in a digital environment.

TECHNICAL SKILL

Library professionals must have LIS Technical Skills, I.T. Skills and Managerial Skills to act in Digital Environment.

LIS TECHNICAL SKILLS

LIS Technical skills include selection, acquisition, processing, including abstracting and indexing and providing services in a library or information centre.

I.T. SKILL

I.T. skills which include computer, hardware, software, key board operation, telecommunication products, data and file management, DTP Word Processing, generation of reports etc. Further skill on information processing, search and retrieval. Retrieval skills include On-line searching as well as searching CD-ROM data bases. The advanced level skill include web and internet skills. Specialized skills like electronic publishing, electronic commerce and marketing. The library professionals need to become part of I.T. with programming skills, system administration, hardware maintenance, networking systems etc.

MANAGERIAL SKILLS

Managerial skills of library professionals is quite vast in the digital environment. Skills for technology assessment and selection of appropriate technology and product skills required to work in team environment and on collaborative basis for resource sharing. Another managerial skill of library professionals is to develop marketing of services. Skills relating to system analysis, self development, creativity analysis etc. Further skills relating to meta competence i.e. skill to communicate orally and in written form.

These three groups of skills are equally significant for library professionals in the digital environment and in the e-world.

NEED FOR LIS CURRICULUM AND TRAINING

Librarianship is going to have much wider sphere of operation in the 21st century and LIS has a greater role to perform in the digital environment. The Universities and institutions have a challenging task ahead to develop their curriculum requirements for education, research and training programme of library professionals in I.T. and digital information environment.

Most of the universities and institutions of European and other Western countries have already implemented their changed curricula with emphasis on I.T. education, research and training. But in India efforts are slowly going on. Many universities and Institutions have introduced I.T. as a special paper in LIS education and are giving training by conducting continuing education programme. Some other institutions and organizations have also involved in imparting I.T. education and training to the Library Professionals. They are NISCAIR, DRTC, DESIDOC, NCSI and others. The courses on Library Automation, use of UNESCO package CDS/ISIS, INTERNET and other I.T. related training Programme.

TRAINING RECOMMENDED BY NATIONAL TASK FORCE

A National Task Force on Information Technology and Software Development was set up in the year 1988 to chalk-out a national I.T. Policy who have suggested the following action plan "As NII (National Information Infrastructure) takes shape we may expect a massive amount of electronic information to be created and make accessible. If relevant information has to be found quickly adequate cares need to be given in proper structuring, categorization, Indexing and Classification of information, library and information professionals have traditionally handled those tasks in the print environment. Content creation strategy needs to recognize this and suggest incorporation of Library and Information Science (LIS) Professionals in Content Creation Teams of Organizations".

Further emphasizes that "If Library and Information

Professionals are expected to play a significant role in content creation, quality of training imparted in LIS Schools in Indian Universities needs to be improved drastically."

TRAINING RECOMMENDATION BY U.G.C.

The University Grants Commission of India has given due importance on University and college Libraries together with teaching in Library and Information Science. Curriculum committees have also appointed from time to time to review the existing standard of teaching and research and suggest recommendations for their modernization. The Karisidappa Committee on Curriculum Development appointed by U.G.C. in the year 2001 has formulated a model curriculum in library and information science recommending I.T. and other information systems to be taught in LIS education and training programme.

In spite of the above recommendations no such effective measures have been taken to provide I.T. education and training in all the universities and institutions except a few running under the control of Central Government of India. Especially the state level Universities and Institutions are far behind to implement these recommendations in their LIS curriculum.

SUGGESTIONS

The following suggestions may be given top priority for training Library Manpower to work effectively in a Digital Environment.

- The Universities and Institutions imparting LIS education and training in different states and union territories of India should incorporate I.T. teaching into their LIS curriculum as a compulsory subject instead of optional subject.

- Professionals already in work in the Library and Information centers should be deputed to acquire up-to-date knowledge and training on I.T. and Software Development availing Study Leave.
- LIS professionals should be allowed to participate in the State and National level Seminars, Symposiums, Workshops, Conferences, Refresher and Orientation Programme conducted throughout India in-order to enhance their practical knowledge on I.T. and other digital systems.
- Provisions for adequate funds be made for infrastructural development of digital libraries and information centers including training the manpower engaged in it.
- A high level body consisting of LIS and I.T. experts and representatives from both the State and Central Government of India be constituted in each and every state to examine the nature, scope, problems and prospects of digital libraries and suggest recommendations for their over all development.

CONCLUSION

The curriculum of library professionals in a digital environment need enhanced and integrated skill development through continuing training programme for the diffusion and mutual exchange of knowledge in-order to bring a harmonious and cohesive relation between library and information science and information and communication technology. Suitable steps should be taken in this direction at an earliest.

REFERENCE

1. Johnson, Peggy, technological change in libraries. Encyclopedia of library and information science., Vol. 53 edited by Allen Kent. New York Marcel Dekker, 1994 p.p. 182-202.
2. Klobas, Jones E. Managing Technological Change in Library and Information Science. The Electronic Library, 1990, 8(5).p.p. 334-349.
3. Mohapatra M & Ramesh D.B. Ed. Information Technology, Application in Libraries (A text book for beginners), 2004, p.p. 590-593, 597-604. Bhubaneswar, Orissa.
4. Palmer Judith. Effectiveness and Efficiency. New role and New skills for health librarians in the future of information professionals (Proceeding of the Aslib Conference, 28-29 May 1996, London.
5. Petti New Mark and Elliott David. Student I.T. Skills, New York, Gower, 1999.
6. Ramaiah L.S. Levels of training for LIS professionals in information technology in India, Paper presented at the XV IATLIS National Seminar, University of Maysore, 1997.
7. Ramiah L.S. & Veeranjaneyulu K. Training and training modules in LIS/. Schools, Paper presented at the XVI IATILS National Conference/ Seminar, Sri Venkateswara University, Tirupati, 1998.
8. Somaraju P. Teach the Teachers : Train the LIS. Teacher in I.T. paper presented at the XVI IATILIS National Seminar, Sri Venkateswar University, Tirupati, 1998.
9. University Grants Commission. UGC Model Curriculum. Library and Information Science, New Delhi, University Grants Commission, 2001.

24
Financial Management of Indian Academic Libraries

Rabindra Nath Mohanta
Rajesh Kumar Mishra

INTRODUCTION

Finance is a critical resource for sustainability and growth any institution including libraries. Traditionally, the higher education institutes and their libraries are supposed to be established for social development as scientific organizations, but now it has been well established as a large market in the developed economies which is also taking shape in India. Role of academic libraries, in the prevailing and proposed model of higher education system, has already been well defined and accepted by educational policy makers around the globe. In the recent past, significant developments have been reported in library and information system and services in the western word and the Indian academic libraries are also supposed to shoulder newer responsibilities in higher education system along with ensuring their sustainability. Traditionally the classroom has been accorded the primary source of learning, and libraries were having a supplementary status in the academic system but the rapidly expanding learner-centric educational environment is leading towards the role reversal. No doubt, the approachable role reversal is depends on the rational planning, management and proper financial input for development of Indian academic libraries.

CONSTRAINTS IN GROWTH OF INDIAN ACADEMIC LIBRARIES

Literature and observation reveals that the major challenges in the development of the libraries are lack of finance, poor collection management, deficiency of ICT skill, unavailability and non-implementation of national standards for libraries, impotency of library associations, lack of library cooperation, ineffective planning, absence of library marketing in competitive environments, meager excellence of library education, dearth of professional literature in Indian languages, lack of professionalism, inadequacy of quality continuing education facilities, scarcity of leadership and team spirit, etc. In states like Uttar Pradesh and Bihar a major constraint of electric supply is also hindering the IT penetration in academic institutions, libraries and civil society at large.

Present Financial State

At present the academic libraries of public sector are receiving financial resources only from the respective governments via their parent institutions. Other minor financial sources of the academic libraries are as library membership fee, fines, photocopying charges, audio copying charges, and CD-ROM duplication charges, Internet charges, inter library loan charges, sale of publications and revenue from auction of obsolete articles. But it is a matter of fact that no academic library can sustain its existence without external financial support. In this situation it is need of the time to explore and exploit the alternative sources of the finance not only to sustain their existence but also to offer improved services.

Alternative Sources of Finance

Marketing of library and information services and product has been proved as an effective way of financial resource generation in the developed world, which may be applied in our country with proper modifications in the line of economic and social conditions of the country.

Marketing of Information Services and Product

Marketing of information organizations is a process in which customers' needs for information and knowledge are met through matching them with appropriate information resources and services. Marketing is a management process which anticipates, determines and supplies product and services to fulfill users' requirements efficiently and profitably. Since libraries are non-monopolistic and nonprofit organizations, hence their profit is user satisfaction rather happiness. Indian libraries face the challenge of marketing due to competitive environment in terms of internet mania and decreasing number of potential clientele, increased pressure to secure funding, etc. At present marketing of LIS in India is in its babyhood stage and there is no specialized course of LIS marketing in our country.

Process of marketing the library and information services and products involve several steps:

- The library should clearly understand the mission of

the organization and then define the marketing objectives and goals.

- The library then understands the market through investigating the customer needs wants, demand and the potential demand as well.
- The market is segmented on the basis of various characteristics and the behavior of customers.
- Marketing programs are planned for target market segments with the process of developing and maintaining a viable fitness between organization's objectives, skills and changing marketing opportunities.
- Select proper marketing mixes, tactics; and implement them.
- Rearrange the strategy in accordance with the changing user need and implement again.

Some other means of alternate financial sources are:

- Fee Based Library Services
- Interactive and Dynamic Web Site
- Donations from Well Wishers
- Community Radio
- SDI through SMS
- Toll Free Help Line Numbers

PRE-REQUISITES FOR A SUSTAINABLE LIBRARY

If we want to run libraries as corporate houses then we have to put that level of human and financial resources, national and local level policies, and standards for restructuring of library and information profession and academic libraries. Some more prerequisites are as follows:

- De-stressing and face lifting of the libraries

(Computerization, networking and effective web presence, weeding out, library consortia)

- Compilation and Use of L-MIS reports in decision making and problem solving.
- Identification and out sourcing of less productive services like Internet and photocopying, website management etc.
- Library Advocacy (To ensure penetration of library profession in other disciplines and in the society at large)
- Re-modeling of library science courses
- Better coordination between Management, ICT, LIS departments and libraries.
- Establishment of a separate marketing section in the libraries.
- Identification of measures to increase outreach of the libraries:
  - Industries have emerged as significant information seeker on payment basis due to increased industrialization and increasing population base of information and knowledge society. Library involves recurring expenditure, most of the industries will prefer to subscribe the quality information products and services as the establishments and maintenance. Academic libraries have not to restrict the users to the faculty and students only but can also extend their services to the society on payment basis. In a city, if there are more than one university can provide access to the resources of the library to other university students and faculty by realizing fees from them. In this way membership can be increased.

CONCLUSION

Globalization can not afford the higher education, merely for social development, anymore. If it is not possible for a democratic government to develop it as profit making sector then they have to design and implement the sustainable model of higher education system in the country to keep pace with the developed economies. At the same time the corporate houses and higher education sector of developed economies have very well explored the vast market of higher education in our country. They are coming in a big way to grab this market. Therefore it's high time to work as a true professional for the cause of profession and country.

Can we just think of "How many academic libraries can **sustain** if the government cease the grant from tomorrow? " Perhaps very few libraries can accept the challenge. The presumption may be not true in the near future but in coming days libraries may be **asked to generate funds**. So, libraries must think for alternative sources of finance other than government grants.

REFERENCES

1. Abbot, Christine. (1994). *Performance Measurement in Library and Information services*. London, Aslib. p. 57

2. Brophy, Peter (2005). *The Academic Library*. London: Facet Pub. pp. 184-196.

3. Brophy, Peter (2001). *The Library in the 21st century: new services for the information age*. London: Library Association Publishing. pp. 73-86.

4. Kent, Allen, ed. (1978). Encyclopaedia *of Library and Information Science*. New York: Marcel Dekker, Vol 39, pp. 203-221.

5. NAAC. (2007) *Guidelines on Quality indicators in Library and Information Services*, Banglore: NAAC, p. 5.

6. Report of the National Knowledge Commission on Libraries. *www.nkc.org*

7. Poll, Roswitha (2003). Measuring Impact and Outcome of Libraries. Performance Measurement and Metrics, Vol. 4 (1), pp. 5-12.

8. Rowley, J. E. (2006). *Information Marketing* (2nd ed.). Burlington: Ashgate Publishing. p.3

25
Internet and Library Capacity Building

Sasmita Brahma
Rabindra K. Mahapatra

INTRODUCTION

Library, the pivot of teaching and research is changing its services from traditional to electronic form. The capacity of library is highly revolutionized in the Internet era. The term "Capacity Building" refers to the enhancement of physical infrastructure in terms of space and building, furniture equipments, information resources and human resource. Libraries need to employ appropriate strategies to enhance their capacity building in tune with the recent diversified demands of users. Planning from top managerial level with adequate budget and co-ordination is highly essential for the proper implementation of the capacity building. The capacity building of the library will be certainly realized if the use of internet is harnessed and the following facets of internet are utilized in real sense.

In the light of capacity building of the library in internet age the following points are required to be elaborated.

- Search Engine
- Electronic Information Sources
- Electronic Databases
- Networking
- Open Access Publishing
- Institutional Repositories and digital library
- Collection Development

INTERNET

Contemporary advancement of computer, communication and networking technology has given new meaning to the arena of capacity building in Libraries and knowledge centers. Through networking various institutions are sharing their information content. According to Venkatesh and Talawar "the network of networks on the global scale is known as internet, the information superhighway". (Jha, Mishra, Sinha; 1994; P59-64)

The Internet or Web or WWW is a treasure of Information. The Internet "is a reference tool and has a searchable online database of thousands of journals and table of contents"(Sarasvatathy,Giddaiah;2007;p207).The Information Super Highway lay down convenience to locate information through World Wide Web Virtual Libraries, Subject Specific Sites, General Web Sites (Academic, Corporate/Government Sites) Access to Journals etc. Internet help to search information, available in farway Organizations or Countries. Primary as well as Secondary sources of information can be located through internet.

Internet is intrinsic for scientific research, current news, database searching, entertainment, conferences, electronic publishing or simple chat. Various utilities of internet for the knowledge building process are communication, document or file transfer, Interactive browsing, Reading and posting to bulletin boards.

WWW support in education and research by providing preprints of research articles, discussion forum, tables of contents of scientific journals, technical report, electronic journals Library catalogue, patents, standards, directories of institutions, associations, universities, reference sources, course work and distance education, (Shiva Sankar, Venkatesh, Talawar; 2003;P 395).

SEARCH ENGINE

By the amplification of information technology, search engines are the most comprehensively familiar tool to come across information on the internet. Assorted information sources are obtainable on the internet, and probing of appropriate piece of information is rather unimaginable without a suitable Search Engine. (Biradar and Kumar, 2006; P232). "Search Engine is a database of Internet files, searched through computer program called spider, robot, crawler, worm, wander etc. Spider/Crawler is the program that travels web from one link to another, identify relevancy of query and return results in a schematic order (by title or by full text or by size or by URL etc.)"(Mukherjee;2005;p483). It is interactive and help the User to locate the information available via WWW. It acts as a interface between the user and the underlying database.

Search Engines are more useful when looking for very specific or obscure information. It can search the whole web and bring the required document. Therefore, an efficient tool for capacity building.

ELECTRONIC INFORMATION SOURCES

The commonly available electronic information resources are, CD-ROMs, online databases, online public access Catalogue (OPAC) and the internet and other networked information sources.

Users access information irrespective of geographical location and time. As they are frequently updated, users get current and advanced information. Electronic resources support teaching, research, learning and extension activities. They provide access to full text and bibliographic data. They cannot be stolen or mutilated, easy to maintain, availability of networking facility, solves the problem of space and time, convenience to search and use.

NETWORKING

User's changing need and growing expectations could be solved by computerized network or consortium. Provision of automated library activities and operations is fundamental requirement for networking. The National Commission of Libraries and Information Science (NCLIS) defines a library network as " two or more libraries or other organizations engaged in a common pattern of information exchange through communications, for some functional purpose".

The meticulous implementation of networking promotes sharing of resources and preparation of bibliographic database. Accordingly networking has proved its dominance, in the field of capacity building.

OPEN ACCESS SCHOLARLY PUBLISHING

Increasing number of publishers are using the internet as a global way to offer their publications to the International community of Scientists and technologist.

Suber aptly distinguished Open Access (OA) journals than others by two characteristics, "Firstly, it is free of charges to everyone, Secondly, the copy right holder has consented in advance to unrestricted reading, downloading, copying, sharing, storing, printing, searching, linking and crawling"(Mukharjee;2008;p 213)

Open Access Journals broadly cover subjects of interdisciplinary research and specifically computer oriented issues accumulating contemporary user's demands.

In India, where almost all academic libraries undergoes insufficient funds and budgetary constrains, open access journals are one of the potential remedies for the confrontation of serials pricing. Leading Universities and R & D Organizations around the globe are coming forward to publish their research outputs in their websites, even if they publish it in conventional journal, enabling people to access it free of cost.

The time lag in between production and access of OA is reduced in comparison to its printed counterparts, thus enhancing its utility and capacity building.

INSTITUTIONAL REPOSITORY AND DIGITAL LIBRARY

Institutional Repositories as defined by Crow "as digital collection capturing and preserving the intellectual output of a single or multi-university community" (Hirwade; 2006; p147). Institutional Repository collects digital content of intellectual output of faculty, staff and students at an institution for utilization and preservation. Capacity building has geared up through this type of storing, archiving, preserving and making scholarly material available.

According to Arms" Digital Library is a managed

collection of information with associated services, where the information is stored in digital formats and accessible over a network" (Venkata Raman;2008;p 147).Textual, multimedia and hyper media images include photographs, drawings, illustrations, artwork, sound and video etc. can be called as digital resources.

Venkataraman (2008;p147) has elucidated some advantages of institutional repositories made through Digital Library." Digital Library provides easy, convenient and comfortable access to wide range of information resources and delivery effective need-based and value-added information services to the users at their desktop. Digital collections have some special features like multimedia content, compact storage, convenient and comfortable search and retrieval, 24x7 accesses to remote resources".

COLLECTION DEVELOPMENT

In the growing population of information on the Web, the selection and procurement information and importance is very crucial as studies and research are now- a- days highly rely on Web based resources

"Most current collecting practices for material on web can be categorized in their approaches

- Web site specific collection.
- Domain specific collection.
- Topic or subject- specific collection

(Schmidt,Shelburne,Vess;2008;p186)

The process of collection development of printed material is more or less symmetrical to that of digital collection from internet. Due to the transitory nature of the web the information should be preserved for anticipated future use as well as present need. Still lots of studies are to be undertaken in this emerging field of capacity building from WWW.

CONCLUSION

Usefulness of Internet as a communication media and as a source of information is incredible. Libraries must be active in participatory networking. The technologies such as blogs and wikis are coming closer to the community and knowledge generation. Libraries should be the heart throb of information society only through engaging upcoming technologies. The significance of web in capacity building is eminent from a statement of Lankes (2007; P.17) "Participatory librarianship is an opportunity not only to enhance the mission of the library, but proactively to position librarians at the forefront of the information field." It is needless to say that internet is very productive to users for carrying out research work in their field of specialization as well as to gather general information.

REFERENCE

1. Birdar(BS), Kumar(S). Internet search engine: A comparative study and evaluation methodology.2006. *SRELS journal of information management*, V.43 n.3.p231-241.
2. Crow(R). The Case for Institutional Repositories: a spare position paper*http://WWW.Url.Org /Spare/IR/ir.html*
3. Das(S).A Text book of Information.2005;NewDelhi,p13.1-13.45.
4. Hirwade (M), Hirwade(A). Institutional Repositories:Challenge and oppurtunity for LIS Professionals in Digital Age.2006. *Library Herald*,V.44 n.2,p146-151.
5. Jha(KN),Mishra(V).Internet Emerging technology for Information generation and its services to users.1999. *Annals of Library Science and Documentation*, V.46 n.2,p59-64.
6. Lankes(RD).Collection Conservations in a Massive-Scale

World.2007. *Library Resources and Technical Services,V.52 n.2 p12-18.*

7. Mukherjee(B).Open Access Scholarly Publishing in Library and Information Science.2008. *Annals of Library amd Information Science,*V.55, sept. p213-217.
8. Mukherjee(B).Users'query through Search Enginrs:Librarians' View.2005. *SRELS journal of information management,* V.42 n.4.p483-492.
9. Sarasvathy(p) and Giddaiah(D).Internet a Wealth of Information.2007. *SRELS journal of information management,* V.44 n.2.p391-400.
10. Schmidt(K), Shelburne(W) an Vess(D). Apporaches to Selection, Access and Collection Development in the Web world.2008. *Library Resources and Technical Services,V.52 n.3 184-191.*
11. Shivashankar(NP),Venkatesh(Y),Talawar(VG).Internet in Pharmacy Education and Research .2003. *SRELS journal of information management,* V.40 n.4.p391-400.
12. Suber(P). Removing the barriers to research:An introduction to open access for Librarians. Available at *http://WWW.earlham.edu/Peters/writing/acrl.htm.*
13. VenkataRamana(P). Development of Digital Library:Issues oppourtunities and challenges.2008.*Pearl,*V.2 n.2, p146-156.

26
Capacity Building and Library User Education

Monisha Mishra
Rabindra K. Mahapatra

INTRODUCTION

Libraries support the teaching and research need of the academic institutions. Hence library is regarded as the backbone of every educational institution. It is the responsibility of every library to make the effective utilization of its resources for the benefit of the users. Information explosion, as well as emerging new technologies and at the same time changing information needs has given rise to a lot of variable library resources such as print, non print, as well as different kinds of e-resources. Traditional librarians instructed the end users to locate and use the print copy of books and journals which they found difficult to locate. But with the advent of Information and Communication Technology (ICT) the use of internet, search engines, e-journals, subject gateways, mailing lists, and discussion groups has become an integral part of study or scholarly research. Hence to train the users with such skills some sort of instruction or training to the users is necessary which may be named as "***user education***". To make the library user friendly the user education program is essential as it provides the users appropriate skills to search the documents in the library which can guide them in their learning process.

Tacatlian, Director of UNESCO General information program mentioned that "User Education is to include any effort or program which will guide and instruct existing and potential users in the recognition and formulation of their information needs in the effective and efficient use of information services and their assessment".

Fleming (1990) defines "user education" as various programs of instruction, education and exploration provided by libraries to users to enable them to make more effective, efficient and independent use of information sources and services to which these libraries provide access.

USER EDUCATION IN CAPACITY BUILDING OF A LIBRARY

Acquisition of large collection of resources is not the sole motto of a library. Only acquiring those resources but not utilizing the same for the benefit of the users is something like decorative items kept in the drawing room for better look. Libraries just like business centers need to focus on building their capacity if they want to maximize their effect on the research and development community. For that the library and information centre professionals need to dedicate themselves to raising their capacity building to the same level of importance as that of their organizations critical functions. Similarly users or researchers using the library resources play a vital role in building the capacity of a library. Educating the users by the library professionals is the result to improve information consciousness of users and their ability to make the best use of the library and the available resources which are kept for their use. The satisfaction of the users is the prime goal of every library. Hence every library should dedicate more and more time to enhance user attendance in libraries which can be possible through the designing of various user education programme.Through this process the libraries have to devote more and more time in organizing training programs/workshops, preparing handouts, arranging demonstrations, lecturing etc.

The various user education programmes will ultimately benefit all librarians by helping them in the field of knowledge acquisition and enhanced professional performance. This will increase the status of librarians. The relationship between the user and the library professional will be improved considerably.

Library capacity building is a whole concept and the library professionals, users and the resources are the major component of every library. If a balanced relationship is maintained between the users, professionals and the resources by a suitably designed user education programme this will directly affect the capacity building of a library.

NEED OF USER EDUCATION

The library's growing strength within the academic community becomes possible by creating a strategic plan that would respond dynamically to the declining fiscal environment; create an appropriate research library role; take advantage of electronic opportunities; and further strengthen relations with users through collaboration and partnerships. These initiatives required a strategic approach, incorporating lower level decision-making, staff flexibility, and responsiveness to quickly changing user needs and also designing a good user education program for its users.

Besides those things certain other points also makes us feel towards the need of user education in libraries. Those are:

- Emerging growth of information and communication technology in all field of knowledge
- Development of several new methods in the transfer of information.
- Multidisciplinary subject approaches
- Tremendous advancement in the computerized storage and retrieval of information.
- Lack of awareness among users relating to various forms, types, and sources of information.
- Inculcate the habit of self study in every user
- Marketing of the library resources and services.

OBJECTIVES OF USER EDUCATION

Library is a service institution and the users are its customers. Organizations that offer goods or services for sale recognize the importance of making the customer aware of the resources and also the opportunities to use those resources. Similarly the library should make its users aware of its resources and services that are offered, where to find them and how to exploit what is available. The main Objectives of user education are:

- To make users independent library users
- To make the library centre of user activity
- Educate the users about the various IT Tools, information sources and how to exploit those resources effectively and efficiently
- To introduce the resources and facilities inside the library

COMPONENTS OF USER EDUCATION

The user need is multi faceted. Library may also be considered as an association of technology, manpower, resources and users. Users need specific help in information gathering, necessary sources and technique. Hence user education program should include necessary bibliographic instruction, library orientation, user awareness and interest profiling. User studies and user education programs improve the professional competencies of the librarians.

a) Library Orientation

Orientation is concerned with introducing the freshman to the general techniques of the library usages and services made available in the Library. It aims at a) familiarize the users with the physical layout and the procedures for using the library relevant to their needs b) to make users aware of the staffs who are available to help to assist them c) to inform users about the basic library holdings such as card catalogue, Web OPAC , Serial List, e-Resources etc.

b) Bibliographic Instruction

Bibliographic instruction is meant to help the users take maximum advantage of library resources to meet their information needs. It improves skills for effective use of library collections, service and staffs. It enables the user independent to use the resources.

c) User Awareness

The aim of user awareness is to increase alertness about the library as a primary source of information and an agency to which users may turn for assistance. The user awareness can be attained by adopting the following steps

- Organizing seminars, workshops, exhibitions etc.

- Circulating Library brochures
- Marketing of Library as well its resources and services
- Developing a library website of your own describing about its resources, written policy and services.

d) User Profile

The users' profile is one of the components which provide the answer. The user profile consists of creating profile of the users who are to be provided with bibliographic instruction. The profile consists of keyword that collectively characterizes the subject interest of an individual or group. A performa is designed for the purpose. Each user is requested to fill up the proforma against which the information generated is matched and answered to the user.

CHANGING FACES OF USER EDUCATION

There are many methods of user education. Some of the commonly used traditional methods of user education are:

- Users guidance desk
- Lectures
- User manual
- Audio-visual program
- Guided Tour
- Computer aided instruction
- Display of Books
- Exhibitions

Apart from that there is a necessity of Web based user education. The methodology adopted for e-environment changes are:

- Train the users to handle internet.
- Make them aware about the different search engines
- Giving them little knowledge about HTML and XML as the case may be.
- Train them about the searching techniques
- Awareness about the different subject gateways
- Imparting Knowledge about Institutional Repository

USER EDUCATION IN A TECHNOLOGICAL ENVIRONMENT

The noticing on libraries has changed drastically. The traditional libraries are being converted to digital Libraries in most of the cases due to the introduction of internet, cdroms, databases, online search engines, web based resources etc. So now a days librarian are acting as information scientists as they have to handle the traditional queries of the users as well as the system handling queries in the computer. There are many methods of traditional user education. The advent of information technology in libraries has necessitated changes in user education. Lectures, Library tours, Seminars, Workshops, Printed Booklets, Display and audio video aids are some of the techniques of user education. Earlier card catalogue was referred by the users to locate the documents in a library. But in the new system the card catalogue has been replaced by the Web OPAC (Online Public Access Catalogue). Software supplier should send the training kit for OPAC module for the users to know the search technique. In the Web environment the user education is required in the following areas.

INTERNET AND E-MAIL SERVICES

Through the internet and E-mail service user can locate

the desired article from the website. Then he/she can request the author through the mail to send a soft copy of the desired article as attachment. Through E-mail user can request for inter library loan, document delivery services etc.

CDROM SEARCH SERVICES

Libraries provide abstracting and indexing services through CDROMS which are best, powerful, cost effective tool for information storage and retrieval. Many libraries subscribe to online databases as well as CDROM databases which are not only cost effective but also facilitates quick and speedy search by the researchers.

ONLINE JOURNALS

Many libraries subscribe to online journals for the sake of their researchers. A vast collection of online journals are available on the net for free. The users of those libraries should have necessary knowledge for finding out those articles from the journals.

KNOWLEDGE OF SEARCH ENGINES

The basic function of the search engines is to search the required information from the vast collection of unorganized resources. Different types of search engines are there such as main search engine and meta search engine.

KNOWLEDGE OF BROWSERS

It helps to find and retrieve by moving from one resource to another glued together with hyper text pointer that by clicking the link or pointer within the page.

KNOWLEDGE OF WEBSITES

How to locate the websites which exclusively deal with particular topic and encourage users to discuss in the discussion forums, chats, talks etc.

RESOURCE SHARING

The development of electronic networked environment has led to the resource sharing among libraries. The users should have the knowledge of the same so that they can avail the benefit from other libraries wherever the required information is made available.

LITERATURE SEARCH TRAINING

Through this programme users are trained in information search skill in all types of information sources like primary sources, secondary sources, tertiary sources etc. They are also trained about different other areas like how to choose a research topic, method of citing reference, style of writing dissertations/ projects/ thesis selection of books , research communication and how to search information over the internet using different search engines.

CONCLUSION

Capacity building in libraries certainly makes for an interesting topic. However it is a vast and complex topic which encompasses collection development, introduction of ICT in libraries, proper professional development of library staffs, designing proper user education guides to make effective utilization of its resources. Capacity building can be achieved at the maximum level by carefully including all the above roles and responsibilities with a properly designed user guide or user education programme.

Training is one of the most essential needs for end users at library in order to access information. If users are given some initial training it will save staff time in the long run. A trained user is more independent than an untrained one who could take up a lot of staff time. The users of the 21st Century are more aware of his information needs and more enthusiastic while coming to the library. Therefore, keeping in view the interest and needs of the users it becomes necessary to instruct them in such a way that they never feel handicapped while using the system as well as the resources. At the same time it will also prove helpful in Library Capacity Building.

REFERENCES

1. *Satynarayana, M* "Library user education in the digital era: A study of academic Libraries", *All India IASLIC Conference, 2009, KIIT Deemed university, Bhubaneswar, No 48, pp 425-432*
2. *Kanamadi Satish, Kadhi Jagdev etal* "Capacity Building in the Knowledge Environment: a Human resource development approach" , *2007, Inflibnet Conference proceedings*
3. *Sharma U.C and Madaan Priya "Users* education Programmes and its utilization within academic Libraries of Digital Era", *All India IASLIC Conference, 2009, KIIT Deemed university, Bhubaneswar, No 48, pp 433-444*
4. *Natarajan, M* "User education Programme in Digital Era", *All India IASLIC Conference, 2009, KIIT Deemed university, Bhubaneswar, No 48, pp 455-463*
5. *Townley, Charles,T* "User-focused strategic services for technological university libraries" *ITAUL Conference proceedings*

28
Building of Library Capacity through Consortium Approach for the Special Libraries

M. K. Seth
P. S. Patra

INTRODUCTION

The impact of ICT has revolutionized the world in multiple angles and that has brought about sweeping changes in the library and information discipline. Though the professionals in the country are also experiencing the virtues of internet, web and electronics information highways, our libraries have not gone much farther than the computerization of in-house operations and availing same databases in electronics media. It is a fact that no libraries even those in developed countries can claim completeness in their collection, and this is more so for libraries in a developing country like India. User expectations are too high especially in academic libraries. The desire to provide users with information to meet their research interests despite a limited budget has always been the prime motivation to librarians[1]. The proliferations of e-publishing across the world have also brought in a revolution in scholarly journal publication, subscription, access and delivery mechanism. E-journals are electronic equivalents of their print counter parts possessing many added features. E-journals offer a range of potential advantages to libraries and end-users: multiple simultaneous access to the same issue, remote access, in-built searching facilities, multi-media capabilities and reduced storage concerns. As a result of the above, libraries today buy licenses for an ever-increasing number of e-Journals from a range of different publishers and providers. Over the last several years, much of the periodical literature has become accessible electronically over the Internet. At the same time computers, reasonable communication bandwidth and access to the Internet have become available to most of the libraries. This availability is expected to increase enormously over the next couple of years because of the initiatives undertaken by various public and private sectors organisations.

WHAT IS CONSORTIA

A consortium could be described as a group of organizations who come together to fulfill a combined objective that usefully requires co-operation and the sharing of resources. And need to have a clear mutual goal in order to ensure their success. One definition of library consortia could be the "coming together of libraries to achieve a common goal that is beyond what an individual library could achieve on its own[2]". According to the *Oxford English Dictionary*, consortium means a "temporary cooperation of a number of powers, companies etc. for a common purpose. It is an association of similar type of organization/institution who are engaged for producing and servicing the common things/for providing services for a specific purpose of its users." According to the *Cambridge Online Dictionary* (Cambridge Online dictionary, *http://dictionary.cambridge.org/*), a consortium is "an organization of several businesses or banks joining together as a group for a shared purpose". The aim of consortia is to achieve what the members of the group cannot achieve individually. A library consortium is a collective activity to provide shared expertise, access to new electronic and print resources, professional development, and new sources of funds. A library consortium formation can be local, regional, state, national and inter institutional level[3].

IMPORTANCE OF CONSORTIA AND ITS VARIOUS ISSUES

The consortium is needed for libraries because of e-journals are becoming increasingly in demand both as a means of rapid desktop access to current research materials and as a way to view past volumes[4]. E-journals offer a range of potential advantages to libraries and end-users:

- To provide better library services
- Can be used simultaneously by more than one user
- Provide timely remote Access
- Supports different searching capabilities
- Save physical storage space and its maintenance cost
- Can support multimedia information
- Optimum utilization of funds due to financial crunch
- Impossibility of self-sufficiency

As a result of the above advantages, libraries today buy licenses for an ever-increasing number of electronic journals from a range of different publishers and providers, and use a diverse set of technologies for information delivery. In addition to the above advantages it has also its own limitation like:

- The library consortium activity is a complex process, which involves the wholehearted support and concerted efforts of the librarians, their management and the publishers. They form an important role in the new scholarly information environment.
- Identifying the most suitable product which is agreed upon by all the members of the consortium is more or less a difficult proposition. This is mostly because each and every member will have their own wish list of information products and services.
- There are various access methods offered by publishers towards accessing their resources and it varies case to case. Access authentication could be User ID / Password based or IP based which are popular among them. Uninterrupted and hassle free access to the scholarly content is the ultimate objective of the consortium.
- As against the print paradigm, the e-Journal subscriptions and access models allow only licensing of the content / product for a stipulated period of time which has several restrictions and bindings on the licensee. There are number of issues which are under debate between librarians, users and publishers which need international attention and solution.

But, the various issues can be manageable with proper standard and negotiation among libraries, venders and suppliers. In most cases cost of the journals are out of reach of many of our libraries and only a consortia approach could provide some meaningful practical solution. Publishers are invited for negotiations and asked to offer their best prices to the consortia.

FACTORS RESPONSIBLE FOR CONSORTIA

Various factors to be taken for an effective functioning of a successful consortium. like:

- Proper cooperation among libraries, suppliers and publishers
- Resources identification on the basis of usage and usability
- Long run planning of the technology infrastructure
- Copyright and licensing
- Aarchival and pricing issue should be economically favorable.
- Last but not least, designing and launching a library consortium should be long term sustenance and robust models towards achieving the above goals.

DIFFERENT TYPES OF CONSORTIA

The types of consortia identified are generally based on various models evolved in India in varity of forms depending upon participations' affiliation and funding sources.

1. Open consortia : This type of consortia is very flexible and it is the wish of members of consortia can join and leave any they please. INDEST Consortium is an example to this.

2. Closed group consortia : It is within defined group. This kind of consortia emerges either by affiliation and collaboration among them like CSIR, DAE, IIM consortium. And the formation and operation of the consortia guidelines and its administration are fairly simple and easy.

3. Centrally funded model : In this model, consortium will solely depend on the parent body. A few examples are INFONET by UGC, ICMR, and CSIR by DSIR.

4. Shared-budget model : In this model the participating libraries take the lead and form the consortium. IIM and FORSA are examples of this model.

5. Publisher initiatives : The Emerald Full-Text Library published by the Emerald Publishing Group (formerly MCB University Press) is recent example. Here, the consortium members will get deep discount price to the participating libraries

6. National consortium : The end of this model is , national level licensing of products. and in this regard are INDEST-AICTE, UGC Infonet.

CONSORTIA INITIATIVES IN INDIA

Consortium based library subscriptions to e-journals and electronic full-text databases are picking up good momentum in India, since the early 1900s; though it was termed differently, the idea was the same, as it is understood now. Today, many libraries are already a part of one or more consortia, and those that are not are rapidly taking steps to develop these strategic partnerships with other libraries[5]. The consortium movement initially was most pronounced in academic libraries and special libraries. Over the past five years more than ten national level consortia have come into existence and started playing around in the country. Some of the notable Indian initiatives on consortium are:

- CSIR Library Consortium- http://www.niscair.res.in/ ActivitiesandServices /Major Projects /majproj.htm#
- ICMR Library Consortium- http://www.icmrinform india.co.in

- INDEST Consortium (http://paniit.iitd.ac.in/indest/)
- UGC INFONET (http://web.inflibnet.ac.in/info/ugcinfonet/ugcinfonet.jsp)
- FORSA Consortium (Astronomy and Astrophysics Libraries) (http://www.iiap.res.in/library/forsa.html)
- DAE Library Consortium (http://www.tifr.res.in/~libws/)
- ISRO Library Consortium- http://www.isro.org
- IIM Library Consortium-http://www.iimahd.ernet.in/ , http://www.iimb.ernet.in/, http://www.iimcal.ac.in/ , http://www.iimidr.ac.in/, http://www.iimk.ac.in/ , http://www.iiml.ac.in/
- HELINET (Rajiv Gandhi University of Health Sciences, Karnataka) (http://www.rguhs.ac.in/hn/newhell.htm)
- ICICI Knowledge Park (http://www.iciciknowledgepark.com/)

CONSORTIUM APPROACH BY CSIR

Journals are a vital source of information for the scientific research and development. The number of periodicals at present is estimated to be ~250,000. Of these, ~ 25,000 are scientific, technical and medical (STM) journals, ~15,000 are refereed scholarly periodicals and ~12,000 are refereed scholarly periodicals which are available online. Journal titles are growing three folds every 15 years and their cost, 2.5 times every 10 years. Obviously, no single library can afford to procure all journals even in a single discipline. With the emergence of IT applications, particularly Internet, there has been a major shift from traditional print journals to electronic journals (e-journals) in view of many advantages of the latter, i.e. fast, easy, 'anywhere-anytime' accessibility, sharability, hyperlink facility to related texts, cost-effectiveness and obviation of the storage problem encountered in the case of print journals. As a result, the number of e-journals is fast growing and at present ~15,000 are available in S&T areas alone. The continuous escalation in price of journals has adversely affected the information resource base of R&D/academic organizations. CSIR labs too have witnessed a steep decline in the journals information base during the past 10-12 years. On comparing CSIR journals base with some of the other leading institutions of the world and taking into consideration the modern IT modes available, it was felt that there is a tremendous scope for enhancing the information base within the constraints of existing resources, through the consortium approach, and the project 'CSIR e- Journals Consortium' was launched[6]. The objectives of this network project are:

1. To provide CSIR S&T personnel electronic access to world S&T literature through strengthening the facilities for pooling, sharing and electronically accessing the CSIR information resources.
2. To nucleate the culture of electronic access with a view to catalysing the evolution of digital libraries.

Following formation of the Consortium, CSIR constituted a negotiation committee, which met on 9-10 January 2002 at Pune to hold negotiations with M/s Elsevier and Springer Kluwer, and on its recommendations, CSIR entered into agreement with M/s Elsevier on 10 June 2002. Encouraged by the tremendous success of this initial move (the e- access of 400 unique titles, which were being earlier subscribed in print form only, became 11 times over a span of just two and a half years), the CSIR e-Journals Consortium team took steps to achieve the set target of about 4500 world class e-journals. Over 60 odd publishers were identified as relevant to the CSIR needs. Selection and prioritization criteria of publishers were evolved. The aspects given due consideration included: need for maximum coverage of journals to all(38)labs, relevance of the journals covered by the publishers to the labs, the total number of labs relevant to such publishers, and economics of various pricing models offered by the vendors for consortium access to e-journals. After a careful scrutiny, 14 most relevant publishers were identified and prioritized. The consortium team organized several meetings of various negotiation committees, nodal officers of the various CSIR labs, pre-bid meeting with publishers, etc. After this long exercise, and available budgetary allocation, CSIR finally entered into agreement with 11 publishers to access about 3316 international journals across the labs. Thus, the expansion of information base of CSIR labs/ Institutions has increased from 20 -200 print journals to 3316 e-journals for its every user. In addition, CSIR labs/institute can access 1500 ejournals from Directory of Open Access Journals (DOAJ) which are free for every one. This all provides an opportunity to CSIR users to access about 5000 e-journals of international repute.

MAJOR PUBLISHERS OF E-JOURNALS

Elsevier Science : Science Direct is the world's largest electronic collection of science, technology and medicine full text and bibliographic information. Investing in ScienceDirect in an evolving solution to refer larger number of STM journals.Since its launch in 1997, ScienceDirect has evolved from a web database of Elsevier journals to one of the world's largest providers of scientific, technical and medical (STM) literature.

SpringerLink : SpringerLink is one of the world's leading online information services for scientific, technical, and medical (STM) journals. SpringerLink is a preferred data source for researchers in academic and corporate institutions and other vital knowledge centers.

The American Institute of Physics : AIP is a society publisher chartered in New York state in 1931 for the purpose of promoting the advancement and diffusion of the knowledge of physics and its application to human welfare. It is the mission of the Institute to serve physics, astronomy, and related fields of science and technology by serving its member societies and their associates, individual scientists, educators, R&D leaders, and the general public with programs, services and publications.

Blackwell Publishing : Blackwell Publishing is the world's leading society publisher, partnering with more than 600 academic and professional societies. Blackwell publishes over 750 journals and 600 text and reference books annually, across a wide range of academic, medical, and professional subjects. Blackwell Synergy is the online journals service from Blackwell Publishing. It holds the content for most of Blackwell's journals, the majority of which are published on behalf of international scholarly and professional societies.

American Society of Chemical Engineering : The ASCE Online Research Library is a comprehensive tool for locating articles of interest across all disciplines of civil engineering. The research library provides you with unprecedented access to more than 18,500 full-text papers from ASCE journals and proceedings published since 1995—that's over 175,000 pages! Approximately 4,000 new papers will be added each year.

Cambridge University Press : Cambridge University Press is the printing and publishing house of the University of Cambridge. It is an integral part of the

University and has similar charitable objectives in advancing knowledge, education, learning, and research. For centuries the press has extended the research and teaching activities of the University by making available

Wiley Inter Science : Wiley is a global publisher of print and electronic products, specializing in scientific, technical, and medical books and journals; professional and consumer books and subscription services; and textbooks and other educational materials for undergraduate and graduate students as well as lifelong learners. Wiley publishes in a variety of print and electronic formats. It features over 1,000 journals, major reference works, online books, Current Protocols laboratory manuals, and databases as well as a suite of professional and management resources.

Oxford University Press : Online access for most of OUP journals is available to institutions for an additional charge to a print only subscription. Alternatively, online-only access may be purchased at a discount. Many of our personal and society subscription rates include online access for free with a print subscription. More details on the Prices and Ordering information pages.

American Society of Mechanical Engineers : ASME conducts one of the world's largest technical publishing operations, holds numerous technical conferences worldwide, and offers hundreds of professional development courses each year. ASME sets internationally recognized industrial and manufacturing codes and standards that enhance public safety.

E-ACCESS TO JOURNALS/DATABASES/BOOKS

There are some tips and access mechanism (How to access) in each of the publishers site. Like -Content-Journal and book information, set up-librarian tools and support, using-researcher tools and support, subscriptions-of the publisher's products available. The CSIR E-Journal Consortium division, NISCAIR has developed web based monitoring system to act as an interface between the users (CSIR Labs) and e-journals publishers. The system has three different interfaces i.e. CSIR labs, Publishers and Administrator of the consortium. It can be accessed at http://202.54.99.7/ejournal/ejournalhome1.htm. The system executes various tasks such as complaint registration, response to complaints and monitoring of both complaint and response. The system generates various reports also. E-access to journals/databases/books of the below mentioned Publishers through CSIR (IMMT)IP address: Access to all the BIS and ASTM standards is also available.

CONCLUSION

We conclude that consortium plays a vital role, especially in developing countries and the success of consortia very much depends on the members of consortia. The published literature and the discussion above give every indication that special libraries will continue to form consortia. The library consortium, on the basis of strength of numbers of institutions, offers strong and healthy business growth opportunities to the electronic publishers and attracts the best possible price and terms of agreement. It is in our interest to work together if we believe there is value in the roles we play or that the scholarly community will be worse off for our absence. At present more than 15 national level library are live and operational in the country. As the consortium initiatives demand active involvement of the LIS professionals as well as the promoting / beneficiary institutions, it normally evolves and grows with hardships

Table-1

Publisher	URL to access	Allowed years of access of full text	No. of full text journals allowed
Elsevier Science	*http://www.sciencedirect.com/*	*Current year + 10 years back files*	**1860**
SPRINGER	*www.springerlink.com*	*Current year + 5 years back files*	**1211**
Blackwell	*www.blackwell-synergy.com.*	*Current year + 5 years back files*	**815**
John Wiley	*http://interscience.wiley.com*	*Current year + 5 years back files*	**408**
Royal Society of Chemistry	*http://www.rsc.org*	*Current year + 5 years back files*	**73**
American institute of Physics	*www.scitation.org*	*Current year + 5 years back files*	**16**
Oxford University Press	*http://www.oxfordjournals.org*	*Current year + 5 years back files*	**184**
American Society of Mechanical Engineering	*http://scitation.aip.org*	*Current year + 5 years back files*	**19**
Cambridge University Press	*http://journals.cambridge.org*	*Current year + 5 years back files*	**93**
American Society of Civil Engineering	*http://scitation.aip.org*	*Current year + 5 years back files*	**30**
Taylor & Francis	*http://journalsonline.tandf.co.uk*	*Current year + 5 years back files*	**613**
American Chemical Society	*http://pubs.acs.org*	*Current year + 5 years back files*	**35**

New Scientist	*http://www.newscientist.com/home.ns*	*Current year*	
Nature	*www.nature.com*	*Current year*	
Web of Science & Derwent Innovations Index(Thomson Scientific)	*http://www.isiknowledge.com*		***1987 +***
METADEX database	*www.csa.com*		***1966+***
MaterialsNetBase (Taylor & Francis)	*http://www.materialsnetbase.com*		***221 E-books***
Ebrary	*http://site.ebrary.com/lib/immtbhubaneswar*		***3100 E-books*** *in S& T and Engineering*

and bottlenecks. At times we find that the movement draws its strength even from its weaknesses, problems and from its own hard-learnt lessons. It is also to be noted that e-journal subscription itself is a complex and complicated process, which adds up problems to the consortium activity in multiple ways. Naturally, there will be a host of issues and problems that keep haunting libraries involved in consortia activities. At the same token and more importantly, the consortium approach brings in numerous benefits to the participating libraries - a steep increase in the resource base at a nominally higher investment burden; ensuring uninterrupted access to the array of e-journals; enabling perpetual access to the previously subscribed scholarly content for future; increasing the institutional intellectual capability and scientific productivity; opportunities for long term preservation of scholarly materials through state-of-art archiving strategies.

REFERENCES

1. Kopp, J., 1998. Library consortia and information technology: The past, the present, the promise. *Information Technology and Libraries* **17** 1, pp. 7–12.
2. Ghosh, M., & Jambhekar, A. (2003). A plan for the establishment of a library network or consortia of management and engineering libraries in western India. Papers presented at International Convention on Mapping Technology on Libraries and People. CALIBER-2003, Ahmedabad, India.
3. Goudar, IRN. and Poornima Narayana. 'Emerging pricing models for E-Journals Consortia and Indian initiatives'. Proceedings of the International Conference on Digital Libraries (ICDL 2004). New Delhi. 24-27 February 2004. 333-341.
4. Janakiraman, S., 'Thoughts on Library Consortium', Proceedings of the Round Table on Sharing of E-journals through Consortia in Indian Libraries, Bangalore. 28-29 November 2002.

5. Arora, Jagdish (et al.) 'Library Consortia and Resource Sharing Initiatives in India: A white paper'. HELINET Consortium. Rajiv Gandhi University of Health Sciences, Bangalore, May 1, 2004.

6. http://www.csir.res.in/External/Utilities/Frames/pressroom/main_page.asp?a=topframe.htm&b=leftcon.htm&c=../../../Heads/pressroom/RnDNewsLetters/econsortium.pdf

29
Building of Modern Library Capacity: From Librarian to Cybrarian

Sudhir Kumar Jena
K.C.Das

INTRODUCTION

LIS professionals need to change their roles as information infrastructure has changed drastically compared to the past. The new information infrastructure has enabled information professionals to meet the needs of the information age. Information explosion, exponential growth of literature (Print & digital), unprecedented and unpredicted end-user requirements for just-in-time information and advancement of Information and Communication Technologies (ICT) are changing the information seekers behavior and trends. Librarians have key roles to play in developing the new information infrastructure. It is important that they should have a vision of the information infrastructure which correlates between users and that encompasses and embraces the internet and digital information resources.

Thanks to the advancement of Information Technology, that proved very handy for the contemporary Information professionals in collecting, organizing and disseminating information with speed and ease. This would not have been possible without the advent of technology revolution that is influencing every domain, professional area including Librarianship.

WHAT IS CYBRARIAN?

A Cybrarian (pronounced sai-BREHR-i-uhn, a compound of *cyber* and librarian) is a library and information science professional that specializes in using the internet as a resource tool. The term has gained currency among many librarians who use the internet. The American Library Association hosts a section called Cyberlib.net, written by Pat Sensor, author of *The Cybrarian's Manual.*

The word "CYBRARIAN" is difficult to be found in dictionaries and possible way to extract its meaning is to track the use of this word on the internet. Taking a quick look at what CYBRARIAN means- answers.com says – "Librarians who do most of their research and information retrieval via the internet and other online services".

According to the Chronicle of Higher Education's I.T. Jargon Monitor – A Cybrarian is-'A Librarian who can maneuver through cyberspace with ease, plucking information form its farthest reaches. The term was coined according to library legend, by Michel Bauwens, an entrepreneur and founding member of a Belgian think tank called the FourthWave, which considers the implications of the digital revolution'. In other words we may conventionally say a CYBRARIAN is a cyber librarian or digital librarian.

MANAGEMENT OF LIBRARIES IN THE 21ST CENTURY

Maintaining a library today is not like what it was two decades ago. With new information technologies, satellite communication systems, intellectual property rights, networking systems like INTERNET, the library environment is becoming more complex and complicated. Added to these developments budgetary constraints, inadequate infrastructure, falling human resource standards are all making the library management more difficult. Also the raising expectations of the users and the management, external and internal administrative problems, client relationships are all adding to the tensions and anxiety of the modern day librarian.

COLLECTION DEVELOPMENT IN THE DIGITAL ERA

Various types of digital resources may be available in the core subject areas of a library. The LIS professional's job is to identify subject materials and information resources in all formats, prior to buying. These resources include reference sources such as handbooks, technical dictionaries, encyclopedias, standards and patents etc in the form of CD-ROMs; on-line journals subscriptions either on an individual basis or through consortia; on-line or CD-ROM databases (either bibliographic or full text); e-books; on-line maps, OPACS and several interactive tools and software, especially in a public library environment. The LIS professionals has to be aware about the problems and pitfalls associated with these digital resources and provide a seamless integrated services to his clientele, incorporating both the traditional and digital resources. Networking and resource sharing with other local libraries in the same subject field can also enhance the library's services. Frequent assessment of users' needs and monitoring trends in R&D are also required.

CAPACITY BUILDING

Due to bio-genetics revolutions, man began to talk, think and communicate through language, script, reading and writing. He has used many formats for communication of his ideas and feelings such as clay tablets, bones, parchment, papyrus, birch bark, palm leaves, textiles and paper. Man creates information in the crucible of his mind, uses it and consumes it. He has struggled across the centuries of time to live less brutishly, think more wisely, amass more knowledge and make more and more information available to more and more people for more and more purposes. It is, therefore, Karl Popper said that the man lives in three worlds, the physical world, the mental world and the information world.

Information is in the man and around him. The man who creates the information may die but the information created by him is deathless. It may become sometimes obsolete, but it is immortal.

The movable type invented by Johann Gutenburg in the fifteenth century made the information-flow faster and quicker in the medieval ages. Libraries of different types were established everywhere with enormous book collections. Thus the printing was a big revolution in the middle ages. Its impact is still there. Few decades back the information (Inplosion) explosion had come upon us. In this context the LIS scholar Prof. Lancaster predicted a paperless future. Technologies growth is not static. Microfilm and analog technologies followed each other, and these are succeeded by the Digital Technology.

Information, both the print and electronic form, has occupied today the center of the stage of the human activities. It has come to be regarded as the most-powerful and profitable resource. There is a dichotomy among the countries of the world today as the information rich and the information poor. Quickest access to information has become pivotal for everyone and everywhere.

The Digital Technology and its sequential development, the internet are the latest revolution in the Information Communication Technology (ICT). The internet (the long Network Tail) is like the proverbial cow tail in the Hindu Mythology to cress the mythical river Vaitharani to reach swargam (Heaven). The internet provides today to the users the same access to information across the globe cutting short of space and time. Digital and digitized information which is accessed on the internet is created and managed by using three technologies viz The Digital Computer, The Digital Communication and The Digital Storage Technologies. The Digital Technology brought forth a new concept of Cyberary (Cyber + Library). The creation, development and management of the cyber libraries with successful websites / platforms and WWW is the need of the hour for students, teachers, research scholars, policy makers, administrators, scientists, managers, businessmen and all other users and information seekers to browse, surf and navigate the seas of information. Cyber libraries and the internet enable the netizens to access the information from one end of the globe to the other end within seconds of time. The ICT enables the information to reach out the unreached in the remote inhabitations in the country. Our astronauts navigating the cyber space may also use the Cyber Librarians in future. A day is not far away when our Librarians to become the *Czars* of information *per se*.

PHILOSOPHY OF LIBRARIANSHIP

Though we are in electronic age, the Philosophy of Librarianship presented by S.R. Ranganathan under the Five Laws of Library Science still holds well with stress on collection –Use –User-Delivery of Services- Growth/ Development. The five laws of library Science have been interpreted by Walt Crawford and Michael Gorman in their publication Future Libraries: Dreams, Madness and Reality (ALA, 1995).

Dr. S.R. RANGANATHAN	WALT CRAWFORD & MICHAEL GORMAN
Books are for use	Libraries save humanity
Every Reader His /Her Book	Respect ALL FORMS by which knowledge is communicated
Every Book its Reader	Use Technology Intelligently to enhance service
Save the Time of the Reader	Protect free access to knowledge Honor the past and create the future
Library is a Growing Organism	

TRANSFORMATION OF COLLECTION

New Technology has transformed the library collection considerably. Libraries with only print resources started procuring wide range of electronic sources resulting in transformation of collection into hybrid collection.

Print Sources	Electronic Sources
Books	E-Books
Pamphlets	E-text archives
Rare Books	On-line text collection
Journals	e-journals/on-line journals

Theses	Databases
Reports	Websites
Conference Proceedings	CD-ROM Databases
Training Manuals	DVDs
Case studies	Microfilms
Specifications	Microfiche
Standards	Audio Cassettes
Patents	Video Cassettes

SHIFT IN LIBRARY SERVICE

For a long time the library services confined to issue and return of books. That was followed by reference, lending, referral, reprography, bibliographic services etc. With the development of documentation and awareness of the importance of current information made the libraries to undertake services such as CAS, SDI, indexing, abstracting, translation, literature search, state of the art reports, bibliography and documentation etc. Now a days the libraries are proving On-Line services, Internet, Electronic Databases, E-Journals, E-Books with 'Any Time, Any Where Access' to information. The conventional catalogue is now On-Line Public Access Catalogue (OPAC) for on-line availability of documents and reserving.

Broad categorizations of services into traditional and present day services are:

Traditionalservices & Related Duties	**New Services & Related Duties**
Lending Services	
Circulation of books etc, Inter library loans, Book Bank Services	Circulation of Electronic products : CD, DVD, etc, Web 2.0, web 3.0

Collection Development	Development of e-resources
Acquisition Book Selection Book Ordering	e-acquisition
Manual Processing of Books	Computerized Processing
New Book Display	OPAC Services
Stack Maintenance	Computerized Stock Maintenance
Preservation	Digital Preservation
Journals Acquisition	Acquisition of e-Journals and search for information
Information work (manual)	Internet Access
Reference Service	Searching databases for Information CD-ROM Search for information
Audio-visual Services	In-house use of Audio-Video collection Borrowal of Video cassettes, VCDs
Reprographic Services	Photocopying, Document Scanning , Laser Printing
Statistics & Annual Report (MIS for decision making and Feedback to the Management)	M I S
Readers Orientation (Assistance in consulting Catalogue to full-fledged programmes)	ON-LINE Catalogue (OPAC)
HR Management (management library staff)	Line Management and Co-ordination with the 'TEAM'
Notice Board (communication with readers/clientele/customers)	Bulletin Board
Rapport with Book Trade	Rapport with Software & Hardware suppliers
	Library Automation
	Library Web Administration to

	develop web pages and update
	Computer software, Hardware
	Library database design and development Systems support and maintenance

LIBRARIAN IN PAST SCENARIO

Earlier the information was available in library-centric model. Librarians during past years were busy in handling the traditional role of the librarian like collecting, organizing, and disseminating information. Networking of libraries was not in much use. Use of internet and its resources were used rarely. Orientations to all these resources were very much on demand for both library and information professionals as well as user communities.

CHANGING SCENARIO

While identifying, collecting, organizing, processing and disseminating information are the crucial skills of a library professional, the advancement in ICT is providing challenges and opportunities to the present day Information Professional. The expectation has been to play the crucial role of an information intermediary in the true sense by conceptualizing and abstracting the exact needs the user. The transition is to elevate the role of Information Professional to the Information Consultant. This is on the lines of moving up from Training Manager to Learning Consultant. This scaling up of the role requires us to be flexible, adapting to change, capacity to learn, interpersonal skills and innovation.

Charles Darwin in his Natural Theory of Evolution had propounded three postulates that reflect the concept of Change Management. They are: Struggle for Existence,

Inheritance of acquired characteristics and Survival of the Fittest. Struggle for existence signified intense global competition for resources and opportunities. This scenario encourages us to be adaptable to changes and building up of new skill-sets, perspective and positive attitude towards the whole industry that takes us to the next level of transition i.e. inheritance of acquired characteristics. The ones who are flexible, adaptable and competent in acquiring the current learning/characteristics would ramp up to the next level of change which is crucial i.e. Survival of the Fittest. Only those who inherited or developed acquired characteristics and competencies would eventually survive as fittest individuals in the evolution of organisms. Therefore the contemporary library professional needs to be a Techno-Savvy Information evangelist and consultant who advise and connect the user-information in just-in-time manner.

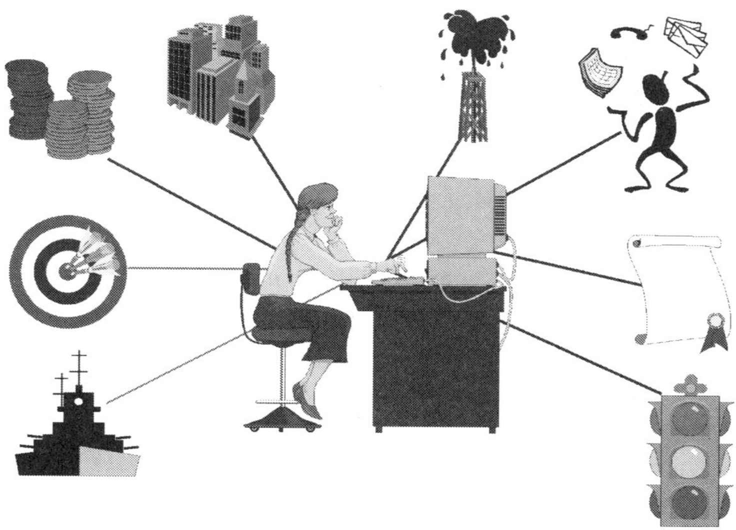

Cybrarian (Digital Librarian) In ICT Environment

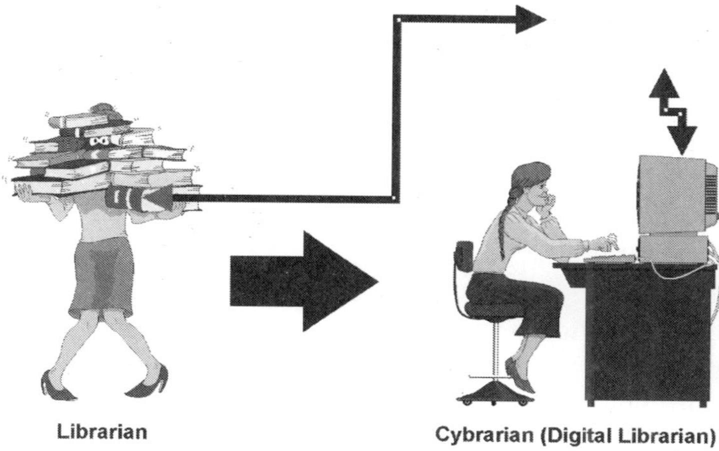

TRANSITION IN ROLES ON INFORMATION PROFESSIONALS

This activities discussed above illustrate some of the new roles which librarians have taken on in the past years and are busy in handling the traditional role of the librarian in collecting, organizing and disseminating information. But the challenges in technology in the past decade have been truly astonishing and the scope for building new information services and new ways of representing content seem unlimited. It is important that all information professionals keep abreast of technology trends and that they try to determine the opportunities that they present for the development of new types of content and services.

Roy Tennant, a leading proponent of developing digital libraries suggests certain skills for librarians to create and manage digital collections and services. These skills are knowledge of:

- Imaging technology

- Optical Character Recognition (OCR)
- Markup languages, including HTML, SGML and XML
- Cataloging and metadata
- Indexing and DB technology
- User interface design
- Programming
- Web technology
- Project Management

Information professionals have received transition in their roles and according to the roles played/job profiles they got different designations from time to time. Librarian, IT Librarian, Curator, Archivists, Records Managers, Information Technologists, Knowledge Managers, Virtual Knowledge Navigator , Web Manager, Information Architect, cyber Consultant, Cybrarian. To cope-up with these profiles, one should also consider changes in the curricula of LIS education. Hence the LIS curriculum has included in its syllabus various new and emerging concepts like-Knowledge Management, Web Designing, Hosting, Application of Information Technology in libraries, Semantic Web, Ontologies, Taxonomy,etc from time to time. With the help of these concepts Librarians from traditional library can reach to the Cybrarian of Cyber World.

CHALLENGES FOR INFORMATION PROFESSIONALS

Nowadays, the new organizational configurations are being improved by professionals that reinvented their own work (Dufy, 1994). The "post –employment organization" are not only based on ordinary positions, functions and careers. They request uncommon styles and professional training, if compared to traditional jobs from labour market.

In this way, the professional career has also different structures, and gives special importance to communication abilities. Its path is like a growing and enlarging spiral of professional value and excellence.

The information handling is an activity with high value added. It includes scanning (data collection), interpretation (data given meaning) and solution (information product and service/action taken/new content). This is a typical function of a new generation of professionals, called by Peter Drucker (1995) knowledge workers. They could be engineers, technologies, managers, systems analysts, information analysts, archivists, librarians, economists. It is also related to any professional class that has in knowledge and information the raw materials for its work. The necessary attributes of the knowledge workers are:

- Know-how to think, how to find information and how to communicate it ;
- Dominium of the " art of the debate" (negotiation and brokerage);
- Management of KM events;
- Purposeful and implementful of solutions;
- Information share;
- Sense of responsibility with partners;
- Pleasure of challenges,
- Mental curiosity and self-control;
- Capacity of identifying opportunities in new business contexts.

Knowledge workers must know how to use different approaches and processes of information handling oriented to solve problems. Librarians need to face the following challenges by inculcating new skills so that they can transit from Librarian to Cybrarian easily:

- Move from Holdings to Access
- Change from Print to Electronic
- Skills to meet the new Challenges
- Knowledge Management Issue
- The Virtual Librarian concepts

CONCLUSION

The opportunities for information professionals' performance through IT innovations and digital environments are promising. They include from classic support activities to teaching, researching and managing electronic information systems, the shaping and delivering of new products bundling until different partnering arrangements. It is a "golden opportunity" to people who desires to follow new paths or refresh their own professional careers. It is necessary to invest and to make efforts to change the situation. IT innovations and the new markets of digital information sector bring new horizons to information professions. It is also necessary to motivate academic researches and to perform market studies to know better about the subject.

In today's technology world, the role of librarians or information professionals is deviating from traditional libraries' librarian role to virtual or digital libraries' Software Librarians, Cybrarians, Configuration Librarian or Librarian-Knowledge Management. Information Professionals are becoming Webmaster and Intranet Coordinators, combining technical expertise with information management ability. The development of electronic media and networks significantly will alter the way in which professionals work. Access to high speed, national or international computer network will significantly alter the way in which professionals will work in the coming decade.

Information professionals enjoy a role of growing importance in society. We should use our position to share new technologies with the public, and lobby together to have these improvements implemented. The role of the information professional of the future will be determined by the actions we take and examples we set today. In the interest of giving them a challenging role to inherit, "We must embrace change, and embrace it as we never have before" (Reuben, 1992).

REFERENCES

1. Alison McNab & Ian Winship: Internet: Use in academic libraries; library Association Record Vol98 No12, Dec 1996
2. *www.la-hq.org.uk*
3. Bhojraju,G. : knowledge Management: why do we need for corporate? Malaysian Journal of library & Information Science, Dec 2005
4. Hunnicutt, Susan C: Defining Cybrarian: *http://www.mlaforum.org*
5. *http://www/whatis.com*
6. *http://www/yourwindow.to/information-security/gl_cybrarian.htm*
7. *http://whatis.techtarget.com/definition/0,,sid9_gci213634,00.html*
8. *http://durak.org/sean/*
9. Harvard Business Review; Drucker, P. The information that executives truly need.
10. SR Ranganathan- The Five laws of library science, 2nd ed.
11. Walt Crawford and Michael Gorman- Future Libraries: Dreams, Madness & Reality New Tak; ALA 1995
12. http://www.ariadne.ac.uk
13. *www.cybrarian.com*
14. *www.cybrarian.community* programmes.org.uk
15. *www.becomealibrarian.org*

16. Handbook of special librarianship and information work ed. By Wilfred Ashworth, London
17. Deegan, Marilyn and Simon Tanner. Digital Future: Strategies for the information Age
18. Find, Soren. Changing the culture –job design, work process and qualifications in the hybrid library, proc.of 68th IFLA general conference.
19. Kalam A.P.J, Challenges for knowledge society Convocation Address at the 11th convocation of Bundel khand university. University news Vol42(37)
20. *http://www.libraryjournal.com*
21. Developing Cyber Libraries, Babu, T. Ashok, Ramaiah, L.S.
22. UNESCO.

List of Contributors

Dr. Rabindra K. Mahapatra
Chief Librarian
Orissa University of Agriculture and Technology
Bhubaneswar-751 003
rkm_02@yahoo.com rkmahapatra60@gmail.com

Prof. K. C. Panda
Prof & Head
P.G.Department of Library and Information Science
Sambalpur University, Orissa
krushna52@yahoo.co.in

Dr. D.B.Ramesh
Head, Library and Documentation,
Institute of Minerals & Materials Technology, Bhubaneswar
db_ramesh@yahoo.com

Dr. K. C. Das
Principal
College of Library & Inf. Science
(Berhampur University)
S.M.I.T., Ankushpur-761100
Ganjam District,Orissa
dr_kcd@yahoo.com

Dr. P. S. Kawtra
Librarian & Head,
DLDI, NCERT
New Delhi
E-mail : *ps_Kawatra@yahoo.co.in*

Dr. Bibhu Prasad Panda
Sr. Librarian
KIIT University, Bhubaneswar

Dillip K Swain
Assistant Librarian
KIIT University, Bhubaneswar

Dr. Kamal Lochan Jena
Librarian, CET, Bhubaneswar
kljena@rediffmail.com

Nirmal Ranjan Mazumadar
Assistant Librarian
GIMT, Azara, Guwahati-17, Assam
E- Mail: nrmazumdar@gmail.com

Prasanna Kumar Barik
Librarian
C. V. Raman College of Engineering, Bhubaneswar
prasanna_barik@yahoo.co.in

Dr. M. K. Seth
Institute of Minerals & Materials Technology CSIR,
Bhubaneswar

Partha S. Patra
School of Hotel Management,
SOA University, Bhubaneswar

Dr. (Mrs.) Puspanjali Jena
Reader
P.G Deptt. of Lib & Inf. Sc.
Utkal University, Vani Vihar.
Bhubaneswar – 751 004

Mr. Dipak Kumar Khuntia
Librarian -cum- Documentation Officer
Xavier Institute of Management
Bhubaneswar – 751 013

Prof. (Dr) P. K. Dutta
Principal
Durgapur Institute of Management and Science
(Affiliated to West Bengal University of Technology)
Sahid Sukumar Banerjee Sarani, Bidhannagar,
Durgapur-713212, WB, India
Email –*askpkd@yahoo.com*

Mr. Promod Kr. Hota,
Librarian
Central Library
Bengal College of Engineering & Technology
Sahid Sukumar Banerjee Sarani, Bidhannagar,
Durgapur-713212, WB, India

N. K. Dash
Silicon Institute of Technology
Bhubaneswar

Dr. Jyoshna. Sahoo
Asst. Librarian
Orissa State Museum
Bhubaneswar

Rosalien Rout
Lecturer in Lib& Inf.Sc
AWDI, Rourkela

Dipen Deka
SRF, DLIS
Gauhati University
dipendeka@gmail.com

Apurba Jyoti Majumder
JRF, DLIS
Gauhati University
apurbajyoti@gmail.com

Bulu Maharana
Lecturer
P. G. Department of Library & Information Science
Sambalpur University, Jyoti Vihar-768019
bulumaharana@gmail.com

Mamata Mishra
MLISc Student
P. G. Department of Library & Information Science
Sambalpur University, Jyoti Vihar-768019

Priya Ranjan Mahalik
Professional Library Assistant
N.K.C. Centre for Development Studies
Bhubaneswar-751013
mahalik_priyaranjan@yahoo.com

D.R. Meher
Asst. Librarian
HKM State Library, Bhubaneswar
meherdebraj@gmail.com

P.N. Mishra
Librarian
A S College, Tirtol, Jagatsinghpur (Orissa)
mishrapn@xmail.com

Arjuna Jena
Librarian
Christ College, Cuttack, Orissa.
arjuna_j@rediffmail.com

Dr Sunil Kumar Satpathy
Sr.Librarian
C.V.Raman College of Engineering, Bhubaneswar-54
drsksatpathy@gmail.com

Dr (Mrs)Bijalaxmi Rautaray
Sr.Librarian
KIIT University,Bhubaneswar-24
rautaray_b@yahoo.co.in

Chandra Kanta Swain
Librarian
Regional College of Management, Bhubaneswar, Orissa
ckswain1969@gmail.com

Monisha Mishra
Librarian
Orissa University of Agriculture and Technology (OUAT)
Bhubaneswar
monishasilicon@gmail.com

Sasmita Brahma
Librarian
Orissa University of Agriculture and Technology (OUAT)
Bhubaneswar

Dr. Rabindra Nath Mohanta
Librarian
Vasanta College for Women
Rajghat Fort, Varanasi – 221001
rnmohanta@hotmail.com

Rajesh Kumar Mishra
Documentation Officer
Central University of Tibetan Studies
Sarnath, Varanasi – 221007

Govind Gopal
M.Phil. Scholar
P.G. Dept. of Library & Information Science
Sambalpur University
govind.gopal77@gmail.com

Ms. Sabitri Majhi
Junior Research Fellow
P.G. Dept. of library & Information Science
Sambalpur University

Mr.Prabhu B. Gaddimani,
Asst Librarian
Sir Dorabji Tata Memorial Library
Tata Institute of Social Sciences
P.B.No.8313, Deonar, Mumbai – 400 088
prabhug@tiss.edu

Mr.Ravi Pothare,
Professional Asst
Sir Dorabji Tata Memorial Library
Tata Institute of Social Sciences, P.B.No.8313,
Deonar, Mumbai – 400 088
rpothare@tiss.edu

Dr. Muttayya Koganurmath,
University Librarian
Sir Dorabji Tata Memorial Library,
Tata Institute of Social Sciences,
P.B.No.8313, Deonar, Mumbai – 400 088
muttayya@tiss.edu

Dr. Banamber Sahoo
Asst. Lib & Inf. Officer
Regional Medical Research Centre(ICMR)
Chandrasekharpur, Bhubaneswar.
sahoo@icmr.org.in

Sudhir Kumar Jena
Librarian
Orissa University of Agriculture and Technology (OUAT)
Bhubaneswar

Kunwar Singh
Senior Library Information Assistant
Central Library, Indian Institute of Technology Madras,
Chennai-36
rawatks@iitm.ac.in

Mrutyunjay Sethy
Professional Asst., Central Library,
IIT Madras, Chennai-36
sethymrutyunjay@gmail.com